Shig

The True Story of
An American *Kamikaze*

Shig

The True Story of
An American *Kamikaze*

A Memoir
Shigeo Imamura
今村茂男

American Literary Press, Inc.
Baltimore, Maryland

Shig: The True Story of an American Kamikaze

Copyright © 2001 Isako Imamura

Library of Congress
Cataloging in Publication Data
ISBN 1-56167-660-8

Published by

American Literary Press, Inc.
8019 Belair Road, Suite 10
Baltimore, Maryland 21236

Manufactured in the United States of America

CONTENTS

Editors' Foreword

Professor Imamura wrote this memoir in the last years of his life. While he was able to complete the entire text, his final illness prevented him from finishing the editing or making the translation into Japanese he planned.

The portions of the text in italics are Professor Imamura's own descriptions of the historical background and the context for his story. The views expressed in the memoir are his own personal views. They are not those of an historian, and may not necessarily comport with those of professionals in that field. Likewise, some of his beliefs or assumptions may be mistaken. However, rather than checking every detail or making every change possible, the editors have chosen to leave Professor Imamura's story in his own personal voice. We let Professor Imamura speak for himself, and he said it best:

> *Readers are reminded that this is not a thesis on history, political science or sociology. If any inaccuracies are found in the finer points of this writing, please attribute them to my ignorance, misunderstanding or loss of memory. After all, most of what goes into this took place half a century ago.*

The editors wish to express their thanks to Lewis Gulick, childhood friend of Shig, who spent years working tirelessly to bring Shig's story to print. Special thanks, too, to Eiji Kanno, who contributed his mapmaking skills, and to Kenneth Kato, whose interest and careful reading of the manuscript prompted many improvements. Please note that because Professor Imamura did not use them, none of the Japanese words transliterated for the text include indications of vowel length.

This story of a remarkable life lived between two countries has a message for those in both Shig's "motherland," the United States, and his "fatherland," Japan. Professor Imamura devoted his professional life to promoting cross-cultural respect and understanding in both his homelands. His story here is a powerful argument with the same theme of his life after the war and his work as an international educator: enduring peace can only come through cross-cultural understanding.

The Editors
Himeji, Japan
San Francisco, California
Washington, D.C.

December 24, 2000

Preface

About a week before December 7 (Pearl Harbor Day), 1978, a call came from Debbie Creamer, a student reporter for the *State News*, the student newspaper at Michigan State University. It was a request for an interview. That was nothing new to me. Almost yearly since I started teaching at Michigan State in 1961, I was made a target of practice interviews by student reporters, most likely because it had somehow leaked out that I was a former *kamikaze* pilot, an object of curiosity among American young people. The interviews sometimes resulted in news articles, small and tongue-in-cheek, in one of the back pages of the *State News*.

There was something different this time. Not only did Debbie appear very serious about the interview but she also brought along a photographer who wanted to take pictures of me during the interview. "Why all this fuss?" I thought. "The 30th anniversary of Pearl Harbor Day was long gone and the 40th was still years to come." Then it dawned on me. A few weeks before that day, over nine hundred Americans had committed mass suicide in Georgetown in Guyana, South America. "Why did they have to kill themselves just because their leader told them that that was the thing to do?" This thought must have flashed through the minds of many American people. And then, "Now wait a minute. Didn't something like this happen before? Sure, the Japanese *kamikaze* pilots. They were told to save their country by killing themselves and they willingly did it. Hey, there's a *kamikaze* pilot right here at Michigan State. Let's go ask him what he thinks about the Georgetown case." This chain of thoughts was my conjecture, of course, of why the *State News* sent Debbie and the photographer to me. But what followed the interview more or less bore out this conjecture.

On the front page of the December 1 issue of the *State News* appeared an article titled, "Kamikaze now a 'U' teacher," with two photos of me, one taken in my office during the interview and another one the photographer asked to borrow from me. It was taken during the war, with me in a flight uniform. The article said that I was born in the United States, was taken back to Japan by my parents at age ten, grew up in Japan and went through the school system up through college, volunteered for the Japanese naval air reserve, trained as a Zero fighter pilot, and eventually volunteered for the *kamikaze* corps but never actually took off on a mission. The article ended with a quotation of something I said during the interview. "We honestly believed in what we were fighting for. Some people seem to think that World

War II is old history and that we now have no reason to believe that such atrocities and self-sacrifices will happen again. Well, it happened in Guyana and more of these may happen in the future."

Just as I finished reading this article in my office, the phone rang. The caller, identifying himself as a United Press International reporter, said that he had read the *State News* article and wanted to ask me some more questions about my past. Although we talked about half an hour on the phone, I forgot about it almost as soon as I hung up. Then, very early in the morning of December 7, I got a call at home. This time, it was from a disc jockey at a radio station in Morgantown, West Virginia, first asking if I wouldn't mind being interviewed live on radio and then proceeding to ask how I was able to survive the war. But that was just the beginning. Obviously, the UPI wire service had spread the article on me all over the world. Throughout that day and in the days that followed, I had telephone calls and letters from friends and strangers who read the article from all over the U.S., even from acquaintances living as far away as England and South America. Not one of them was hostile. They all congratulated me for being alive.

However, I couldn't help but feel, deep inside, that they were also asking themselves: "How could he, born and partly educated in America, ever willingly have volunteered to sacrifice his life for Japan fighting against America?"… "What caused him to change his allegiance?"…"How could he, less than a month after the end of the war, switch his allegiance again and start working for the U.S. Army, even though only as a translator-interpreter?"…"Could something like this happen to other people today?"

I have asked myself these same questions for decades now but never found good answers. After a number of my friends, especially Americans, urged me to write an autobiography, I came to think I might come close to finding the answers if I wrote out my thoughts. And even if the answers were not clear ones, they might help people realize that what they strongly believe in at one point in life, even to the extent of wanting to sacrifice their lives for the cause, may not be so believable in later life. Hopefully this would help lessen the amount of tension that exists around the world today. If only more and more people would come to realize that no arguments, no differences of opinions— political, economic, social, religious or otherwise—are worthy of the sacrifice of human lives, including one's own, the purpose of this writing would be accomplished.

The readers are reminded that this is not a thesis on history, political science or sociology. If any inaccuracies are found in the finer points of this writing, please attribute them to my ignorance, misunderstanding or loss of memory. After all, most of what goes into this took place half a century ago.

HOKKAIDO

Naval Air Base
CHITOSE

Hakodate

Aomori

Akita

JAPAN SEA

Sendai

HONSHU

KASUMIGAURA
Naval Air Corps

Atsugi

HIMEJI

Okayama   Osaka

Hiroshima

Zentsuji

KARASU
Mie Naval Air Station

HANEDA
Tokyo Naval Air Corps

KYUSHU

Amakusa

OITA
Naval Air Corps

MATSUYAMA

SHIKOKU

IZUMI

PACIFIC OCEAN

Chapter 1

The Native Son

Ten Years in San Francisco

My birth certificate says that I was born at 565 North 5th Street, San Jose, California, on August 14, 1922. That was because my parents knew Dr. Ochiai, an obstetrician who hailed from their hometown in Japan and worked at the hospital at that address, commonly known as the Japanese Hospital. A week after my birth, Mother took me back to our rented home on Webster Street in San Francisco. I do not remember anything about San Jose. Among the many calls I received after the UPI press release on me was one from a San Jose journalist, who opened the conversation with, "Hello, Shigeo. This is your hometown newspaper calling." When I told him that I considered San Francisco to be my hometown because I have no memory of San Jose, he seemed very disappointed.

My father, Keijiro, was born into a farm family in Ishii Village, now a part of Matsuyama City, the capital of Ehime Prefecture on Shikoku, the smallest of the four major islands of Japan. Although the family was well off and grandfather owned much farmland, mostly rice paddies, Father knew that he would inherit only a small portion of the land because he was the second son. His older brother would inherit most of the land in accordance with the Japanese tradition. Father finished primary school right around the turn of the century and advanced into secondary education, something very few farm boys were able to do in those days. While attending Matsuyama Middle School, he visited friends in Kobe, one of the largest overseas trading ports in the country. There, he was impressed by the many foreign vessels moored in the harbor; eventually he decided to go to America. Part of this urge seems to have come from his realization that, even with a secondary education, he would have to find a job upon graduation because the small farm he would inherit would not be enough to make his living.

Around the close of the 19th century and the beginning of the 20th, quite a number of young Japanese boys, mostly second, third or fourth sons of farmers and fishermen, found their ways to America. Their dream was to work hard, make a fortune and return to Japan for an easy late life. Father had a boyhood friend who worked as a farm hand in Fresno, California. This Mr. Muneta wrote to Father saying that while life in America was not as easy as folks back home might think, jobs were available. So, Father hopped on a freighter in Kobe and headed for Fresno via San Francisco. That was around 1905.

Even though he was from a farm family, Father had little real farming experience, because tenant farmers did most of the work. And he found the farms and orchards in Fresno vast, compared to the small patches of rice paddies in Ishii Village. He just couldn't bear the hard work and moved to San Francisco within a year. In the big city, after several years working as a houseboy, he found a steady job as a clerk at a Japanese-owned Taiseido Book and Stationery Shop on Post Street. By 1921 he was ready to rent a house and raise a family. He was in his mid-thirties.

It was quite common for eligible Japanese immigrants in the United States to send their photographs to their friends and relatives in Japan and have them circulated among eligible women. In turn, some of the women would send their pictures to the men. It was usually the men's decision which women they wanted to marry. Most of the women traveled by themselves to the United States and the couples would meet each other on the pier of the port of arrival for the first time in their lives. It is said that some of the men, and some of the women for that matter, sent photographs taken when they were a bit younger and were aghast to see how different the real persons were from the pictures they had seen.

Father had to do it differently. Generations of the Imamura family served as mayors of Ishii Village, as did my grandfather. To maintain this social prestige, a bride from the "right" family had to be chosen for him and a formal wedding and wedding reception had to be held. A "picture bride" and a ceremony in far away California just wouldn't do. The then head of the family in Ishii, Father's older brother, settled on the third daughter, Hisako, of the Tachibana family in Masaki, a neighboring village. The Tachibana family also produced generations of leaders for that community. Hisako's father was the principal of the elementary school in Masaki. Hisako herself was a registered nurse at the local Red Cross Hospital. Father was told to return to Ishii for a proper wedding there. This was in 1921. The newlyweds spent a few months in Ishii, and by early 1922, when they took a ship back to San Francisco, Hisako was pregnant with me. They moved into a house Father had rented before leaving for Japan. The house was on Webster Street in San Francisco.

I remember very little about life in and around the house on Webster Street, because we moved to a house on Cedar Avenue when I was four or five. I am guessing this from the snapshots taken around that time. Cedar Avenue no longer exists. It used to run one block, from Octavia on the east and Laguna on the west, between Post and Geary. It is all built up now. When I visited the area in 1953, on my way back to Japan after a two-year course at the University of Michigan, the avenue was still there but the buildings were beginning to be torn down. But our old two-story house (we lived on the second floor and another family occupied the first floor) was still there. I rang the doorbell. I told the lady who came to the door that I used to live in the house and asked if I could see the inside for old time's sake. But she looked scared, refused and said she would call the police if I didn't go away right then.

This general area of uptown San Francisco is known today as Japantown, in contrast to Chinatown further downtown. Even in the 1920s, the Japanese-American population in San Francisco was concentrated there. The adults were first generation immigrants, the *isseis*, and we children were the *niseis*. Post Street was lined with various stores operated by the *isseis*. Taiseido, where Father worked, is gone now, but some of the same stores are still there today. Uoki, where Mother used to take me along to buy fish and groceries, was operated in the 1990s by old men I remember as the young sons of the owner. Soko Hardware Store is still there and so is the barbershop where I used to get haircuts for 25 cents.

Cedar Avenue was a rather new area for Japanese-Americans and not many of them lived there yet. It was a mostly white neighborhood. Right across Cedar from our house was the backyard of the Sakuyama family, whose house faced Post Street. They had four girls, Takuko, Taneko, Taeko and Takeko, who were two years apart from one another. The second oldest, Taneko, was my age. They were the first friends I made in that neighborhood and we went back and forth between our homes and played. Their parents were from Northern Japan and spoke a dialect quite different from ours, making it a bit difficult for me to understand. But we children spoke a kind of neutral dialect and got along fine. Next, I got to know Minoru, about my age. His parents were from Wakayama in Western Japan. His family, the Nishiokas, lived in an apartment house on the corner of Cedar and Laguna. Then the Iida family moved into the first floor below us. Akira, the younger of the two sons, was also my age. As I got to know more and more *nisei* kids, we developed our own lingo, a mixture of Japanese and English.

One of the things I vaguely remember from going to other children's places is that in some of those homes portraits of the Japanese Emperor and Empress were hanging on the walls. The Imamura household never had such a thing. I wouldn't be surprised if some of the *issei* parents tried to indoctrinate their children in royal divinity and some other ultra-nationalistic thoughts to which I was exposed in my later life but never got from my parents while in the United States. Perhaps these kinds of things caused the American authorities to become suspicious of the Japanese-Americans' loyalty to America and motivated them to relocate the *isseis* and their families during the early part of World War II. The mistake the U.S. government made in doing so was simply assuming that the Japanese-Americans as a whole were basically not loyal to the United States. Their loyalty to the country they lived in was later amply verified by the number of *niseis* who fought and died for the country, notably the 442nd Division.

At age six, I started going to Raphael Weill School, one of San Francisco's public primary schools. It was a few blocks down on Buchanan Street and as a child I used to think it was a pretty long walk each way. The pupils there were of a real racial mixture. There were Chinese, Filipinos, French and Russian students, but the Japanese made up the largest ethnic group because of the school's proximity to Japantown. There were only a few blacks there at the time. We all spoke English at school, of course. I don't think any of us ever thought of ourselves as anything but Americans. We pledged allegiance to the American flag and sang the national anthem every morning like any other American children and thought nothing of it. Incidentally, the national anthem we sang was, "My country 'tis of thee," not, "Oh, say, can you see."

There was one thing different about the *nisei* kids from the others, however. Our *issei* parents made us *niseis* attend the Japanese language school as well as the local public school. My circumstances were a bit unusual, however. Since I was born on August 14, I had reached the full age of six when school started in September 1928. But since the Japanese language school would not enroll students who have not reached age six by the end of March, just as in Japan (where the school year begins on April 1), I had to wait until the following fall to be admitted to the Japanese language school. But, starting in the fall of 1929, I began the double duty of a typical *nisei* kid in San Francisco. On weekdays, I was at Raphael Weill from about 8:30 to 2:30, and then from 3:00 to 5:00, I attended *Kimmon Gakuen* (Golden Gate Institute) on Bush Street, about four or five blocks from Raphael Weill. The *Kimmon Gakuen* teachers were all trained educators who taught us two subjects, reading and writing of the Japanese language and Ethics. The textbooks were the same ones as those used in the public schools in Japan, published by the Ministry of Education.

Some of the *nisei* boys and girls did not like going to *Kimmon Gakuen* because it gave them an extra load of studies and took away some of their play time. Most of us enjoyed the experience, however. Since we all spoke the language to some extent, it was not too hard to learn to read and write it. Ethics, however, was a little different. The lessons were about historical figures known for hard work, thrift, bravery and other moral values: role models. Most of them were not hard to understand, some even enjoyable, and made it easier for us to understand why our parents said some of the things they said when trying to discipline us. Only after World War II were we, as adults, told that some of those stories were historically unproven or even fictitious.

There was a small, asphalt-paved yard behind *Kimmon Gakuen*. It was too small for ball games, so we played leapfrog, hide-and-seek, tag and the like between classes. One thing I remember about playing in that yard is that when one side won in a game, whether a person or a group, that side yelled, "*Nippon katta, Nippon katta. Rosha maketa,*" meaning "Japan won, Japan won. Russia lost." The Russo-Japanese War had ended in 1905 and this was around 1930. Our fathers must have brought this battle-cry from the old country. There were touches of such nationalism in our Ethics stories too, as I recall. For example, one story was about General Nogi befriending the Russian General Stoessel after the former defeated the latter in one of the major battles of the Russo-Japanese War.

I'll continue with just a few "snapshots" of life in San Francisco. In fact, it is the survival of some snapshots from that time that has helped me remember these vignettes.

The Doll Exchange. But for the professional group photograph I still have in one of my albums, I probably would not have remembered this. I started at Raphael Weill in September of 1928 and at *Kimmon Gakuen* a year later. During that interim year, my parents sent me to the kindergarten at *Kimmon Gakuen*. One day, the one hundred or so of us children were assembled in the auditorium. We were there for a welcoming ceremony for eight of the many Japanese dolls that had been sent to the United States on a friendship mission. From the picture, the beautiful *kimono* clad dolls appear to have been about three feet tall. We all faced the dolls, Principal Suzuki spoke some words of welcome, we sang some Japanese songs and then lined up in front of the dolls to have the picture taken. About a year or two later, American dolls were sent to Japan as a reciprocal offer of friendship, and the song, "*Aoi me wo shita oningyo*" (The Doll with

Blue Eyes) became very popular with Japanese children. The song went, roughly, "The doll with blue eyes, is an American born celluloid. When she arrived at the port, she was full of tears. 'I don't understand the language. What shall I do if I get lost?' You kind children of Japan, be nice to her and make friends."

It is a pity that in just a few years such grassroots efforts at mutual friendship disappeared as relations between Japan and the U.S. rapidly deteriorated into mutual suspicion and antagonism.

Some of my other clear, snapshot-type memories of impressive events from those days in San Francisco:

Bad News from Afar. Father was quite a heavy drinker. His favorite watering hole was Sushigen, a sushi shop owned by the Ideno family. It was right next door to Taiseido, the bookstore where Father worked, on Post Street. I think Father spent the evening there once a week. Mostly, though, he drank *sake* over dinner at home. It was during a typical dinner at home one evening that Father received a telegram from his brother in Ishii. I think I remember the exact wording because of the unusual sentences. It just said, *"Haha shisu. Shirasu."* A literal translation would be something like, "Mother died. Notified." It is considered a sin in Japan for a person not to be at the bedside of a dying parent. The "Notified" probably meant, "I'm letting you know because you have to know, but we know you can't be back here in time for the funeral." Grandma was in her eighties but we had all thought she was doing quite well. I think her unexpected death was quite a shock for Father. And I think he also must have felt very guilty because he had no way of getting to her funeral in time.

Bad News from Nearby. Father had a good friend by the name of Sozaburo Takahashi. They called each other "So-san" and "Kei-san." Although So-san was a little older than Father, they both were from the same general area of Ehime and were distant relations. So-san worked as a live-in butler for a well-to-do white family in Menlo Park and came into San Francisco about one weekend a month. So-san loved Mother's cooking. The adults sat up until very late at night, talking and drinking. So-san slept on the sofa in our parlor Saturday night and went back to Menlo Park on Sunday. One Saturday evening, when So-san was not expected, Father got a call with the news that So-san had been run over by a car and killed. That was the only time

I remember seeing Father cry; not even when he learned of his mother's death did he cry. We later learned that So-san had gone out drinking at a tavern in Menlo Park and was walking across a highway on his way home when he was hit. Father officiated at a modest Buddhist funeral for So-san, had him cremated and sent his ashes to his sister in Japan.

Excursions with Father. Father liked to go fishing. Once in a while on Sundays, he would come home with what seemed to me huge fish, sea bass or striped bass. Mother made them into sashimi and other goodies. Occasionally when the sea was calm, he took me to Tiburon, north of the Golden Gate, to catch rock cod. I used to enjoy it immensely, and my fishing hobby is still with me today. Father never had enough money to buy a car. So it was only when he, or we, would get a ride with his car-owning friends that we went fishing.

Excursions with Mother. Mother was a strong-willed person who more or less dominated Father. She worked hard at home, sewing and knitting, to supplement the family income. She had never studied English in Japan. As a matter of fact, very few women learned English in Japan in the early 20th century. But living where she was in San Francisco Japantown, she didn't have much trouble getting around with very little English. When I was eight or nine, something must have motivated her to try to learn English. She started to go to an adult school, probably what we know today as an Americanization program. One day when I came home from *Kimmon Gakuen*, she said," Shigeo, I want you to listen to what I learned in school today and see if it sounds right," and she said, "Mr. Bonelli has no woik." "No, Mother, it's 'work,'" I corrected her. "But the teacher said 'woik.' She went to a university in New York, so she ought to know what she is talking about."

Perhaps because she didn't understand much English, Mother hardly ever listened to the radio except the occasional music program. But movies were different. She was able to watch and tell what was going on, especially comedies. Once in a while she took me to Saturday matinees at Temple Theater on Fillmore Street, about a ten-minute walk from home. I remember mostly comedies with Charlie Chaplin, Buster Keaton and Harold Lloyd. One of the last movies I saw there was the original version of Frankenstein, which really scared the devil out of me.

Childhood Illness. I cannot leave the San Francisco scene without touching upon my allergy problems. Mother used to tell me that she learned very early that she could not feed me any milk other than her own. I was one of those children whose bodies did not accept lactose. When I was old enough to eat solid food, Mother discovered that every time she fed me something with mayonnaise on or in it, I would throw up. At age seven or eight (I still remember this well), I had a severe attack of asthma. Dr. Kiyasu, our family doctor, came and looked me over. He then pasted a layer of mustard all over my chest and covered it up with a woolen cloth. "Now, that should clear it up by morning," he said and left. I almost immediately began to feel a burning sensation, then a severe pain on my chest. I started to cry, and as the pain grew I cried very hard. Staying with me at the bedside, Mother must have felt my pain as though it was her own. Not being able to stand watching me any more, she removed the cloth from my chest. I still remember the yell she gave out, as though someone had stabbed her. She ran to the phone. Dr. Kiyasu came right away, took one look at me and said something to Mother. My memory fades right there, but as I learned afterwards, I was allergic to mustard. Mother told me that my chest was blistered as though a bucket of boiling water had been thrown on it.

Commercial mayonnaise contains a small amount of mustard. That's why I threw up when Mother fed me sandwiches or potato salad with mayonnaise. As I grew older, my allergic symptoms to mustard have grown milder. Yet as recently as the summer of 1992, shortly after finishing a fabulous French dinner, which unbeknownst to me contained mustard in the steak sauce, I had a violent reaction. I still can't drink milk, but I am glad that mustard is the only other food I am allergic to.

My life in San Francisco came to a swift and, to me, very surprising conclusion. My life had been progressing quite normally and pleasantly. I was proud that I was allowed to skip a semester at Raphael Weill and go on to one level higher. In the fall of 1931, I skipped 4A and was put into the 4B class at Raphael Weill. At the same time, I started my third year at *Kimmon Gakuen*. In February of

1932, I was in 5A. It was then that I learned of my parents' decision that Mother and I would leave for Japan that March, and that Father would follow us a year later. Mother told me that the decision to leave in March was made so I would be in Japan before the school year there started in April.

There were a lot of people on hand to see us off at the pier in San Francisco. Snapshots show that they all looked happy, except Father, who was not coming with us. The ship was ***Tatsuta Maru***, a 15,000-ton twin vessel. Its sister ship was called the ***Chichibu Maru.*** They were flagships of the Japanese NYK Line. Both were converted into military vessels during the war and were later sunk. If my memory serves me right, we set sail at noon on March 9, 1932, and arrived in Yokohama on the 23rd, exactly two weeks later, with a dawn-to-dusk stop in Honolulu on the way. As we sailed out of the Golden Gate Bay, we saw two foundation-like structures on the shores. We were told that those were the beginning of the now-famed Golden Gate Bridge. Who would have known that I would be sailing under it in the opposite direction on a U.S. army transport ship 19 years later?

Sailing was smooth until past Honolulu. Mother and I weren't able to afford anything but third class, which meant living in a small cabin with something like six double-level bunk beds. With luggage and whatnot strewn around the narrow aisles among bunks, we kids had to go out into the hallways or on the decks to play. Out on the decks, we occasionally saw porpoises swimming along the ship and whales in the distance. The meals were good, with choices of Japanese and American dishes. A few days out of Honolulu, we hit a big storm. The ship pitched and rolled for a couple of days. It was fun for the kids, but some of the adults, including Mother, got badly seasick. We also learned that two seamen were seriously injured trying to prevent the company flag from being torn away from the bow by the waves.

If I have bored the reader with all the details of my childhood life, please bear with me. It was an attempt to show that I was more or less an average American child with Japanese ancestry before leaving for his fatherland. To me, the United States is still my motherland.

Chapter 2

The Returnee

MATSUYAMA

Bancho Elementary School

Arriving in the port of Yokohama on March 23, 1932, we were met by Kazuko, the daughter of Father's older brother, and her Tokyo University professor husband. Mother had last seen Kazuko when she stayed in Ishii Village for several months just after marrying Father. But Kazuko had been a very young girl then. Once down on the pier, Mother wasn't sure at all who to look for. Then, we heard a voice ring out, "Auntie!" It was Kazuko with her scholarly-looking husband. They took us to a hotel in Tokyo. I remember it was a Japanese-style inn but have no idea where in the city it was. For the next couple of days, Kazuko showed us around Tokyo. The only places I remember visiting were the Mitsukoshi Department Store on the Ginza and Yasukuni Shrine. I probably remember Mitsukoshi because I was so impressed: I had not realized that there could be such a huge store, much bigger than the Emporium on Market Street in San Francisco. The shrine had no particular meaning to me then, except that it was the first real Shinto shrine and the biggest wooden structure I had ever seen. How would I have ever known that I would almost end up being enshrined there among the spirits of those who fought and died for the country?

On our fourth day in Japan, Mother and I took a special express train from Tokyo to Osaka. Called the *Tsubame* (Swallow), it was the fastest train in Japan at the time. It took eight hours to cover the distance of about 350 miles. Today, the super express *Shinkansen*, running between the two metropolises on new tracks laid in time for the 1964 Olympics held in Japan, takes no more than three hours. And Japan's engineers promise that the travel time eventually will be cut to one hour with magnetically levitated super trains.

From Osaka, we traveled by ferryboat across the Inland Sea to Matsuyama. For the overnight trip on the 2,000-ton vessel, we again became third class passengers, this time sleeping in blankets laid on the floor Japanese style instead of in bunk beds. As dawn came, Mother took me up on deck, and, oh, what a view! I marveled at the beautiful scenery all around me of small islands floating on the calm sea. There were small fishing boats in shapes I had never seen. They looked "Oriental," I thought. The ferry finally came to rest alongside a floating dock and we were met there by the Nishiokas — Mother's oldest sister, Yoshie, and her businessman husband. I later learned that the dock was in the port of Takahama, an area within the city limits of Matsuyama. It was where I would spend a good deal of my life from that point forward. The Nishiokas took us on by streetcar (my first experience) to Matsuyama City Station, from where it was a ten-minute walk to the Nishioka home.

Several generations of the Imamura clan lived in a house on an estate rather large by the Japanese standard in Ishii Village outside Matsuyama. They also owned a house in the city that the family members used when they came into the city. Mother and I were to live in the city house, but because it needed repairs we stayed with the Nishiokas for several weeks.

Like the Sakuyama family in San Francisco, the Nishiokas had four girls; the second oldest, Ikuko, was my age. All four of the girls seemed to shy away from me and I soon found out why. It was customary in Japan in those days for boys to have their hair cropped very short, their heads basically shaven. All boys wore school uniforms with short, upright collars around their necks and golden buttons down the front. The uniforms were light gray in color from June 1 through September 30 and black for the rest of the year. Boys also wore military-style caps. Well, there I was with my long hair, just like any other American school kid. And when I arrived in Matsuyama, I wore a suit with a necktie. Maybe a few boys of rich families in big cities like Tokyo dressed like that, but this was simply not done in a rural city like Matsuyama. Even when I wore just a shirt or a sweater, people stared at me because of my long hair.

Both the Nishioka home and the house in Yanai-machi into which Mother and I were to move were in the same school district. So Mother went to Bancho Elementary School to consult with the principal. She explained that I had officially finished fourth grade in a San Francisco public school and had started fifth grade, although my age would place me in the fourth grade in the Japanese system. Surprisingly, at first the principal said that I could start as a fifth grader if Mother and I wanted it that way. After learning that I had completed only the third grade materials at *Kimmon Gakuen*, however, his advice was for me to join the fourth grade. For one thing, starting at the fifth grade would give me only two years to prepare for the entrance exams for secondary school. Mother wanted me to go on to Matsuyama Middle School, the best boys' school in the area, and Father's alma mater. Of course, I wanted to go there too. So, of course, we followed the principal's advice.

Although the official school year in Japan begins on April 1 and ends on March 31, schools do not actually open until about a week into April. In Japan, the academic year for elementary and secondary schools is divided into three semesters, or trimesters, and the first day of each semester is spent on ceremonial functions. Mother took me to Bancho Elementary School and left me with Miss Tatsukawa, a pretty, young lady who was to be my class teacher. Miss Tatsukawa asked me many questions about my past life until the siren signaled the call for everyone to assemble in the auditorium.

Bancho Elementary School had six grades with three classes in each grade, and each class had about 50 pupils. So the total number of pupils at Bancho Elementary must have been about 900. When I appeared in the auditorium, all 900 of them stared at me. Since all the teachers were there too, the kids behaved politely but they were obviously very, very curious. They had never seen a little suited gentleman with combed long hair.

The first event of the opening ceremony was the singing of the national anthem, the *Kimigayo*. Because I had learned *Kimigayo* at *Kimmon Gakuen*, I had no trouble singing along with the others. Next, the principal went to the back of the raised platform and took a deep bow. I noticed for the first time that there was a shrine-like fixture on the wall, with wooden doors to pull open left and right. The principal opened the doors. There appeared two oval-shaped portraits of the Emperor and the Empress, much like the ones I saw in some of my friends' houses in San Francisco. The head teacher, who was serving as master of ceremonies, ordered, *"Saikeirei"* (Deepest Bow). We all hung our heads very low for about five seconds until the MC ordered us to raise our heads.

Then the principal came forward and stood erect in front of a small table, on which was an oblong wooden box. He bowed low before the box and then opened it. He took out a neatly folded piece of Japanese rice paper. When he unfolded it, it took his full arm's length to hold it open. It was the Imperial Rescript on Education, supposedly written by Emperor Meiji and promulgated in 1890. It was read aloud by the head of all educational institutions at each year's opening ceremony, and on some special holidays such as the Emperor's Birthday. The Rescript's content emphasized the necessity of obedience to parents, love for the country, and harmony among brothers, sisters and friends, among other things. At the time of its promulgation, Japan was entering the third decade of its contact with the outside world, which had followed three centuries of total isolation. Japan's School Law was adopted in 1872 and schooling was made compulsory through the sixth grade. Public education needed directions, thus the Rescript.

The Rescript was written in Japanese, of course, but its language was somewhat archaic. Some of its vocabulary items were reserved for use exclusively by the Royalty. Principal Tomihisa started reading very slowly and deliberately, with a highly exaggerated intonation pattern. As soon as the reading started, I heard some giggles from the back of the auditorium where the children in the lower grades sat. But I was more awe-struck than amused by the strange situation. Principal Tomihisa was a very solemn person. (I don't think I ever saw him smile during my three years at Bancho.) Here he was, reading aloud, dead seriously and in an exaggerated manner, something I didn't quite understand. The teachers were lined up on both sides of the room, bowing their heads slightly and looking very serious. For the upper-grade pupils standing in the front half of the room, this was the umptieth time to listen to this. It was perhaps more boring than amusing for them. The reading couldn't have lasted much longer than five minutes, but it seemed very long to me. Finishing the reading, the principal carefully folded the paper, put it back into the wooden box, put the lid back on, took a step back and made another deep bow. He then turned around and closed the doors on the royal portraits. The whole room took another deep bow.

The fact that the portraits of the Emperor and Empress were displayed to us while the Rescript was read probably meant that we were supposed to imagine the presence of the imperial couple. The principal's voice was supposed to be heard as His voice. Now that the Rescript was back in the box and the doors to the portraits closed, the imperial couple was to have left the scene. The Japanese are pretty good at these things – one only sees what one is supposed to see and doesn't see what one is not supposed to see. Go to a Japanese *bunraku* puppet show. The puppet handlers, who do their job on stage, are dressed all in black from head to toe. Only their eyes are not covered. At first, one cannot help but notice their movements. But as the show progresses, one's mind concentrates on the puppets and one does not notice the handlers at all. Returning to the table on the platform and clearing his throat, Principal Tomihisa began his own talk. I think it was a usual speech for such occasions, full of typical advice for school children – keep in good health, study hard, etc. I hardly remember anything he said, because my mind was occupied with thoughts of the strange ceremony I had just witnessed. What did the Rescript mean? Why all the formality? Why such seriousness? What was the purpose of this whole event anyway?

That was it for that occasion. But during the recess hours that first day and the next few days, I was the object of attention, and a magnet for my curious classmates. I was quizzed thoroughly. They wanted to know if my parents were Japanese or Americans, why I spoke Japanese if I was born and brought up in America, if I really spoke English, etc., etc. There were also a great many demands that I say something in English.

The three classes at each grade level at Bancho were named *"Tsuki"* (Moon), *"Yuki"* (Snow) and *"Hana"* (Flower). I was placed in 4-*Hana* under Miss Tatsukawa. There were about 50 pupils, about half boys and half girls. The boys were seated on one side of the classroom and the girls on the other half. (This was the usual seating arrangement in most schools until after World War II.) There is an old Confucian saying, "Boys and girls do not share seats after age seven." Actually, Bancho attempted to separate the fifth grade boys and girls. But, because there were roughly 150 pupils, the best the school could do was make one boys' class, one girls' class and one mixed class. In fifth grade, I was placed in 5-*Tsuki*, the all boys' class.

We can't say that the Japanese were undernourished in those days, but the menu for the average family consisted of lots of rice, vegetables and modest amounts of fish. Chicken was not a rarity on the dinner table, but pork and beef were considered luxuries. Children who drank milk were far fewer than those who couldn't afford it.

The first period of the first day of class was Reading. From the brand new satchel hung on one side of the desk, I pulled out the *Kokugo* (national language) textbook Mother had bought for me. It looked exactly the same as the ones we used at *Kimmon Gakuen*, except that this one said "Book 4" on the cover. In Lesson 1, there were some *kanji* (Chinese characters) I never saw before. But after Miss Tatsukawa gave the lesson a once-over model reading, I knew all the words. When you already understand the meaning of the word when you hear it, then it is fairly easy to be able to read it. *Kokugo* is not going to give me much trouble, I thought to myself. The next period, the class moved to the auditorium, which doubled as the music room. There was a grand piano that looked brand new. Mrs. Ito, the music teacher, said that we were going to review some of the songs the pupils learned in Grade Three. Now, I was in trouble. We didn't have any music lessons at *Kimmon Gakuen*, so I didn't know any of the songs. As they started singing, I had the textbook open but it was no use. I opened and shut my mouth pretending to sing with the class but using no voice. But when some of the songs were sung for the second time, I was able to sing along a bit. It was then that I realized that I had a pretty good ear for music. I can usually remember a melody after hearing it just once. The lyrics in the school text were simple and easy to understand. But a part of one song went,

"*Iraka no nami to, kumo no nami*"

Now, *nami* is wave, *kumo* is cloud. That I knew. But what was *iraka*? When I went home and asked Mother, she explained to me that that meant roof tiles, for which the usual word is *kawara*. "Why call it *iraka* in the song, then?" I asked. Mother couldn't quite explain it to me.

The third period of the day was Science and the fourth Arithmetic. Science was taught for the first time to 4th graders. It was as new a course for the rest of the class as it was for me. So no problem. Arithmetic I never liked. But since I had had it at Raphael Weill and Mother had helped me a lot on it at home, it didn't seem so hard. Then lunch. At Raphael Weill, we used the school cafeteria. We ordered what we wanted to eat, mostly spaghetti in my case. Following the Japanese custom, Mother had packed me a box lunch. Pupils brought aluminum lunch boxes with them to school. The boxes were about 4 x 7 x 1.5 inches. Usually about three fourths of the box was packed with rice. The rest of the space was filled with vegetables, fish and other small tidbits. When lunchtime came, a few pupils, on a rotation system from day to day, went to the custodian's room and brought kettles of tea to the classroom. Sitting at our own desks, we ate our lunches. The school lunch system was unheard of in those days. After lunch, we all went out to the playground and played. That, of course, was the best part of the school day.

The after-lunch class was Physical Education. First, we did a lot of calisthenics. The boys and the girls were separated. The boys' favorite sport was dodge ball and the girls' volleyball. We all did broad jumps and high jumps too. The last class for that day was Ethics. I am not sure what the first lesson was on, but, as I think back, there were more and more lessons on nationalistic themes as the grades progressed. When classes were over, our day at school wasn't finished yet. Again, on a rotation basis, with everyone taking a turn, the pupils swept and mopped our own classrooms. Some of us cleaned the schoolyard. The most hated task was cleaning the school toilets. We had to bring bucket-loads of water and clean the entire inside of each booth. They weren't flush toilets in those days either. Incidentally, the custom of having elementary and secondary students clean school toilets was banned by the Allied Occupation Forces in 1946. It was said that this was to keep young people from being exposed to harmful germs.

Back then, public school children usually got home from school around four P.M. and had plenty of time to play outdoors. Children today are not so lucky. With entrance exams to pass and what not, many, if not most, of them go to cram schools where they study for another hour or more. A fairly large number of them also take private lessons in piano, violin, ballet, etc. They come home for dinner, do their homework or review their next day's lessons and go to bed around ten. High school students who are preparing for entrance exams for colleges often stay up until way past midnight to cram. Families that can afford to do so often hire tutors (usually college students) to help their children in their studies.

A few days after the first day of classes, the other pupils still stared at me but they kept their distance. I was no longer bothered. Then, one day, I went home after school to find Mother waiting for me at the door of the Nishioka house. She said, "I'll take the school bag for you. Here, you take this money and go to the barber. Be sure to tell the man to give you the same haircut as all the other school boys." I went to the barbershop and told the man exactly what Mother had told me. He said, "Aw, that's too bad. You have such a nice head of hair. But I suppose a school rule is a school rule."

On my way home from the barbershop, I kept rubbing my head with the palm of my hand, because it felt prickly and funny. And the April breeze felt awfully cool on my bare head. When I got home, Mother took one look at my head and burst out laughing. She said it looked like a blue melon. Then she took me into the room the Nishiokas were letting us use and said, "Try this on." It was my brand new school uniform. I put it on and turned toward Mother. She said, "Now you look like any other kid on the block." Hearing the commotion, a couple of the Nishioka girls asked if they could come in. They took one look at me and laughed their heads off. "You're not Shigeo-san anymore." When I went to school the next morning, nobody seemed to notice anything about me. Some of the girls said, "Oooh, you had your hair cut," but nobody said anything about my new uniform.

In pre-war Japan, Science and Japanese History were added to the curriculum at the fourth grade level. The first class in History started with what is today considered mere mythology. Then it was taught as historical fact. The first story was about the creation of the Japanese Isles. From high above the clouds in the sky, a god and goddess dipped their spears into the sea and stirred the waters. As they lifted the spears, the droplets from the spears turned into islands, four of them large ones. The god and the goddess had two children; a daughter who later came to be known as the Great Sun Goddess *Amaterasu* and her brother Prince *Susano*. *Susano* was a violent person, who did a great deal of damage to people and animals. One day, Princess *Amaterasu* became so outraged at her brother's behavior that she hid herself in a rocky cave and pulled a great rock in front of it to block the entrance. The world became dark. Many gods and goddesses gathered in front of the cave and begged *Amaterasu* to come out. Finally, the gods and goddesses decided to pull a trick on Princess *Amaterasu*. They began to sing and make merry. Princess *Uzume* danced to a chorus of songs. Overcome by curiosity, *Amaterasu* pulled the rock door slightly open. A prince whose name would translate as "Strong Arm" pulled the door wide open and pulled *Amaterasu* out in the open. The sun suddenly reappeared and the world became bright again, restoring life to normal.

All this is supposedly symbolic. The forming of the isles from the water droplets represents the breaking away of the Japanese Isles from the main Asian Continent. As far back as it can be geologically traced, at least the islands now known as Russia's Sakhalin and the southern Japanese island of Kyushu were directly connected to, or were part of, the Continent. The myths go on. The additional stories are thought to be connected to the various internal conflicts and tribal battles of the Continent.

One day, Princess *Amaterasu* looked down at the islands from above and said to her son, Prince *Amenouzume*, "Those islands are beautiful and fertile. Go, son, and rule them." So the son descended on the large western isle now known as Kyushu, fought his way eastward with his army through the present Seto Inland Sea area until he reached the general area now known as Nara. There he faced his last but strongest enemy. As he was fought into a tight spot, a golden bird flew down from heaven and alighted atop his bow. Suddenly, the clouds parted and the bright sun shone on the bird. The golden bird glistened so much that it dazzled away the enemy. Thus Prince *Amenouzume* cleared the land of foes, named the region Yamato and ascended the throne to become the first emperor. As Emperor, he was known as *Jimmu*. Some archeologists confirm the story of an eastward invasion and the establishment of the first capital in the general Nara area. Others argue that the first capital was set up in Northern Kyushu, where the army first landed. Recent archeological findings are producing evidence to support these hypotheses, but nothing is definite yet.

All this was supposed to have taken place in the late B.C. era. The myths seemed to indicate that the Japanese Isles were first sparsely populated by aborigines, who were invaded by people from the continent, either Chinese, Koreans or both, with unification into one loose-knit nation following. Looking back on what I was taught, it becomes obvious that this was an attempt by the government to indoctrinate the nation's children to believe that Japan was a divine nation of chosen people. This led to the belief that the then emperor, known to the Westerners as *Hirohito*, was the 126th generation of a direct hereditary, divine monarchy. My tender ten-year-old mind took in all this. I began to understand and appreciate the solemnity of the opening ceremony. The newspapers and the radio of the day were reporting that the Japanese army was in China for a sacred war, trying to bring peace and prosperity for all the peoples of Asia. I began to believe in all that too.

When Mother and I returned to Matsuyama, the Imperial Army was already in China. The Kwantung Army, as the corps was called, was there purportedly to protect Japanese assets, especially in Northern China, the location of the Manchurian Railway, which was built and owned by the Japanese government. The protection, we were told, was necessary to prevent the damage that might be caused by the warring Chinese military factions.

Domestically, Japan had been suffering economic depression since the early 1920s, as part of the aftermath of World War I. Then came the second punch with the Great Depression of the United States in 1929. On the world stage, Japan was humiliated at the London Conference on Naval Limitation, where Japan had to agree to a treaty limiting the size of the Japanese navy to less than 70% of those of the other major naval powers, Britain and the United States. To make a long story short, these and other factors gave rise to popular dissatisfaction with the civilian government and spurred the military to seize domestic political power.

While China was far from politically united as a nation, there was a widespread anti-Japanese sentiment among its people. The Chinese central government announced a confiscation of all Japanese assets in that country. This heightened a sense of crisis among the leaders of the Kwantung Army. They secretly planned to take over Northern China. In September 1931, Chief of the General Staff Kanji Ishihara ordered demolition of the roadbed of the Southern Manchurian Railways on the outskirts of Mukden, the provincial capital. He blamed the incident on the Chinese and used it as an excuse for military action. This was the beginning of what was known as the Manchurian Incident. Prime Minister Wakatsuki and his cabinet attempted to contain the conflict, but the Kwantung Army ignored the government's wishes. Seeing that the sentiment of the Japanese people was behind the army, Wakatsuki resigned and Premier Inukai, a rightist, took his place. It took no time for the Kwantung Army to occupy most of Northern China. In March 1932, the "independence" of Manchuria — the five provinces of Northern China — was declared. A puppet government was set up by the Japanese, using the then stateless Pu Yi, the last emperor of the Ch'ing dynasty, as its emperor.

I relate these stories only to show how fast domestic and international events moved in the early 1930s. And all during this period there was an intensification of government propaganda with militaristic and ultranationalistic aims. There were slogans, posters, songs and movies, for both children and adults; everything was aimed at extolling the emperor and the military. Anyone saying, writing or doing things that went against this trend was arrested and punished. At about this time, some Western nations, with the leadership of the United States, expressed publicly their displeasure with the actions of Japan on the Continent. They demanded an "Open Door Policy" for China, and that Japan coordinate with other nations on economic and diplomatic policies toward China. In retrospect, I think the Japanese leaders took this not only as an interference with national policies, but also as an intrusion into Asian solidarity and independence. Very soon, anti-American and anti-British slogans surfaced in Japan.

As war clouds gathered over Manchuria, troops from regiments and divisions from all over Japan were mobilized. The 22nd Infantry Regiment of Matsuyama was no exception. Usually early in the morning, when there was little traffic, troops left the south gate of the regiment compound and marched to Matsuyama Railway Station to board the trains which took them to the port of departure. The people of Matsuyama, including the children, lined up on the sidewalks to see them off. Some of the spectators were seeing off their fathers, sons or brothers. A few of them tried to walk along with the troops but were pulled away by the military police. No personal emotions were to be displayed in public. No sorrow of parting was allowed. Those days, people had confidence in the military strength of the country. After all, only a few decades before, Japan had defeated China and Russia, two of the world's great military powers. At least on the surface, there was little sorrow in sending off the men. People shouted, "*Banzai, banzai* (Hooray, hooray)!" as they waved their hands or small rising sun flags. Troop departures like this from the Matsuyama Regiment continued through the war.

After about a month's stay with the Nishiokas, Mother and I moved into the Yanai-machi house. Father returned to Matsuyama from San Francisco in the summer of 1933. I remember Mother scolding him for not bringing back anything with him from the Cedar Avenue house. She also complained about the small sum of money he brought back with him. He probably drank away some of his earnings while living by himself for a year. Father seemed a bit surprised to see me looking as good as I did. I was no longer the thin, pale weakling he used to know. I wasn't the American kid he knew before either. I needed no coaxing in speaking highly of the nation's military strength and the nobility of the Japanese people. Father was also surprised at how the country itself had changed during the eleven years he had been gone. The rise of nationalism and militarism was quite obvious to him — in the newspapers, on the radio and in everyday topics of conversation. Although a cease-fire was put into place in China in May of that year, the Kwantung Army was still in Manchuria, "seeking to counter Chinese aggression."

I have never been a studious type, but I had to try pretty hard during the fourth grade year to catch up with my classmates. In those days in Japan, about 10% of the students in one class were given the title *"yuto-sei"* (honor students) and about another 5% the title *"karyo-sei"* (semi-honor students) at the end of each school year. I was made one of the semi-honor students at the end of the fifth and sixth grades. As the graduation from Bancho School approached, I had to brace myself and prepare for the entrance examination for the next step.

When schooling was made compulsory for all Japanese children in 1872, school was required through Grade Six. By 1935, when I was to leave elementary school, an additional two-year higher elementary education was also obligatory. At that point, however, pupils were given choices. Boys could advance into a middle school or one of the commercial, technical or agricultural vocational schools. Girls could attend a five or four year girls' high school or a vocational school. In any case, applicants had to pass entrance exams. Those who failed to pass the exams for the special schools had to attend the higher elementary school. Those who failed but who wanted to try again could wait until the next year.

Most large cities had several boys' middle schools and girls' high schools as well as vocational schools. However, the academic hierarchy was quite clear, and the vocational schools were usually easier to get into. Very often only one boys' middle school and one girls' high school had the highest rank – they were, of course, the hardest to get into. (Boys and girls were completely separated after elementary school, except at a few of the most exclusive private schools in the major cities.) Matsuyama Middle School was the best school for boys in that area. My parents very much wanted me to go there, but they were a bit unsure that I could pass the entrance exams. Mr. Sasaki, who took over our class from Miss Tatsukawa when she decided to quit teaching and get married at the end of my fourth grade year, was also a bit reluctant to let me take the exams. In the end, though, he encouraged me to try it and, should I fail, go for the second ranked Hokuyo Middle School. I took the exams at Matsuyama Middle School and, luckily, I passed.

One final story about my first days in Matsuyama, in some ways perhaps the most important story from those days: A few months after our arrival in Matsuyama in 1932, a Mr. Ichiro Yamauchi came knocking on our Yanai-machi door. He introduced himself as a teacher of English and music at Matsuyama Middle School. He had heard that a child named Shigeo Imamura had come to Matsuyama from America, spoke fluent English and was attending Bancho Elementary School. He told Mother that if I didn't keep using English I would lose it altogether, and that that would be a shame. He said he would be glad to introduce me to an American family living in Matsuyama, and told us that the family had expressed their willingness to let me come and visit them once a week. Mother and I gladly accepted the offer. The following Sunday, Mr. Yamauchi took me to the Gulick home, which was right across from Bancho Elementary School.

The Reverend Dr. Leeds Gulick was a Methodist missionary, perhaps in his mid-forties. His wife was a kind lady who treated me just like another member of her family. The oldest child was a son named Merle (later known by his middle name, Lewis). He had two sisters. Merle was ten years old too, but much taller than me. We became good friends. We played together almost every Sunday from then on. Sometimes we climbed Castle Hill in the center of the city. It is about a 400-foot high hill, on top of which stood Matsuyama Castle, a typical Japanese castle built by a feudal lord more than 450 years ago. There wasn't any particular reason to go up the hill, except to watch the Russo-Japanese War era cannon go off (firing a blank, of course), signaling noon to the citizens below. My visits with the Gulicks went on for about ten years until the Gulicks had to be evacuated to Kobe because of impending war with the United States.

A few months after I started going to the Gulicks', I was persuaded to join the vespers service held by the Reverend Gulick every Sunday evening. The sermon, the singing of hymns and the after-service chats were all conducted in English. Some of the Japanese congregants were there because they were believers, others because they wanted to listen to and speak English. I was not a believer; I still am not. But I thought some of the things the Reverend said made good sense, and I loved to sing the hymns. By the way, Leeds Gulick was the third generation of Gulicks to serve as missionaries in Japan. In fact his father, I understand, was the very person who initiated the goodwill doll exchange between the United States and Japan that I was part of as a pupil at *Kimmon Gakuen* in San Francisco.

Here I was, a boy born and bred in America, back in Japan, being more Japanized by the month, and yet attentively listening to Christian sermons by an American missionary and feeling no contradiction whatsoever. One might say, "Well, a child is a child." Maybe so. One fact is that, had it not been for Mr. Yamauchi and the Gulicks, I probably wouldn't have retained enough of my English to be writing this story.

Chapter 3

MATSUYAMA

Botchan

Matsuyama Middle School

The Wider World: Militarism Triumphant in Japan

The Japanese army continued its aggression in Northern China, eventually succeeding in establishing the Japanese puppet state of Manchuria in 1932. In the same year, Japanese marines clashed with Chinese troops in Shanghai. With superior air control, it was victory after victory for Japan. Or so it seemed, because the Imperial Headquarters never disclosed unfavorable battle results, as we learned after the war. This progressive military momentum heightened the people's confidence in the nation's might, which, in turn, caused a rapid rise of nationalistic sentiment. Not only did newspapers splash the news of these victories across their front pages, but novels were written and movies produced extolling our brave soldiers. Biographies of old war heroes from the Sino- and Russo-Japanese wars were popular. Artists even produced paintings of war fronts, paratroopers and combat airplanes. Symphonic music gradually gave way to brass bands and military music. Particularly popular were pieces such as "The Battleship March" and "The Patriotic March."

On the other hand, in the post-World War I period of the 1920s and early 1930s, Japanese statesmen made efforts to accommodate the Western powers by signing arms limitation treaties. Notably the treaties signed in Washington, D.C. (1921, 1922) and in London (1930) *severely limited Japanese naval power. These and some other events put right-wing extremists on the offensive. There were several attempts to assassinate top conservative politicians, culminating in the coup of February 26, 1936, during which about 1,500 soldiers in Tokyo led by radical young officers attacked and occupied the Prime Minister's residence, the Tokyo Metropolitan Police Headquarters, etc. Although the coup failed and Prime Minister Okada survived, Finance Minister Takahashi and the Lord Privy Seal Saito were assassinated.*

In February of 1936, I was still in my first year at Matsuyama Middle School. I remember the large photographs that appeared on the front pages of newspapers. One showed soldiers in overcoats huddled together on the snow-covered ground. Another depicted a column of soldiers marching back to their barracks. It took four days for the military authorities to quell the coup. I suppose I was too young to really know what was going on, but I do remember having a grave feeling that something very critical was taking place in my country. By the way, rumors circulated years later that most, if not all, of the men who took part in the coup were sent to the battle fronts in China and eventually killed in combat. They could not be court-martialed, since they were simply following the orders of their superiors.

According to the history books, there was a sudden surge in exports, especially textiles, from Japan in the early 1930s. On the other hand, Japan was heavily dependent on the import of items such as cotton, petroleum, scrap iron and machine tools. Western nations, which had previously dominated the textile markets, naturally became increasingly wary of the Japanese. In addition, the Western powers, which had been continually warning Japan since the Nine Nation Pact of 1922 to respect the autonomy of Nationalist China and to maintain equal trading opportunities for all nations in that country, had become increasingly suspicious of Japan's motives.

In 1934, Japan broke away from the Washington Treaty on Naval Limitation and began to move rapidly toward building a powerful naval fleet. In February of 1937, there was a particularly severe clash between the Japanese and Chinese armies. As one result of that, the then Prime Minister Konoe attempted to curb the expansion of hostilities, but failed. The front-line army continued to advance. Later in the same year, the two factions that had been warring against each other for years, the Chinese Nationalists (Kuomintang) led by Chiang Kai-shek and the Communists led by Mao Tse-tung, declared an alliance to fight against the Japanese. Toward the end of that year, the Konoe Cabinet declared a "New Order for East Asia" policy, which featured the Nationalist Chinese, Manchuria and Japan as equal partners. This implied that Japan was going to ignore the other Chinese factions and establish a new government under Japan's influence.

Schools at all levels in Japan could not be and were not immune to the rising national and international tensions. Young children were told to finish breakfast early, assemble at certain spots in their neighborhood and march to school in formation. Secondary school boys were made to wear military-style leggings when coming to school and to salute any military officers they might pass on their way. School rules were tightened and new rules added. Looking back on those days, I recall some teachers who scrupulously avoided talking about the Imperial Family, the war on the Continent or anything to do with the military. They must have been liberals. The others, however, seemed quite willingly to go along with the tide of the time. In short, schools became semi-army camps, in form and in atmosphere.

Education in Pre-War Japan

As mentioned in the previous chapter, boys and girls went to separate schools for secondary education in pre-war Japan. And girls had to consider themselves lucky if their families allowed them to go beyond grade school. Only a very, very few women went on to higher education. And compared to today, not even many boys continued their education beyond what was required. Since the school system was rather complicated, let us take a few simplified, fictitious examples.

Ichiro was the top honor student at his elementary school. He had no trouble entering the best middle school in town, where he was again an honor student. While most students took five years to finish middle school, Ichiro succeeded in passing the entrance examination to high school at the end of his fourth year. A high school in pre-war Japan, called "Koto-gakko," was a three-year institution dedicated solely to preparing students to pass university entrance exams. It attracted only the brightest. Each koto-gakko had two divisions: liberal arts and science. Ichiro elected liberal arts. He still stood at the top of his class and passed the exams for Tokyo University, the top institution of higher learning in the nation. He majored in political science and graduated in three years.

Jiro made it all the way up through middle school with Ichiro. Since his grades were not as good as Ichiro's, he decided to settle for a private college instead of trying for a high school. He succeeded in entering a private university in Tokyo and majored in Economics.

Saburo was a semi-honor student in elementary school. Luckily he made it into a middle school, where he was at about the middle of his class scholastically. He knew he was not cut out to enter high school, so he went on to a local commercial college, a three-year institution like a high school. He majored in Business Administration.

Shiro did pretty well in elementary school but was not anywhere near the honor roll. He always wanted to be a teacher because both of his parents were teachers. He went on to higher elementary school for two years, then to the two-year prep course for normal school, and then finished the three-year normal school.

Of course, many boys quit school after finishing higher elementary, middle or vocational school and started to work. Whether they went to school or worked, all Japanese males were obliged to take a physical examination given by the local draft board at age 20. Those who passed were drafted into military service, but those enrolled in higher education were given deferments until graduation. More about military service later.

Matsuyama Middle School saw its first class of students graduate in 1879. Since then, it has produced a large number of national leaders in the fields of government, politics, education, business, motion pictures, etc. The school was made particularly famous through a novel written by a scholar-turned-novelist Kinnosuke Natsume. Natsume, better known by his pen name *Soseki*, taught at Matsuyama Middle School from 1895 to 1896. His novel *"Botchan"* is based on his experiences living in Matsuyama and teaching English at the school. The novel is full of anecdotes about students and colleagues

– some quite humorous and others redolent of Soseki's disdain for his surroundings. Evidently, he did not find the local character simpatico. That is probably why he left Matsuyama after only one year. At any rate, *Botchan* is still widely read and has been made into a movie.

According to my Japanese-English dictionary, *"Botchan"* is an honorific term used for someone else's son. It is also translated as "sonny," "greenhorn" and "youngbuck." A Tokyo University graduate, Soseki probably intended to depict himself as a naive young teacher, brought up with his nose buried in books, someone who had never learned to get along with people. Despite his unflattering comments about Matsuyama, the locals are grateful that Soseki made their city and the school so famous.

Matsuyama Middle School is *Matsuyama Chugakko* in Japanese, which for everyday use is shortened to *Matsuchu.* Unlike my first days at Bancho School, I hardly remember anything about my first days at *Matsuchu.* I remember, though, how proud I was to wear the *Matsuchu* uniform, especially the hat. Right above its brim, my military style cap sported a bronze pin with the Chinese character *Chu* for *Chugakko*, and it was trimmed with a white band. Anyone seeing me, even from afar, could tell that I was a *Matsuchu* student.

Matsuchu was located at least twice as far as from my home as Bancho Elementary School. It took me 20 to 25 minutes to get there. On the way to school, I had to walk the length of *Okaido*, the main shopping street of Matsuyama. There, students going to the Prefectural Girls' High School and the private Saibi Girls' School walked in the opposite direction. The ten-minute walk along *Okaido* was a real pleasure. It must have been so for the girls, too. As many of them stole glances at us as we did at them. Among the girls I passed every day were some of my classmates from Bancho. In the beginning, we would exchange broad smiles, but new self-consciousness caught up with us: *Hey, we're middle school and girls' high school students now. We're not supposed to do that kind of thing anymore.*

As a matter of fact, fraternization between secondary school male and female students was strictly forbidden by school rules. School rules applied to many other things too. Students had to wear uniforms, and each school had its own style and color of uniform. For girls, the skirts had to have a certain number of pleats and had to be a certain number of centimeters below the knee. Shoe styles were prescribed as well, and for physical education we wore a particular type of canvas shoes. There were rules, too, for the school bags we carried, and for how they were to be carried: with the strap on one shoulder and the bag itself on the back hip. I think it was at the beginning of my fourth year at *Matsuchu* that the rules were tweaked: we had to have the strap on the right shoulder on our way to school and on the left shoulder on the way home. We thought the school authorities were going a bit too far on this, but we were told that it was for the balanced growth of our young bodies.

We were strictly forbidden to enter movie theaters or other entertainment establishments. Once or twice a year, we were allowed to go and see movies recommended by the Ministry of Education or other educational or cultural institutions. We were not supposed to go into restaurants or coffee shops unless accompanied by our parents. Smoking and drinking were totally out of the question. Of course our hair was cropped short. Uniformity and conformity, in appearance and behavior, were the thing. These rules got increasingly stricter as Japan approached and entered World War II.

English classes started the first year of secondary school. You can imagine that my experiences with English were rather unusual. In the second or third week of the first trimester of the first year, Mr. Kashiwagi, our algebra teacher, turned to me in the middle of his lecture and said, "Imamura, I hear you came back from America. Can you still speak English? Ah, so. OK, come on up here. Now, face the class and recite the story of *Momotaro* (a Japanese fairy tale) in English." I had to comply. After I was through, he said, "I didn't understand a word you said, but it sounded good."

In *Matsuchu's* official English classes, we began with pronunciation. The teacher taught us how to pronounce each vowel and consonant, along with the phonetic symbol for each of these. We then moved on to reading the phonetic symbols of some vocabulary items, then to writing some words in phonetic symbols the teacher read to us. One day, when we reached this last stage, we were given a quiz. Among the words the teacher read off was a word which sounded to me like "ber." Now, wait a minute, I thought. There is no such word in English. So, I raised my hand and said, "Excuse me, sir, but would you kindly repeat that word facing my way?" He blushed but did comply. Sure enough, the shape of his mouth for the last consonant was formed to produce the sound "r." So, I wrote down the symbols for "ber." When we got our papers back the next week, I found the symbols for that word crossed off as wrong. Obviously, my guess that he was trying to pronounce "bell" was correct. Did I protest? Oh, no, not in a Japanese school ... probably not even today.

Otherwise, I had no trouble getting all "As" in my English classes, even without any preparation. But when we started English grammar in the third year, it was a different story altogether. Of course, I had never studied English grammar at Raphael Weill grade school in San Francisco. Having picked up both Japanese and English the "natural" way, I had no need to know grammar to understand English, put English into Japanese, or vice versa. The grammar lessons turned me off and I didn't study. It was a mistake: I got "Bs" and "Cs" for that course all the way through my last year at *Matsuchu*.

Another class new to the *Matsuchu* students was Martial Arts. We had to take an hour of *judo* or *kendo* (Japanese fencing) every other week. The *judo-kendo* class went on for two years, and at the end of that period we had to choose one or the other to continue for the next three years. During the middle school years, most of the students interested enough to join the *judo* or *kendo* club reached the black-belt stage before graduating. But I was not among them. We practiced *kendo* in our phys ed outfits of long-sleeved undershirts and long, white trousers. We had to purchase special pads and protectors and keep them at school. For *judo*, we had to have our own *judo* outfits. Being short, I was at a disadvantage in both, especially in *kendo*, where even though the head gear protects the face and the top and the sides of the head, the back of the head is exposed. The swords used in *kendo* are made of bamboo slits, tied together with leather cords to form a roundish surface. When a tall opponent struck the top of my head, the pliable sword would bend to hit the back of my head. It hurt.

Another new subject for us was Military Training. Every boys' secondary school had retired army officers and non-commissioned officers on the faculty. In the first year we had mostly basic training:

marching, handling of the rifle and the like. The rifles we used were Model 38 Infantry Rifles, the same ones used by the army. The training was very strict and in compliance with army regulations. On rainy days, the officers lectured to us in classrooms on bits of military history and strategies. We didn't necessarily like the training, but we all took it seriously as a matter of course. Speaking out against it in any way would have been interpreted as a traitorous act. In our fifth year, we were marched about an hour to the Matsuyama Regiment's shooting range to practice shooting with real bullets. We also took part in a full-day maneuver involving all the senior students from all the boys' secondary schools in the city. The thousands of students were separated into the Red Force and the White Force to engage in mock battles. When the "battles" concluded, we assembled at the Regiment's parade ground for a review by the Regiment commander. Thus, the military spirit was well ingrained into us by the end of secondary education.

Once drafted into the army, secondary school graduates were promoted a little faster than those with only compulsory education. Those with college degrees were encouraged to volunteer for officer cadet programs. Such volunteers went through intensive training while rising rapidly through the non-commissioned ranks and, in about a year, were commissioned as second lieutenants. Most college graduates went through this course. I know some did not because becoming an officer inevitably meant a longer term of military service.

Mother brought me to Matsuyama from San Francisco in 1932. Father joined us in 1933. From birth, I was brought up as my parents' only child. One hot summer night in 1934, I somehow woke up in the middle of the night and overheard my parents talking in the kitchen. I was sleepy and was drifting back to sleep when some of their words caught my ears. "Baby." "This place is going to be too small for us." "Can we afford it?" I couldn't suppress my curiosity. I got up and went to the kitchen. "Are you going to have a baby, Mother?" "You'll have a brother or a sister this fall. Are you happy?" Well, I wasn't sure how I felt, but going back to sleep was more important for me at the time.

Takao was born on October 5, 1934. The fifth of October was the eve of the Matsuyama Fall Festival, "*Omatsuri*." Takao was known as the "Omatsuri Boy" for years. He and I were born twelve years apart. The oriental zodiac has an animal assigned to each year, in a twelve-year cycle. Both of us were born in the "Year of Dog." After being the only child in the family for twelve years, it was a strange feeling, somewhat uncomfortable, to have a baby brother. And the big age difference played a role in many later events.

Matsuchu had a music club. While a few students studied piano, violin or other solo musical instruments, the majority of the members of the club were the boys in the brass band. Mr. Yamauchi, who was the teacher who introduced me to the Gulick family in 1932, sought me out shortly after I entered *Matsuchu*, and got me into the club. He suggested that I take up the saxophone, but somehow the trumpet seemed more attractive to me. Back then, students simply didn't buy musical instruments for themselves. They couldn't afford it. *Matsuchu* music club owned a trumpet, a cornet, a trombone, a baritone, a bass, a clarinet, a peti-clarinet, a flute, a piccolo, a snare drum and a drum, as well as the piano in the music room. I wanted the trumpet, but, no, a senior student already had that. I had to settle for the cornet. In a couple of years, I got pretty good. Then my fate called. One day in my third year, one of the military officers assigned to the school called me out of class to tell me, "Imamura, if you can play the cornet, you can play the bugle. From now on, you are the school bugler."

This new assignment had advantages. If I had not been the bugler, I would have been at the tail end of a long marching column. Japanese military tradition always put the tallest at the head of a marching column and the shorter ones at the tail end, probably to have the longer-legged fast walkers set the marching pace. The tail end tended to lag behind, scurry to catch up, lag behind, scurry to catch up. This was very tiring. As the bugler, I was always at the head of the column, keeping a swift but a steady pace. During military maneuvers, my friends went crawling on the ground, falling into trenches, shooting blanks and charging into "enemy" lines. As bugler, all I had to do was to stand by the commanding officer and blow the bugle when needed.

Being the bugler involved another duty, although this was not necessarily an advantage. The send off of soldiers to the front from the Matsuyama Infantry Regiment continued. As years went on, the departures became quite frequent. The very first column of soldiers was led by a mounted officer, followed by a batch of buglers. And the following columns were led by school brass bands. Playing our instruments while marching to the railway station was not an easy thing to do, especially when it happened three or four times a week. But there actually was one advantage. Many of the girls' school students were in the crowds lined up to send the soldiers off. The girls would cheer us as much as they cheered the soldiers, maybe even more. That posed one danger, however, for those of us playing instruments like the trumpet and the cornet. We would be stealing glances to the side at the girls as we played and marched. If the column came to a sudden stop, due to traffic, for example, we would run our horns right into the backs of those in front of us and cut our lips.

Admittedly, the history of the 1920s and 1930s touched upon up to this point is overly simplified. There may be some misinterpretations of events involved also. My personal experiences may not necessarily be set down in strict chronological order either. This is because it is very difficult to trace my failing memories. After all, I am trying to describe what happened to me, how I felt, and what circumstances surrounded me some 50 to 60 years ago. Still, I shall try to continue putting into words as accurately as possible what comes to my mind.

At about my fourth year at *Matsuchu*, a *Hoanden* was built just inside the main gate of the school. The *Hoanden* was a structure about 7 or 8 feet tall and 3 feet wide, shaped like the main pagoda of a Shinto shrine with slanting roofs. The dictionary says *Hoanden* means "Enshrinement Hall." It was used to store the portraits of the Emperor and the Empress, which were brought out to the auditorium to be worshipped on ceremonial occasions. Now, every time we passed through the main gate, coming in or going out, day or night, we were supposed to take our hats off and offer a deep bow towards the *Hoanden*. It went without saying that the deep bow was to be accompanied by a prayer for the long lives of the royal couple and the prosperity of the country. If we used any of the other gates of the school, we were to stop as soon as we were inside the school grounds, face the *Hoanden* and pay our respects. Some students naturally neglected to perform this ritual when they didn't think anyone was watching.

When pupils and students came to school each morning, it was customary for them to leave their belongings in their classrooms and hurry to the playground for the morning assembly. There, each class lined up in double rows, in neat military style. Each homeroom teacher would stand at the head of his/her class. The principal would get on a three-foot high platform and face the students. At the barked command of the head teacher, the principal and the students bowed to each other with a shout of, *"Ohayo gozaimasu"* (Good morning). At *Matsuchu*, the students' morning formation faced east. The Imperial Palace was to our east. The principal made a right about-face, and, at the head teacher's command, "To the Imperial Palace, deep bow!" everyone bowed deeply.

Occasionally, the principal would make some comments, informing us, for example, of the capture of a strategically important point on the battlefront or a significant diplomatic move. And he would end up with words such as, "You must study hard to live up to His Majesty's expectations." One such morning, after the principal finished his talk, Colonel Matsuura, the head army officer assigned to *Matsuchu*, got up on the platform. Clearing his throat, he said, "Some of you are shirking your most important duty in using the school gates. Imamura of Class 4-1 never does. Let him be your model. You may think no one is looking, but the sky has eyes." I was flabbergasted. Now, my friends all around me were 100% Japanese. Could this have meant that, by then, I was 105 % Japanese?

Chapter 4

Ronin

Zentsuji
MATSUYAMA

The Perplexing Years

During my ten years in San Francisco, the Japanese naval training fleet called at the port there on a few occasions. Each time, my parents took me on board one of the ships open to the public. My memory tells me that the ships were of the size and type of what we call frigates today. I marveled at the vigor of the seamen from those ships, who walked the breadth of the city for sightseeing, from the piers on the Bay side all the way to the Ocean side. The fleet band offered concerts at the music dome in Golden Gate Park for a mostly Japanese-American audience. After the concert, the band members and other seamen mixed with the audience for picnics on the park lawn, with the food supplied by the locals.

Whether or not these events had some latent psychological effect on me, specifically on my admiration for Japan and its Navy, I am not sure. As I grew up, Mother kept saying to me, "What do you want to grow up to be, Shigeo? Kids your age always say, I want to be a policeman, a baseball player, a radio announcer or something. You've never said anything like that." I really didn't know. I suppose I was so happy with and excited about my everyday life that I just had no time to think about my future. Even when one of my best friends at *Matsuchu*, Masao Sasaki, passed the exam and went off to the Naval Academy, I had no particular envy for him.

In April, 1939, I was in the fifth and the last year at *Matsuchu*. Some of my classmates had already gone on to the military academies or Matsuyama High School, the prep school. Late that spring, as late as one was able to wait to decide which higher school to go to, I asked my parents if I could go to a private college in Tokyo. Keio University was at the top of my list and Waseda second, but I kept that to myself. It took Father and Mother several days to come back with their answer, "No. …With the war going on like this, Mother could very well be drafted into the Nurse Reserve Corps. Takao is only five years old now. You are needed at home. Sure you can go to college, but go to a college in Matsuyama." That left me with only two choices, Matsuyama High School or Matsuyama Commercial College.

Then, late in July, my friend Masao came home from the Naval Academy for summer vacation. He and I talked a lot and, gradually, I was attracted by the Academy. Or, to be honest, maybe it was Masao's smart cadet uniform that attracted me: the waist-length short jacket with gold bars on the collars for his semi-officer cadet rank and the dagger in a gold-trimmed sheath on his hip. This was the first time in my life that I felt an attraction for a life career. After Masao went back to the Academy, I asked Mother and Father to sit down with me. I told them that I wanted to go to the Naval Academy. After all, the Academy was just across the Seto Inland Sea, less than four hours away by ferry. And the entire cost was paid by the government. Apparently, given my fraternizing with Masao, they had anticipated something like this from me. They gave me an immediate answer, "No, absolutely no. We're not ready to offer your life to His Majesty yet." That was it. Late that fall, the call for Mother to join the Nurse Reserve Corps did come. She was sent to the army divisional hospital in Zentsuji, also on the island of Shikoku but about a three-hour train ride away.

Father, who had worked as a desk clerk for a machine tool factory since his return to Matsuyama, had to quit to take care of Takao and me when Mother left. Poor Father. He had to do all the household work while I was at school. I helped as much as possible, but that wasn't very much because of all the studying I had to do to prepare for the upcoming entrance exams. I had no confidence that I could pass the exams for Matsuyama High School, but Father talked me into trying it, saying, "If you don't make it this time, you can try any other school you like next year." So, in February, 1940 I took the exams — and failed. I should have applied to the other school, Matsuyama Commercial College, which would have been easier, but I didn't. So, I became a *ronin*.

The term *ronin* originated in the feudal era. It applied to a *samurai* (warrior) who was without a lord to serve. When a feudal lord lost a war or was killed in a battle and his territory confiscated, his warriors became *ronin*. Some of them sought employment with new lords, some went into hiding among commoners, others committed suicide in shame. In the modern era, a *ronin* is a student who does not have a school to go to. If a student cannot pass the entrance exams and is waiting for another chance in the following year, he/she is a *ronin*. A college graduate *ronin* is usually one who cannot find a job.

Most of today's *ronin* go to cram schools to prepare for the next year's entrance exams. Every town and city has cram schools. Some are small with only a few students. In major cities, however, some of the cram schools are huge, with thousands of students. They are all privately run, of course. It was said that there were roughly 400,000 high school graduate *ronin* throughout the country in 1992. Tuition at reputable cram schools is very expensive. Some *ronin* cannot afford cram schools and study by themselves at home. I probably couldn't have afforded a cram school if there had been any, but such things were unheard of in my days.

My yearning to go to the Naval Academy was still with me. Had Mother been home, she probably would have objected to it strongly, and Father most likely would have gone along with her. But it was not too hard to convince Father to at least let me try. After all, he had told me that I could try any school if I failed the exams for Matsuyama High. So I studied day and night. Only in mid-afternoon I would take Takao out for a little exercise. Early on, we just took a walk around the neighborhood, but eventually it became our daily routine to go to Bancho School. I would let Takao play in the sandbox while I ran around the track, broad jumped, high jumped and used the iron bars to build my muscles. The physical exam at the Academy was a very tough one to pass.

Entrance exams were generally held between early February and early March for high schools and colleges, so that the freshman class can start in the new academic year in April. The service academies were exceptions. Their exams were held in November the year before, if I remember correctly. This was probably so the academies could take the cream of the crop before the other institutions grabbed them. It is strange that I don't remember where I went to take the Naval Academy exams, but I passed the physical with no problem at all. Then came the written exams. I found the math test very difficult, and, just as I had thought, I flunked. Just about the only option left to me was Matsuyama Commercial College, so I went back to my daily routine of studying and taking Takao out.

One of those days, I took Takao out a bit further than Bancho School, to the castle moat that surrounded the army regiment compound. As we got there and looked down on the waters of the moat, we saw a school of fish sucking air at the surface. "Look, brother. Look at all those sardines!" Takao suddenly shouted. I put my hand over Takao's mouth to shut him up. At the same time, I looked around to see if anybody was within hearing distance. I felt terribly embarrassed because sardine was the cheapest fish available at the fish market, and I didn't want anyone to think that that was all we ate at home. To five-year-old Takao, any fish was sardine.

Mother came home occasionally on weekends. She told Father and me gruesome war stories she had heard from the hospitalized soldiers — how Japanese troops rounded up Chinese civilians when they overran a village, how they beheaded or bayoneted the civilians to death on the suspicion that they were spies and so on. She also talked about how badly some of her patients were wounded. I particularly remember the case of a man who lost both his arms and legs when he was blown up by a land mine. He needed help doing everything, except sleeping.

This was a long year for me indeed, but 1941 finally came. In February, I took the entrance exams for Matsuyama Commercial College and passed. The name of this school in Japanese was Matsuyama Koto Shogyo Gakko, which translates as Matsuyama Higher Commercial School, but is too long to pronounce even for the Japanese. So it was commonly called *Kosho.* I had finally made it into college.

Chapter 5

Prelude to Glory

MATSUYAMA

College Life

To go back in time a little, what was to be known as World War II had begun back in 1939 with the German invasion of Poland. The Japanese government was at first reluctant to become involved in broader hostilities. It already had its hands full with the goings-on on the Asian Continent. However, as Germany overran Allied territories and occupied Paris, the Japanese army became increasingly belligerent. They were determined to move into Southeast Asia to exploit the area's rich natural resources, even at the risk of provoking the United States. Newspapers were full of defiant editorials. The Navy, we learned later, was more hesitant. They knew the U.S. naval power was greater than their own. In September 1940, Prime Minister Konoe, basically a peace-loving person with a noble ancestry, gave into right-wing pressures and concluded a tripartite military alliance with Germany and Italy, later known as the Axis.

In June of 1941, Germany and the Soviet Union began to battle each other. An Imperial Conference was held in July. The membership of the Imperial Conference consisted of the Emperor, the Prime Minister and his ministers, plus a small number of civilian and military leaders. As a result, the army invasion of Indochina began. All this while, *negotiations between Japan and the U.S. were going on, the U.S. demanding that Japan withdraw its troops to the pre-Manchurian invasion lines and Japan trying to get the U.S. to accept the status quo on the Continent. The negotiations got nowhere. Seeing the Japanese advancement into Indochina, the U.S. turned the threat of an oil embargo against Japan into a reality. This, in turn, incensed Japan's military even more because of the threat of an oil shortage for their war machines. An Imperial Conference was convened again in September, and the conclusion was that war with the Allies was inevitable should the Japan-U.S. negotiations not achieve satisfactory results for Japan by early October. Due to pessimistic forecasts, the Konoe Cabinet resigned in October and General Tojo, the foremost proponent of the "all or nothing" policy, took over.*

*Thus, as I began college life, the air around the world at the time was tense. At home, Japan began to suffer from the lack of raw materials for its industrial and military needs because of the shrinking trade with the West, particularly with the United States. To counteract this situation, Japan began to pressure Southeast Asia for materials such as petroleum, rubber and bauxite (for aluminum). The United States did not condone this, of course, and began to tighten the noose around Japan's neck, in the form of a threat to freeze Japanese assets overseas and an embargo on oil and scrap iron. I think it was about this time that we started hearing the expression, "The menacing threat of the **ABCD** line": the A standing for America, B for Britain, C for China and D for Dutch.*

In Europe, Germany had invaded Poland, and Britain and France declared war against Germany. Closer to home, clashes between Japanese and Russian troops along the Soviet-Manchurian borders were more than just skirmishes. More and more soldiers left Matsuyama Infantry Regiment to fight abroad. More enthusiastic were the citizens lining up on the sidewalks to see them off. It was obvious that the military was gaining power in the running of the country. The Ministers of the Army and the Navy had been generals and admirals ever since the Modern Era of Japan began in 1868, but the prime ministership was in the hands of civilian statesman with very few exceptions. But now, it was General Abe who was Prime Minister. Germany, Italy and Japan seemed closer and closer in alliance against the rest of the world. But even in such circumstances, school life went on more or less normally.

Matsuyama *Kosho* was founded in 1923. It was a relatively new private college. But by the time I was admitted, it had grown to be one of the leading colleges of its kind in the country. Therefore, it was not all that easy to get in. Only one out of 17 applicants succeeded in passing the entrance exams that year. So the 207 of us who attended the opening ceremony were rather proud of ourselves, even if our school did not enjoy as high an academic status as Matsuyama High School. Many of my classmates were from around Matsuyama, but there were others who were from all over Western Japan. Most of the freshmen were a year younger than me because of my one-year experience as a *ronin*.

I had to struggle with classes new to me, such as Introduction to Economics, Business Administration, Bookkeeping, Civil Law and Logic. Quite an emphasis was placed on English classes, due to the assumption that a high percentage of the graduates of a commercial college would work in overseas trade where the use of English was necessary. A second foreign language was obligatory and we had a choice of Chinese, German or French. I chose German. Physical education and military training were also emphasized and the training was tough. I joined the basketball club because I liked the sport, but that was a mistake. I was pretty good at it, but the much taller fellows had me well covered.

We had some interesting characters among the faculty members. Professor Kagawa was an economist by training. I had some economics classes from him, but we were surprised to see him show up at our very first German class. He said, "I was asked by President Tanaka to teach this class because the professor from Germany who was scheduled to teach this class could not get here due to the war situation in Europe. Yes, I learned German in high school and college but that was a long time ago. I will try my best to stay ahead of you, but you must forgive me if I stumble around from time to time." Stumble around he did, perhaps more often than from "time to time." He would wipe the sweat off his forehead and continue on. The teaching was ineffective, but we all liked him because he was so good-natured and humorous. By the way, when we were in our third year at *Kosho*, Professor Kagawa left us for a new teaching job in Taiwan. On his way, the ship he was on was torpedoed and sunk by an American submarine. Everyone on the ship perished.

Professor Takahashi taught us Business English. He was a *haiku* poet by hobby. His poems were *haiku* but without the regular 5-7-5 rhythm. He called them "free-style *haiku*." He would be lecturing along on Business English, suddenly pause, look up at the ceiling and recite a poem. Then he would say something like, "I came up with that one last night as I lay sleeping. What do you think of it?" Not being a particularly poetic type, my usual reaction to his poems was, "Silly, silly." Still, I remember one, which rather struck me. That one translates as, "Wherever you go, you see grass growing." My thoughts went back to my childhood days. There were kids in San Francisco and there were kids at Bancho School. Whichever place I was, kids were kids. That was the thought that came to my mind when I heard Professor Takahashi recite that poem. Much later, as I gained experience of traveling widely internationally, I always remembered the poem and said to myself, "How true."

Then there was Mr. Hoshino, professor of Jurisprudence, who was known for his liberal thinking and sharp wit. Occasionally, he would say something like, "This is what the law says now, but you never know what will happen once 'you know who' takes over," implying General Tojo. These were probably the last days in the pre-World War II period when liberals were still able to make public remarks like this and not be jailed. One late spring afternoon, the whole class of some 200 of us was sitting for his lecture in a large classroom. I was sitting at a desk by the south window, and the warm sun shining in made me very drowsy. Before I knew it, I dozed off. Suddenly, I thought I heard someone calling my name. I opened my eyes to see the professor staring at me. "Imamura, you just had a haircut, didn't you?" True, I did have a haircut the day before. He grinned, turned around and went right back to his lecture. Had he given me a reprimand for sleeping in class, even just a "Stay awake," I would probably have been a bit embarrassed and then forgotten about the incident for the rest of my life. Professor Hoshino became the President of that college shortly after the end of the war.

I had a secret I kept to myself. Masahiro Yoshimatsu, two years my senior at *Matsuchu*, entered Matsuyama *Kosho* and then went on to the Naval Academy. I wanted to do the same thing. I don't remember how I got hold of the application form, but I did. After all, I thought, all expenses at the Academy are government paid. I can save my parents two more years' tuition and the other expenses of attending *Kosho*. They can't be too unhappy about that. I started to fill out the forms thinking I knew how to since I had done it before. When I came to the column to put in my birthday, I noticed the fine print, which said, "Check instructions for age limit." I turned the page back to the instructions, and, "Oh, my gosh!" Applications would be accepted only from those with birthdays on or after November 1, 1922. I was two months overage. My dreams for the Japanese Navy vanished.

Despite the increasing threats of war, far and near, our class was able to enjoy life at *Kosho*, with quite a bit of the taste of the good old days. We had occasional drinking parties, even in the freshman year. The law said drinking was prohibited for those under age 20, but nobody bothered to stop us from drinking, not even the police. Japanese society is rather lax on matters of this kind. Smoking was also against the law for those under 20, but many of my classmates smoked openly. I didn't, because Father was a heavy smoker and I hated the smell of tobacco. Another light side of life at *Kosho* was that, as college students and unlike middle school students, we were allowed to go wherever we wanted: movies, coffee shops, restaurants. We stayed away from bars only because we couldn't afford them.

Then it broke! The year was 1941. Early in the morning of December 8, Father, Takao and I were sitting (on the floor) at our breakfast table. As usual, we were listening to the morning news on the radio. Suddenly, the news was interrupted and a voice broke in. To the best of my memory and my ability to translate, it went, "Here is a special news bulletin. Here is a special news bulletin. The Imperial Navy has entered into a combat situation with the United States at dawn today in the Western Pacific." This was repeated. "*Banzai!*" I jumped up shouting. "We finally did it!" Father sort of half-smiled at me, seemingly in approval. Brother Takao was too young to tell what was going on. The only other thing I remember about that morning is that Father muttered, "It's going to be a long time before Mother comes home." It seems I was 110% Japanese by then.

My second year at *Kosho* began in April 1942. At the end of the first year, I got permission to quit the basketball club. I had come to realize that I was just too short for a sport like that. One of the assigned army officers somehow heard about my quitting the basketball club and approached me at the beginning of the second year. He asked me if I would be interested in organizing a horseback riding club. If I was and I could get about ten students together, he might be able to persuade the army regiment to allow us to practice riding their officers' horses. I asked him if my legs were long enough for me to ride horses. He stepped back, looked me over and said, "Well, I think so." I had never ridden horseback or even thought about it. But then I remembered the beauty of horses from the cowboy movies I used to see — Tom Mix, and who else was there? It wasn't so hard to get about ten men together, all complete amateurs like myself, probably, but they were all very enthusiastic.

One Sunday, the assigned officer took us over to the regiment and handed us over to Mr. Ochi, the riding instructor. Since Matsuyama Regiment was infantry, all they had were about a dozen horses. They were used mainly for officers to ride in parades and for those living in private houses off compound to commute to the Regiment. On that first day, seeing that none of us had any experience handling horses, Mr. Ochi showed us how to bridle and saddle horses and, pretending that the horses were exercised, how to wipe them clean, brush them, and massage their legs.

The next Sunday, we were allowed to take the horses by the reins out to the riding ground inside the compound and ride them around to get used to the feel. In the following weeks, we gradually made it up to trotting, then galloping and eventually to steeplechasing. Of course, it took us almost a year to get to that last stage. After we returned from our summer vacation that year, some of the riding club members began to complain that it was no fun just riding inside the army compound. They wanted to ride through the city, probably to show off. Strictly speaking, the horses were for exclusive use by army officers, but the Regiment was doing us a favor, very likely with a hidden motive of luring us into military service upon graduation. So, it was up to me, the captain of the club, to find some civilian horses. It took quite a while to find even one such horse, but I finally found one in a stable very close to the college. Mr. Miyamoto, the owner, was in the transport business, still using a horse wagon. Because that business was increasingly being taken over by trucks, his horse was often idle in the stable. Mr. Miyamoto was glad to have us exercise the horse. So, even on weekdays, after school, the club members took turns riding the horse, first just near the stable, but later all over the city. It was obvious that Matsuyama-ites had never seen college students riding horses before. They watched us with great curiosity at first but soon became very friendly. Many of them smiled and waved at us as we trotted by.

As college students who would be serving in the military in the near future, we felt the mounting tension indeed. Yet, as in the case of many other people in many other situations, we had a vague feeling that all this was taking place somewhere far away, having little to do with us. On the other hand, our daily life became progressively tougher. The 1939 Civilian Expropriation Act made it possible for the government to draft civilians into war industries. The following year, a coupon system was established so that families could not buy sugar, charcoal, matches and some other commodities without government-issued coupons. The rationing of rice and clothing followed. If the fuel situation for combustion engines was bad for the military, it was worse for civilians.

Late February to early April 1943 was our last spring vacation. But for the full month of March, we soon-to-be-senior students were sent to a naval arsenal in Kure for what in those days was called "voluntary labor service." For eight hours a day we packed solidified gunpowder into shells for 50 centimeter (19.7 inch) guns, obviously for battleship use. It was hard work because the gunpowder and the shells were heavy, but we ate well. The military still had the quality and quantity of food no longer available to civilians. We particularly liked the black tea served during the morning and afternoon breaks. Was it sweet! We hardly had sweet things to taste back home because sugar was a scarce commodity. We lived in a dormitory and were free in the evening. We were not allowed to go out, though. The whole city was blacked out because of the possibility of air raids by American planes. Our Navy was badly defeated in the Battle of Midway the year before, although people were told at the time that the damage to our fleet was minimal. Here and there in the dorm, we gathered to play cards, wrestle and generally have good fun. We were young and full of vigor. We were also conscious of the fact that we were contributing directly to our nation's cause. My memory of that period is a rather pleasant one.

Back to school in April. I had taken the physical exam for draftees, passed it and was given a deferment. In the oral interview, I was asked if I would prefer the cavalry over infantry. Had I chosen infantry, I would have been drafted into the Matsuyama Infantry Regiment. I chose cavalry, meaning I would be in the cavalry regiment in Zentsuji. According to a memoir titled *Naval Air Reserve Students* published in 1988, the Ministry of Navy announced a recruitment of a large number of college graduates to become air reserve students on May 29, 1943. It was probably to supplement the dwindling number of front-line pilots. Something hit me. I had longed so much to go to the Naval Academy and never made it. Maybe this was the chance. I might become a naval officer yet. Hey, flying planes was more exciting than riding horses. So I decided to take the naval air reserve exam in August. Father was a bit reluctant, but he wrote Mother and got her approval. The physical and oral/written exams were held in Takamatsu on Shikoku. I think seven of us from *Kosho*, myself included, passed the exams.

According to the memoir, over 70,000 students took the exams at 19 locations, including Seoul, Taipei and Shanghai. Some 5,000 passed. Roughly half of them were to be assigned to Tsuchiura Naval Air Station north of Tokyo and the other half to Mie Naval Air Station approximately half way between Osaka and Nagoya. The problem was that there wasn't much time left for us to report to the air stations. We were to be there on September 13, 1943. Anticipating this, the *Kosho* administration decided to move up our graduation from March 1944 to September 1943. That meant we were enrolled in college for two and a half years instead of the regular three. Anyway, I think it was September 7 that the seven of us were hurriedly assembled in the President's Office. After some simple formalities, President Tanaka looked into the eyes of each of us and said, "Your diplomas will be sent to your families a little later. Best wishes for a successful military career. Take care of yourselves and come home alive." These last words we only half-believed. At that stage of the war, most people knew that going into the military meant almost certain death. Of course, everyone going in hoped that that wouldn't be the case for himself. But the password of the day then was "the glory of death for the Emperor and the country."

Chapter 6

Hiroshima
Osaka
KARASU
Mie Naval Air Station

The Cadet

Basic Training

To the east, Mie Prefecture faces the Bay of Ise, a part of the Pacific Ocean that washes the southeastern coast of Honshu, the largest of the four main islands of Japan. Mie Naval Air Station (NAS) was located on the coastline of a small town called Karasu in Mie Prefecture. The NAS had a large compound with facilities mainly for on-land training, residential barracks and one short landing strip. In order to get there by nine A.M. on September 13, Father and I had to leave Matsuyama the day before, arrive in the city of Matsuzaka, the closest large urban area, and stay at a Japanese-style inn that evening. I had turned 21 at that time, and was quite capable of traveling by myself, but Father came along to help carry all of my belongings.

Father and I left Matsuyama by ferry. There were many people on the floating dock at Takahama Port: Mother, who had taken a special leave to see me off, nine year old Takao, several *Kosho* friends who were to graduate in a week or so, some old buddies from Bancho and *Matsuchu*, and neighbors from Yanai-machi. There was more pride in joining the military than sorrow of departure in my mind as I waved to them from the deck of the ferry. But as the ferry left the pier and the people looked tinier and tinier, I became sentimental. I would probably never see Mother, Takao and all those people again. I wouldn't see these beautiful islands again either. So long, Matsuyama. So long, Shikoku.

The ferry took us to Hiroshima, where we got on a train. We had to change trains in Osaka, and arrived in Matsuzaka late in the afternoon. It took us almost a full day from Matsuyama to Matsuzaka. After we settled into our room at the inn, Father pulled out a medium-sized bottle of *sake* he had brought all the way from home. He knew that *sake* would not be available at the inn because of the shortages. He called in the maid and asked her to warm it and serve it at dinner. It was one of the rare occasions that Father allowed me to drink with him. We had a long talk, but I hardly remember what we talked about.

The next morning, we had to get up early to take a train to Karasu Railway Station. It was a long walk from the station to the NAS main gate. Only the prospective cadets were allowed to enter the gate. The area in front of the gate was crowded with young men and their families and friends. Since Father and I had talked so much the evening before, we didn't have much more left to say to each other. He grabbed my hands, held them tightly, said, "Stay well," started to say something else but stopped short. As he quickly turned away to leave, I think I saw tears beginning to wet his eyes. Fortunately, that was not going to be the last I saw of him, not by any means. But as I watched him walk back toward the station, I did not expect to see him again.

I struggled to walk through the gate with heavy baggage in both hands and came to a checkpoint. I had my name checked off the roster, and was told that I was in Division 1 and was to go to Barracks 5 to leave my baggage and come out on the parade ground. On the parade ground were hundreds, perhaps thousands, of men in college uniforms. From the badges on the front of their caps, I was able to tell which universities some of them were from. I looked around to see if I was able to find some of my classmates from Matsuyama *Kosho*, but I couldn't. There were just too many people there.

Soon enough, an officer got on the platform and spoke through a loud speaker. "Attention, all men. Line up in rows of three. Division 1 at that end, and Division 12 at that end. All men, assemble!" I scurried toward the end the officer pointed at for Division 1 and fell in line. Each of the three rows for our division looked about 100 men deep. I later learned that Division 1 had 215 men. Twelve divisions should make about 2,500 men. The man on the platform, who we later learned to be the vice commander of Mie NAS, told us that, after the assembly, we were to go back to our barracks and change into the work suits that would be given us. There would be no more use for the college uniforms we were wearing, ever. In the afternoon, we would have drills on some basic matters. For a week starting the next day, we would go through general orientation, including all sorts of aptitude tests.

For the white cotton work suit, which was a pull-over jacket and trousers, we had a choice of "Large," "Medium" and "Small." I chose "S," of course, but it was still too large. I just had to deal with it. "It will shrink down to my size after a couple of washings," I thought, and it eventually did.

After we all changed into work suits, we had a little time to kill. I looked around and saw that our quarters on the second floor of the two-story barracks were just one big, long room with the hallway running in the middle. No partition whatsoever. Large wooden beams ran at right angles to the hallway. On the beams were large metal hooks at regular intervals, obviously for hammocks. All Navy personnel, except officers, slept in hammocks, on land or out at sea. In our case, we were told, we would be sleeping in coarsely made double-bunked wooden beds, because there were not enough hammocks due to a canvas shortage and the short notice on which we were recruited. Wooden tables and benches were set on the floor between the beams. The men were sitting on the benches, chatting and getting to know each other. I started to do the same. The first person I got to know was Tetsuo Kobayashi from Tokyo. He said he had been a long-distance runner for the athletic team at Chuo University. We later got to be very good friends, but unfortunately he died in the war as a *kamikaze* pilot.

The first orientation was held that afternoon. Lieutenant Senior Grade Yamamoto introduced himself as the commanding officer of Division 1. He then introduced Lieutenants Junior Grade Muraki, Kinoshita and Kuwabara. Yamamoto was a Naval Academy graduate. Muraki and Kinoshita were reserve officers, the same as we were.

Kuwabara had made it up through the ranks. One of the first things Lt. Yamamoto explained was that there were other groups of Navy men living and training at the NAS. The largest group was made up of about 2,000 *yokaren*. *Yokaren* was short for *Yoka Renshusei*, or Reserve Trainees. They were boys, 16 or a bit older, who volunteered to be trained to become aircraft pilots. There was no way for me to know at that time that I would be a flight instructor for *yokaren* a year later.

Later in the afternoon, the younger lieutenants took over and drilled us on getting in and out of bed. In the Japanese military, getting up in the morning and going to bed at night were no easy tasks. Compared to using the hammock, getting in and out of the bunk beds was relatively easy. Still, we were made to practice lining up in the hallway, and at the order, "To bed!" we ran to the beds, took our clothes off and got into bed in 30 seconds. Then, at the order, "Reveille!" we jumped out of bed, put our clothes on, made the beds and lined up in 30 seconds. At first it took us much longer, but practice makes perfect, and we were soon able to meet the time limit.

Most families back then slept Japanese style, in bedding laid on the *tatami* mat floors. So many of my comrades were not used to sleeping in beds. Consequently, quite a few of them fell off the bunks, even the top bunks. Especially on warm nights, they would kick off the blankets. The blankets would start to slide off the bunks because there were no side railings on these bunks. When a sleeping trainee rolled over and came close to the edge of the bunk, the weight of the hanging blanket would start pulling the person over the edge, and eventually down to the floor below. This happened to me once too, from the upper bunk, but I was lucky enough to wake up in mid-air and landed on all fours. Some were not so lucky and fell right on their faces. We were so exhausted from the heavy training during the day that some kept right on sleeping on the floor after they fell.

The next few days were spent on detailed physical examinations and aptitude tests. Only later did we learn that the real purpose of all this was to weed out those who were not fit to be aircraft pilots. Quite a few were actually rejected and became cadets for navigation, gunnery or land combat. Special attention was paid to our eyesight. None of us wore glasses to begin with, but one had to have very good eyesight to become a combat plane pilot. One interesting chapter in the physical exams was the dizziness test. One special room had several rotating barbershop-like chairs. We were made to sit in them and spun around very fast for about 10 seconds. The chair was then suddenly stopped and we were pushed off. We were then supposed to walk on the straight, white line about five meters long painted on the floor. I made it to the end all right, but a bit wobbly. Some men stepped off the line because of dizziness. A few that I watched couldn't even walk at all. They fell over to one side right after they were pushed off the chair.

Another highlight was in the mental aptitude tests. We were given a booklet with about six pages. On the pages were nothing but horizontal rows of one-digit numerals. At the signal, "Go!" you added the first and the second numerals of the first row and wrote the sum between and above the two numerals. If the sum was 10 or larger, you just put down the second digit. You moved on to the sum of the second and third numerals and all the way to the end of that row. Then you added all the sums for that row and put down the total for them at the right end of the row. You went down all the rows on that page, added the sums of all the rows vertically and put down the grand total at the bottom right of the page. You went on to Page 2 and did the same. At the end of Page 2, you added the grand total for Page 1 and Page 2, and so on until you were stopped by the proctor. I think we were given three minutes to go as far as we were able to. I do not think anyone was able to do it all. I suppose this was to evaluate our quickness and accuracy in making judgments, a quality essential for aircraft pilots.

During this period, we learned that we were ranked as officers, or to be more accurate, our rank was between petty officer and ensign. As naval officers, we were to behave as gentlemen. We had to always be in our uniforms, neatly pressed, when not in work suits for training. We had to always stand erect when not sitting down. We were to sit only on chairs, sofas or benches, and not on the edges of objects not made for sitting. We were to carry only briefcases or suitcases and never a *furoshiki* (a traditional Japanese cloth used to wrap bundles). We had to always salute any senior officer we saw, and salute back at saluting junior ranks.

I might quote here an interesting piece of information from the aforementioned memoir. It is the result of a part of a survey conducted by the Reserve Student History Publishing Association of former reserve cadets. To the question, "Why did you volunteer to become a reserve cadet?" the following were the responses:

To defend my country and its people	33%
Having to serve in the military anyway, I preferred the Navy to the Army	33%
Because I wanted to fly airplanes	22%
Because naval officers look smart	12%

After the first week, we were put on the regular schedule for basic training. One of the mottoes of the Japanese Navy was "five minutes before." We were to be ready for action five minutes before the time for action for anything. So, the first thing that came to our attention every morning was the voice on the public address system, "Five minutes before reveille." It was customary to sleep in our underwear so we would be able to spring into action in the shortest amount of time in case of an emergency. We were prohibited from making any bodily moves between the five-minute-before call and the six o'clock reveille. The lieutenants took turns watching us to make sure we didn't. Once the reveille sounded, we jumped out of bed, put on our work suits, made our beds, which had to pass inspection later, and lined up in the hallway — in 30 seconds from the last note of the reveille. The lieutenant on duty timed us till the last man lined up. "Good, that was 28 seconds. You're doing better," he would say. Then at his order, the division ran out of the barracks to the parade ground, joined the other divisions, saluted the commander, deep-bowed toward the east and did some calisthenics. Back at the barracks for breakfast at seven, we ate pretty fast. Fast eating was a part of the training, so we would be able to eat fast during combat.

Classes began at eight o'clock: four 50-minute classes in the morning with 10-minute breaks in between. The classes first covered areas of knowledge all naval officers had to have, from marine navigation to gunnery. Then we moved on to more aircraft related areas such as aerodynamics and astronomy. Throughout, we had training in Morse Code communication, audio and visual reception and manual transmission. It was hard at first but became fun once we became more used to it. As we advanced in aeronautics, we were taken out to the hangars to study the bodies and engines of different types of aircraft. In the afternoon, we had outdoor training in gunnery, sailing, cutter rowing, navigation, and so on. We also engaged in sports of various kinds. After dinner at six, we had two more classes between seven and nine. It was very intensive training for four months.

The training went on from Monday through Saturday. We were free on Sundays but couldn't go into town the first couple of weeks. We hadn't been given our uniforms yet. They would not dare let us go out in work suits. I think it was in the third week that we finally got our uniforms along with government-issued daggers. Were we happy! We finally started to look like real Navy officers. The insignia on both sides of the front collar of the navy blue uniform had a golden stripe, showing that we were officers. The blades on the dagger were so dull that we couldn't peel apples with them. Still, with golden trimmings on the haft and the sheath, it looked very handsome hanging from our hips.

The weeks without an outing seemed very, very long to us. Then the Sunday finally came. The walk to the railway station was long again, but it didn't seem as long as the time Father and I walked in the opposite direction. For one thing, I didn't have anything to carry with me this time. At the station, some took the train going north to Tsu City; others took the one going south to Matsuzaka City. I joined some of my friends from Division 1 going south. Our major purpose for going into town was to eat. Considering the shortage of food nationwide, they fed us relatively well at the NAS. Still, military food was monotonous. My group decided to go into a Japanese style restaurant. I don't remember exactly what I ordered, but I think it was noodles, two helpings.

After lunch, we strolled down the main street, window-shopping. We aimlessly wandered into some of the side streets, just to get a taste of what civilian life was like. Occasionally, children playing in the street would say, "Look, Navy officers!" and gather around us. Evidently, they were used to seeing sailors and soldiers walking on their streets, but very seldom Navy officers. They had no particular questions to ask, but they took much interest in our daggers. "Let us see the blade. Does it really cut?" they would say. On one of these streets, we came across a photo studio and decided to have our portraits taken, each one of us individually for our families and some group photos for ourselves. We were to return to the NAS by six P.M., but before boarding the train back, we stopped into a coffee shop and enjoyed the coffee and music. Back in the NAS, we were too full to eat supper. They must have had a lot of leftover food that evening.

A "Family Day" was held on a Sunday in late November. The reserve students' parents, brothers and sisters from all over came for the four-hour get-together. I found Father among the crowd at the gate. He carried a knapsack on his back and looked tired, but he lit up when he saw me. I took him to a nice spot on the lawn that surrounded the parade ground. We just sat down and talked and talked. Mother was to be released from her reserve nurse duties and was due home very soon. Brother Takao was doing fine as a second grader. All the neighbors were doing well too. As noon approached, Father unpacked the knapsack. He took out four sizable wooden boxes neatly wrapped in newspaper. He opened the first two, which were packed with cooked rice, way more than enough for the two of us. He opened the third box, which was filled with all kinds of home-cooked fish and vegetables. He then slowly went for the fourth box. Fried chicken, my favorite! He said he cooked all this in the late afternoon of the day before, took the evening overnight ferry to Kobe and a train to get to the NAS in time. Just then, I spotted Comrade Kobayashi walking nearby all by himself. I yelled out to him and asked if his family was with him. No, it was too far for his mother to come all the way from about an hour outside of Tokyo. I invited him to share our lunch with Father and me. He gladly joined us, and with three of us we didn't let any of the food go to waste. Kobayashi and I walked Father to the railway station and saw him off. Well, I had seen Father once again. Would I have another chance?

The general public was kept in the dark as to what was really going on at the front lines, which, by then, had extended from the

Kurile Islands to Micronesia, including the Dutch East Indies, Southeast Asia and as far west as Burma (Myanmar). Once in a while, people were told that there was a troop movement from Point A to Point B on the front. The government used the term "transfer" for such movements to make people think that they were just normal troop movements. We, as naval officers, were given a bit more truthful information. The army unit defending Point A was overrun by the Allied forces and only the survivors retreated to Point B. As 1943 came to an end and 1944 rolled around, we had a sense that Japan's sphere of military dominance in Asia was beginning to shrink. All the more, however, we were seized by the notion, "Just wait till we get there. We'll take care of them all."

Toward the end of January 1944, we were ordered to assemble in the hallway of our barracks. With a solemn face, Division Commander Lt. Yamamoto said our basic training had almost come to an end, and that he was going to give each of us orders for our next assignment. When I received my form, it read, "Flight training at Izumi Naval Air Corps." I had no idea where Izumi was located, but it didn't matter. As long as I was to be trained as a pilot, I was happy. According to my count in the Reserve Student Alumni Book, my class of roughly 5,200 cadets (half of whom got their basic training at Mie NAS and the other half at Tsuchiura NAS) were assigned to about 15 naval air corps scattered throughout the country. Not all of them were for flight training. Tokushima and Suzuka, for example, were for navigation training. I understood that a small number of my comrades were to be sent to other naval facilities for training in non-aviation duties.

Chapter 7

13th Class

Amakusa
IZUMI

Intermediate Flight Training

Those of us destined for Izumi, some 100 strong, marched from the Mie NAS gate to the railway station in formation. Evidently our belongings were trucked to the station, because carrying our luggage was unbecoming of naval officers. This was early in the morning of early February 1944. Changing trains at least three times on the way, we arrived at Izumi Station late in the afternoon. Altogether, it was a long train ride, from the central part of Honshu to the southern part of Kyushu, the southernmost main island of Japan. Izumi, enjoying the status of a city today but just a small town then, was located in the northern part of Kagoshima Prefecture, the southernmost prefecture except Okinawa. The walk from the railway station to the gate of Izumi Naval Air Corps wasn't so bad. Since it was already getting dark when we arrived, not many townfolks noticed our arrival. It was already past the regular dinner time, but we were served dinner in the barracks. As we were eating, a lanky officer showed up and very informally introduced himself as Lieutenant Senior Grade (SG) Takeuchi, the commander of our division. He said he was a reserve officer, the same as we were. "But," he added, "I'm not going to go easy on you. I'm going to give you the roughest but the best training so the regular Navy guys will have nothing negative to say about us reserve officers." He said all planned orientation would be held starting the next day. We might as well take a bath after dinner, put our belongings in place and hit the sack with taps at ten o'clock.

The five-minutes-before-reveille call and the six o'clock reveille the next morning were no different from the ones at Mie NAS. It was just as dark as it was at Mie, perhaps even a bit darker here since we were a little further west. At the morning assembly, we heard the commandant's voice but could not see what he looked like. On the other hand, it was noticeably warmer than it was in Mie. The eight o'clock orientation began with the history of Izumi Naval Air Corps (NAC). It was a fairly new airfield, built for the specific purpose of the training of flight cadets. It had one runway extending north to south, because the prevailing winds were from the north. As we were listening to the lecture, we heard planes taking off and landing. "Ah, we are finally on an air base," we thought. "The local people here seem to be fond of us and look after us well," Lt. SG Takeuchi continued. "There's another thing the people are fond of, and that is the flock of cranes that migrates here from Siberia during the winter. Be careful of the birds when you fly at low altitudes." He went on to explain the type of plane we would be using for training, the Model 93 Intermediate Trainer.

No matter how hard Lt. Takeuchi tried to act dignified in front of his juniors, we could not help but recognize him as being an informal, friendly and generally nice guy. We had been in the Navy long enough to tell the difference between a basically civilian reserve officer and the professionally trained Naval Academy graduates.

Our class of 5,200-some college graduates was officially called the "13th Class Naval Air Reserve Students." This was because the recruiting of college graduates into the Naval Air Reserve began in 1934, and we were the 13th class to enter the service. Many of the reserve students senior to us belonged to glider clubs and flying clubs while in college. Upon recruitment, they were placed right into intermediate flight training. Those who didn't have any flight experience were sent into basic flight training. For the 13th Class, however, there wasn't enough time for basic flight training due to the worsening war situation and shortage of flight instructors. We were also getting short of high-octane gasoline.

In the afternoon, younger lieutenants took over and drilled us on the use of hammocks. If the reader remembers, we were made to use makeshift double-deck bunk beds at Mie because not enough hammocks were available. Now that we were at Izumi, we had to use hammocks. First, we lined up in two rows in the barracks hallway, shoulder to shoulder. At the order "Readyyy, go!" those at both ends of the rows ran to the ladders at the ends of the room, climbed the ladders to reach the racks where the hammocks were stowed and started throwing them down. Meanwhile, the other men scattered throughout the length of the room. Those close to the ladders passed the hammocks arm to arm until they reached those at the center of the room. As soon as they got them, they hooked them up on the beam hooks and untied the ropes binding the hammocks. All this was supposed to be done in 30 seconds. It took us a full minute to do it at first, despite our training with the bunk beds. Next we were drilled in putting the hammocks back on the racks, going through the same motions in reverse order. Again, a full minute. All the while, the lieutenants timed us on their watches. The hammocks were made of thick canvas and were heavy, but we were made to repeat the drill over and over again. The drill was called to a halt when we cut the time down to 40 seconds. We were amazed at ourselves when we were able to cut it down to 30 seconds in a few weeks. One of the mottoes of the Japanese military was, "Nothing is impossible."

At eight o'clock the next morning, we lined up on the east edge of the airfield. We were all in flight uniforms that we had practiced putting on the evening before. We had flight goggles over the leather helmets. And as all Navy pilots did, whether flying over land or sea, we had our life jackets on. After we were split into small groups of ten each, we were told to sit on the grass, cross-legged, and listen. A non-commissioned flight officer for each group explained where all the gears and instruments were in the cockpit and how to use them. We knew all that from our training at Mie, but just in case. Lt. Takeuchi went from group to group, seeing that all necessary explanations were given. Then, two by two, the instructor took us to one of the planes parked on the tarmac. He pointed out each gear, instrument and gauge to make sure we knew where in the cockpit they were. Now, we were ready to go up for our first flight experience.

The planes we used were Model 93 Intermediate Trainers. This model was a single-engine biplane with a tail wheel. It was a wooden-framed, cloth-covered light plane. It had a big engine which was heavy relative to the body, so it rather easily tipped over, nose down, when accelerated too much on the ground with the elevators not fully pulled up. Its fixed landing gears were not very strong and sometimes collapsed on a hard landing. Still, it was highly maneuverable and easily maintained, making it practical as a trainer plane. It had two open cockpits, the front one for the trainee and the rear one for the instructor. The two were connected with a voice tube through which the two aviators could speak to each other. The throttles, the control sticks and the steering sticks in the two cockpits were linked together so that when the trainee made a wrong move the instructor was able to take an instantaneous corrective action.

When the time came for my virgin flight, I climbed up into the trainee cockpit. My first impression was "Oh, what a big engine." I could hardly see anything in front of me. "You can't see much ahead now, can you, Student Imamura?" came the voice over the voice tube. The instructor told me to crank up the seat but not beyond the point where my feet could still push the steering stick the full length, left and right. "Now, can you see better?" It was a little better, but I still couldn't see anything over the engine cowling. "That's because our nose is up and our tail is down. You'll see what happens when we start to take off."

Model 93 was a propeller-driven plane, of course, and it had no self-starter. Its engine had to be cranked up by the ground crew. When the inertia starter was fully cranked up, the ground crew yelled, "Inertia all right!" The pilot was supposed to yell back, "Switch on!" as he turned the ignition key on. The pilot. Oh, that's me. "Switch on!" The terms "inertia" and "switch" and some other words that were used were English, inherited from the British Navy, but pronounced in the Japanese way. The Japanese Navy used many expressions in English. In contrast, the Japanese Army used nothing but Japanese.

The engine was running smoothly, or at least I thought so. We were ready to go. "Taxi?" I asked the instructor. "Taxi," he answered softly. "Chocks away!" I shouted to the ground crew. As soon as we started taxiing, the instructor reminded me, "The streamer." The ground streamer in the traditional red-and-white cloth indicated north wind. We steered toward the south end of the runway. I suppose I can't quite say "we" here, in that the instructor was doing all the steering. I had my hands clutching the rims of the cockpit as we had been told to do. On this flight, the trainee was not supposed to touch anything and was just to keep an eye, no both eyes, on every movement of the gears and instruments in the cockpit, as well as be on the lookout, all simultaneously. But, as soon as we started to taxi, there was something I noticed. The instructor was swinging the plane slightly to the left and to the right as he proceeded, obviously to see for sure where we were going. So, that's how to do it!

Taxiing up to the south end of the runway and slowly making a left turn to point north, we made sure that no plane was on the runway ahead of us and no other plane was coming in for landing from behind. The flagman's flag changed from red to white. "Takeoff!" I yelled. The throttle moved forward, slowly at first and then a little faster until it hit the front end. Almost immediately the tail rose. As the plane leveled with the ground, I got the whole view in front of me over the cowling. It took not much more than ten seconds for the light plane to lift off. I'm flying, I'm flying! I saw the control stick move back a little and the plane nosed up, perhaps about 30 degrees. The full throttle was also pulled back from takeoff speed to climbing speed. We were airborne! Close to 1,000 meters out, north, the control stick and the steering stick showed movements to make a right turn. As we turned 90 degrees (due east), we just reached the designated altitude for takeoff and landing practice of 300 meters, and leveled off. After going 500 meters east, we turned right, 90 degrees. Now we were flying south, parallel to the runway. Oh, the scenery was beautiful: the Izumi Plain below with the airfield in its center, flanked by low mountains to the east and ocean bays to the west. There were many islands in the bays, pretty much like those off the coast of Matsuyama. My daydreaming was cut short when the instructor made another 90 degree right turn, shortly after which he throttled down a bit. A slight descent began. As the south end of the runway began to come clearly into sight, our plane made another right turn and faced the runway squarely. The throttle lever moved further back.

The Navy always insisted on a perfect three-point landing, in our case on the front two wheels and the tail wheel. This was for the eventuality that, as carrier-based pilots, we could be sure to have the tail hook catch the restraining cords. So as our plane neared the ground, the instructor started to call out, "30 meters, 25 meters, 20 meters, 15 meters....," and when we were down to five meters, he pulled the throttle and the control stick all the way back so the plane would come to a three-point landing. Of course, the rate of descent, wind velocity and direction and other factors would have an effect. These were the things we were to master in the next few months. My instructor made a perfect landing.

From the moment your name is called by the student deck officer and you jump up from the grass, run to the command post, salute Lt. Takeuchi and report, "Student Imamura now departing, sir," run to one of the trainers parked on the tarmac with the instructor already sitting in the rear cockpit, go through all the actions described above including flying, run back to the command post to report the return, it took each student trainee about 20 minutes. With three trainees per plane per hour and ten planes used, we were able to fly only once a day.

On March 6, 1944, just about a month after arriving in Izumi, there was an accident. It happened that a very high ranking naval officer was visiting Izumi NAC to observe how the training of the 13th Class Naval Reserve students was coming along. The visitor sat at the command post on the airfield, so we were all rather uptight. Takeoff and landing practice was going on. I happened to be sitting on the grass waiting for my turn to go up. Suddenly, I heard a scream. Seconds earlier, I had heard someone yelling, "He's coming in too high! Wave him off!" I guess I was looking down, thinking about what I would do if I came in too high. At the scream, I looked up and just caught sight of a trainer flipping up in the air. It then came crashing down, tail first. We all ran over but were told to stay clear because the wreck might burst into flames any moment. Soon enough a fire engine and an ambulance came and took care of the situation. We were later told that it was instant death for Student Horie and the instructor. They never found out what caused the plane to flip up like that. As far as I have been able to find out in the records, this was the first casualty the 13th Class suffered.

Despite the tragedy, which made us feel how fragile our life could be, the training continued. After the first day of hands-off flight, we were told to put our left hand on the throttle lever, our right hand on the control stick and our feet on the steering stick very, very lightly, just to feel how the instructor was handling them. As the days went on, our grips became more and more firm but never to the extent of resisting the movements made by the instructor. About two weeks into the flight training, right after takeoff, the instructor said, "OK, Student Imamura, you're on your own." It took me a second or two to realize that his hands and feet were off the controls. I began to sweat but kept on doing exactly what I was trained to do during the previous two weeks. The turns were smooth. The descent for landing seemed to go well. "Five meters" I yelled, and pulled the throttle and the control stick back. It seemed I pulled the stick back a bit too fast. The plane glided about a meter off the ground for three seconds and then thumped on the ground. It wasn't bad enough to do any damage to the landing gear.

We did this type of flying for three or four days. On the last day or two, I don't think the instructor had his hands or feet on the controls at all. The next day, some of us were told to assemble in front of another command post south of the one we had been using. Lt. Takeuchi told us that we were going to begin our solo flights, that he had confidence in our ability to fly by ourselves, but to pay special attention on the lookout because we were using the same runway as the other trainees. One after another we went up. Once up at 300 meters, oh, what a wonderful feeling it was! I felt very powerful, not only being in full control of one whole airplane but of the whole world! The scenery below looked especially beautiful. I was very much tempted to go into a roll or a loop, but I didn't know how to do those yet, of course. So, I came into the landing nonchalantly.

In a few days, after all of us completed solo flights, we went into advanced intermediate night training—loops, slow rolls, quick rolls, pursuits and dodging pursuits. Nose diving from 1,500 meters and pulling up at 500 meters was fun. The hardest was formation flying. Since Model 93 had a maximum speed of only 75 knots, once you fell behind a bit, it was hard to catch up with the lead plane. Since we did not know at that time what type of plane we would be assigned to fly eventually, we had to be trained to have the basic mastery of all kinds of flights. The more we flew, the more fun it became.

As mentioned earlier, we were all issued daggers, nice to look at on the outside but real duds on the inside. I had written to Father about this, and he had seen the dagger when he came to Mie for Family Day. We had a neighbor in Yanai-machi who dealt in antiques. Father bought a real *samurai* dagger from him, appraised to be about 400 years old. It took time for him to send it off to Kure, where there was a specialist who made *samurai* daggers into naval officers' daggers, adjusting the grip and scabbard to fit Navy specifications. It was sent to me in Izumi in early spring. Did everyone envy me for having that! A real dagger in Navy style casing. The blade was really sharp, but that was not why people were so envious. It was a bit longer and wider than the government issued version.

We did not always sit on the airfield grass waiting for our turn. That was only for the first few weeks of training, for us to get the overall idea of what went on. After that, we were split into squads with only the squads on actual flight training staying on the airfield. The rest of us were engaged in various activities—continued training in Morse Code transmission, studying aircraft engine maintenance, athletics and even training in the use of rifles and bayonets to prepare ourselves for the eventuality of being shot down and engaged in hand-to-hand combat.

Throughout this training, corporal punishment was an everyday occurrence. It usually took the form of getting hit on the cheek with a fist, in full force. Making a poor landing, for example, deserved a blow. It came from the officer in charge of whatever activity we were engaged in. For more serious offenses, such as landing too hard and collapsing the landing gear, or nearly hitting someone with your propeller, or not making proper lookout, we got what we called the "round-trip punches," a one-two on both cheeks. If we even tried to duck a punch, we were sure to get a once-again. Of course, anyone hit with such a force will have a brain concussion to an extent. Early on, some of my friends just keeled over. But as time went on, we gradually got used to it and were able to keep standing erect after being socked. Our cheeks, especially the left cheek, seemed to harden too. After a hit, it would redden a bit, but had no more swelling or any marks.

If you hit someone on the cheek with the full force of your fist, your own hand hurts too. When the whole group does something wrong, such as assembling at a wrong place, it would be too much for an officer to go around socking everybody. So, he would order the group to form two lines, order the front line to turn about face, give the usual "Legs apart!" order and "Go!" We whacked each other with all our might. But when we had a good friend in front of us, our whack might not be as strong as it should be. Pilots have keen eyes. The officer in charge would catch it right away and say, "Students Tanaka, Yamashita, Ogonogi, Minoda and those you're paired with, stay where you are. All others, two steps back. Hup!" This time, everyone was watching the four pairs. There was nothing for them to do but hit each other as hard as they could. And that was it.

These seemingly barbaric acts were not called, or even considered, punishments. This was "injection of the Navy spirit." Some of the officers carried sticks about four feet long. On each stick was written, "Navy Spirit Injection Stick." They were used for various purposes, but one in particular. When a large number of men needed the "injection," and the officer didn't particularly feel like the usual two-row, back-and-forth punchings, he would order the men to form two (or three, or four) rows, about five feet apart, then order, "Take position!" The men would bend forward, stick their behinds out, and raise both arms straight up. The officer would go down the row, whacking once on each bottom. As we did when punched on the cheek, after the whack each one stood up straight, saluted the officer and said, "Thank you, sir." All of this may seem either comical or ridiculous today, even for young Japanese people. But we took it all very seriously. It was comical to us too only when we all went to take a bath in the evening. It was obvious which squad got the stick that day.

Rough training does harden men. We were gradually shaped into fighters with no fear. But roughness was not all of our training. In some large metropolitan areas and around naval bases, there were naval officers' clubs. An officer was able to go there and eat, drink, sleep, use the library and generally relax. We who were stationed in rural areas like Izumi were given what were then called *"Geshuku,"* which would translate as boarding houses. But they were not boarding houses as we know them today. They came closest to what we call host families these days. We were allowed to go into town on Sundays only. About a month into the training in Izumi, we were told that we would be assigned to *Geshuku*, two to a family. We were allowed to pick whoever we wished to form the pair. Kobayashi, with whom we shared the lunch Father brought to Mie NAS, and I chose each other. We were assigned to the Tanaka family in Komenotsu, another small town near Izumi. One Sunday, Kobayashi and I set out. It was something like a 25-minute walk to the Tanakas'. Arriving there in mid-morning, we were greeted with open arms by the whole family in front of the house—Mr. and Mrs. Tanaka, Reiko, the oldest daughter, and her two sisters, the Tanaka baby and the maid.

To make a long story short, the Tanakas became my second family. I never had a chance to pay them a visit after the end of the war, but we corresponded for some years. Mr. Tanaka, who ran a pharmacy, died fairly early and that was when our correspondence stopped. Come to think of it, it was at the Tanakas' that I learned to do some hard drinking. Southern Kyushu and Okinawa are known for their *shochu,* a distilled liquor with 35 to 45 % alcohol content. Mr. Tanaka loved to drink *shochu*, and I drank along with him. Kobayashi drank just a little. As was mentioned much earlier, my father was a pretty heavy drinker. I must have inherited his genes. I did fairly well with Mr. Tanaka, but then I had never had anything so powerful. Some Sunday evenings, Mr. Tanaka had to take me back to the barracks on his bicycle, with Kobayashi trotting along on the side to make sure I didn't fall off.

Reiko Tanaka, a high school student then, was very shy at first. It was probably because Kobayashi and I were the first young men to become so intimate with her and her family. However, she gradually came out of her shell and started to show signs that she liked us, both of us. Her problem seemed to be in making up her mind which one of us she liked better. By the time we were about to leave Izumi, I think she had decided to go for Kobayashi, the more suave, urban type. I bring this up to move on to a related but more serious topic, namely the sex life of the reserve students. While in Mie, we hardly ever talked about sex. Oh, once in a while, someone would get a love letter from a girl friend and people around would tease him. But nothing about sex per se. We were too exhausted from our training anyway. After the first outing in Izumi, however, we started hearing about groups of men going out to hot springs and other places of entertainment. They came back and told us about the good times they had with *geisha* and bar girls. It slowly sank in on me that sex was a part of Navy life. Still, Kobayashi and I were not the type, at least not yet. We were quite happy visiting with the Tanakas practically every Sunday. I would be lying if I said my heart didn't move at all for Reiko, but I knew Kobayashi would make a better boyfriend for her if we were to stay on much longer in Izumi...but we knew we were not going to be there much longer.

One Sunday in April, our division was put on a naval vessel and was taken to Amakusa across the Sea of Ariake. It was a small ship, a minesweeper or something, but it was painted gray and had the conspicuous rising sun flag fluttering at the stem. The purported purpose of the trip was for us to gain knowledge and experience in fleet activities. In reality, it was a sea-faring excursion. Amakusa then was, and today still is, known for a rebellion that took place there in 1635, when a band of farmers and fishermen, led by a teenager, fought against the local lord. Most of the rebels were Christians who rebelled against religious persecution. To get back, all I remember is that a good lunch was served on board and that we all enjoyed the experience. In a way, I have the feeling that the event was planned by Lt. Takeuchi to give us a chance to relax before the boom was lowered, meaning our eventual death. At any rate, that was our first and only experience on a naval vessel. The smell of the paint reminded me of the Japanese fleet visits to San Francisco.

At the end of that month, April 1944, an announcement was made as to which air corps we were to be transferred to. It didn't matter so much as to where our destination was. What was important to us was what kind of aircraft we were to be trained for: fighters, heavy bombers, dive bombers, torpedo planes, reconnaissance planes or sea planes. My assignment was Wonsan (then called Genzan in the Japanese pronunciation) Naval Air Corps in Korea. However, there was a note saying we were to report first to Oita Air Corps. We did not know why. Oita City was in Northern Kyushu, on the same island as Izumi, about four hours away by train.

Mother had been back home since late the year before, after serving for three years as a reserve Red Cross nurse at Zentsuji Army Divisional Hospital. She had written me several times since then. Her most recent letter said she would like to visit me before I was transferred, perhaps to some far-away place. She came to Komenotsu, stayed with the Tanakas and met me at Izumi railway station. Luckily, I was able to get her on the same train we were taking to Oita. We talked a lot during the four-hour train ride. She told me that Brother Takao was in the fourth grade, that Father had returned to his clerical job and that food and everything else was scarce. Mother always was a bit on the heavy side, but I noticed that she had lost quite a bit of weight. Dieting was practically unheard of in those days. It must have been the food shortage that took some of her weight away. Upon arriving at Oita Station, Mother went to the port to take the ferry to Matsuyama, and I went to the Naval Air Corps. I was very glad to see Mother again, even only for such a short visit.

Chapter 8

The Warrior

OITA
Naval Air Corps

Fighter Training

Of the 5,000 some members of the 13th Class of Navy Air Reserve Students, one half received basic training at Mie and the other half at Tsuchiura. For the intermediate flight training at Izumi, there were about 100 of us. For the fighter training at Oita, the number was down to about 50. Of course, there were other naval air bases where fighter pilot training took place, so I have only a vague idea of how many fighter pilots were produced from my class.

We found out two things upon arrival at Oita. In Izumi, we were told that our assignment was to Wonsan in Korea but that we were to report to Oita first. We were never told why. Well, it turned out that Northern Korea, where Wonsan was, had had a very bad winter. The runway was heavily damaged by frost and ice, and we could not be sent there until repairs were complete. We were going to have fighter training at Oita for a little over a month. The other thing was that Oita did not have any of the Zero fighters for which we were supposed to be trained, so we would, for the time being, be using Model 96 fighters. The Model 96 was a rather outdated low-wing monoplane, which was used extensively during the late 1930s on the China front. It became famous for its sturdiness when a Navy pilot by the name of Kashimura flew his Model 96 safely back to his Shanghai base with the right wing half blown off by enemy anti-aircraft gunfire. Like the Model 93 Intermediate Trainer, it had a big engine up front and a tail wheel. Its landing gear was not retractable.

The airfield was located on the shoreline of Oita City, the capital of Oita Prefecture. The prefecture occupied the northeastern portion of the island of Kyushu, facing the island of Shikoku to the east. We were a short train ride from Beppu, famous for its hot springs. Oita Naval Air Corps (NAC) was originally built for intermediate flight training. There were many *yokaren* (air trainees) already into their training when we got there. Because of the arrival of fighter planes, the airfield needed a longer runway. When we arrived, the construction of the extension of the runway was almost, but not quite, finished. There was an army of high school and middle school students working on the runway with the construction workers.

For this training, we had to repeat the process we went through for intermediate training — hands off first, hands on the controls lightly, taking over the flight with the instructor in the rear cockpit, and then solo. This time, however, we needed to acclimatize ourselves to faster speeds and higher rates of ascent and descent. We were exposed to a higher degree of danger. The on-the-ground and in-the-air discipline was tighter than at Izumi. The "injection" of Navy Spirit took place quite frequently.

Yet, there were many more accidents than before. Some came in too fast or too low and practically crash-landed or overshot the runway. One day I was on watch, using binoculars and calling off the numbers on the planes taking off and landing for the record book. As I happened to look toward the rows of parked planes to see which plane was going to taxi to the end of the runway next, I saw a member of the ground crew walking from one side of a plane toward the front end. My yelling would not have done any good because of the distance and the roaring of engines, but I think I yelled. Simultaneously the man disappeared from my sight. Minutes later, I learned that the young recruit was killed by the propeller of the plane, which practically slashed him in half. We had strict orders to always go around the ends of the wings while walking near planes so as not to get into this kind of accident. Evidently the young man forgot this rule.

On another day, I was sitting on a bench at the command post, waiting for my turn to go up. Suddenly, the student on the watch cried out, "No. 48 is coming in too low!" Instantaneously we looked at the blackboard. "It's Tsujimoto!" Sure enough, his landing gears hooked a pole at the end of the runway. As if in a slow motion movie, Tsujimoto's plane continued its forward motion but slowly tipped over, tail first. Then the plane hit the ground upside down and slid forward. All of us at the command post ran over and lifted one wing, hoping to tip the plane over and get Tsujimoto out of the cockpit. When the cockpit was about two feet off the ground, we saw Tsujimoto squirm a bit and then fall to the ground. He had unhooked the seatbelt. He crawled out from under the upside down plane, stood up and said, "What happened?" We replied, "What happened is what we want to ask you." To which he retorted, "Well, I was looking at those high school girls working on the ground. I guess I came in too low." He was lucky. All he had was a nick on the tip of his nose. We had thought he would be decapitated.

I think we had three or four Sundays off while at Oita. There were a few hotels in Beppu designated for use by naval officers. A bunch of us went to one of them every one of those Sundays. Because of the naval designation, the hotels were supplied with extra rations of food and drinks. We ate and drank to our hearts' content. We also dipped ourselves in the natural hot spring baths, both indoors and outdoors, partly to cleanse ourselves and partly to sober up.

In 1944, we did not have any television sets, pinball parlors or anything of that sort to amuse ourselves. One Sunday, we felt a bit bored just eating, drinking and bathing, and decided to explore a *geisha* house. None of us had had the experience and really did not know what to expect. We at least had some idea that there were different levels of *geisha* houses. The top level ones were places for men to eat and drink while listening to the women sing traditional Japanese songs and watching them perform traditional Japanese dances. The most lowly provided mainly sex. The first ones were too expensive for us and probably beyond our tastes. The second ones were below young naval officers' dignity. So we went to ask the hotel manager and had him recommend a house. The women there knew how to handle naval officers. They knew many navy songs and joined us in singing them. Some of my comrades who had gone to colleges in big urban cities knew how to social dance, so they did that with the girls. After we got tired of all that, each one of us went to bed with a girl. That, of course, was my first such experience. I found delight in sex itself, but the experience as a whole left a void in my heart. Through the long talk I had with the girl, I came to realize that she had little personal freedom. She had to have special permission from the owner of the house every time she left the premises, and was only allowed out for limited amounts of time. She had to go through a weekly physical checkup for venereal disease. She had to entertain whomever she was told to entertain, and some of those men were not at all pleasant to be with. For quite some time thereafter, I stayed away from the sex-for-money business.

As we had been notified beforehand, the 13th Class was promoted to ensign as of June 1, 1944. We were still considered to be in the reserve forces, but nevertheless became full-fledged officers. It has long been, and it still is, customary in Japan for those wearing uniforms — students, servicemen, policemen, etc. — to change to summer uniforms as of June 1. So, at the ceremony held for us that morning, we wore our white summer uniforms. Each of us was given our new shoulder straps, with one silver cherry blossom on a golden stripe each, showing the rank of ensign. From that day on, we were addressed as Ensign So-and-So, not Student So-and-So. How proud we were. Our promotion came a bit earlier than normal for two reasons: it was a wartime promotion and we were aircraft pilots. I am sure the next Sunday when we went into town, we showed off even more than before. Young girls couldn't help but take sidelong glances at us, but I am sure more mature adults looked down on our attitude.

In early June, we were told that the repair work on the runway had made Wonsan NAC almost ready to take us on. We thought we would soon be sent directly there, but instead it was announced that we would first be given a three-day leave before heading for the Korean Peninsula. This was probably done out of compassion on the part of the naval authorities, since we, at least some of us, might never return to the Japanese mainland. Chances were that we would be sent directly to the front lines after completing our training and get killed in combat. Anyway, the leave was a total surprise. We couldn't have been happier. Everyone started calling home to give their families the good news. Japan Airlines was in existence at the time, but because of the wartime conditions, especially fuel shortages, their planes were not flying regularly. All travel had to be by train. Those whose homes were in Tokyo or a bit further north barely had enough time for an overnight stay at home. Those who came from further north, Hokkaido for example, had to arrange to meet their families somewhere between home and Oita, perhaps in Tokyo. From Oita to Matsuyama via a ferry from Beppu was only a little over a half-day trip. From Matsuyama to Shimonoseki, our point of assembly on the third day, was also a short one-day trip. I could stay home for two nights.

I got home late in the afternoon of the first day of leave. Oh, it felt good to sit on the *tatami* mat again. Of course, I sat on *tatami* at the Tanakas' in Komenotsu and at the hotel in Beppu. But the *tatami* at home felt different. It was so soothing. I asked Mother for my clothes from my college days and started to take off my uniform. "Wait. Go around the neighborhood in that uniform first and tell them you're back for a short while," she said. She probably wanted to show me off. It was a fried chicken dinner that evening. I didn't know how Mother was able to get that much chicken at that time of food shortage, but she somehow managed. It was the first fried chicken since Father had brought me some at Mie. Father seemed very happy to drink with me. He said he was lucky he had decided to quit drinking for a while and saved the rationed *sake* for a couple of months. We talked and talked way into the night.

After breakfast the next morning, I donned my uniform and set out to visit Bancho Elementary and Matsuyama Middle School (*Matsuchu*). Since Navy officers were prohibited to ride bicycles, I had to walk. I was able to see some of my old teachers at both schools. Without exception, they seemed to have a hard time finding the right words to say to me. Obviously they wanted me to stay well. Yet, they had to tell me to do my best in fighting for the Emperor and for the country. They knew that that meant an eventual certain death. That did not bother me, though. By then, I firmly believed that my death meant survival for my family and all of these good people. I was again probably 110% Japanese. Talking to different teachers during different class hours at the two schools, there was no time left for me to pay a visit to Kosho, my old college.

What we had for dinner that evening and what we talked about during and after, I have no recollection. Probably, at least half of my thoughts were on the Zero fighter we were going to be trained in in a couple of days. Takao had to go to school the next morning. Father, Mother and I had a late breakfast. Mother brought out what was known as a *senninbari. Senninbari* translates as "thousand person needles." It was about a three-foot-long, six-inch-wide piece of white silk cloth, with hundreds, maybe a thousand, knots of red thread sewn on. It was a half Shinto ritual object, half superstitious object given by a girl or a woman to a man going to war for whom she cared. A girl would first go around to the womenfolk in her family and relatives, then friends, and then stand on the street corner asking female passersby to tie the knots. This one was given to me through Mother from Michiko, a girl I used to like a lot in college. I would have wrapped the *senninbari* around my flight helmet or my waist under the flight suit if I ever flew combat missions, which I never did. Supposedly, the *senninbari* would have protected me from enemy bullets. Time flew, Father and Mother accompanied me to Takahama Port, and I got on the ferry to Beppu and sailed away. The same feeling that I had when I sailed out almost a year before came back to me — this is the last time for me to see Father and Mother and this beautiful scenery.

In the late afternoon of that mid-June 1944 day, we all made it to Shimonoseki near Oita, where we boarded the Kanpu Ferry, which shuttled between Shimonoseki and Pusan, Korea. As the ferry passed through the Shimonoseki Straits and sailed into the open ocean, we all leaned on the deck railing and watched the mainland grow smaller and drift farther away. While nobody said much, our thoughts must have been about the same — would we ever see the mainland again?

Guadalcanal had fallen to enemy hands. American troops had landed on the Marshall Islands. The Japanese Mainland was exposed to Allied air raids. Just being on the ferry itself was not altogether safe. But somehow we made it across to Pusan and started out on the long train trip north. I must have slept through the ride till we reached Seoul (which was then called Keijo under Japanese colonial rule, which imposed Japanese names on the Koreans) because I hardly remember anything about the scenery we passed through. We had a little time in Seoul as we waited to change trains; we spent our time sightseeing. The citizens seemed friendly enough, although we were to later learn how much the Korean people hated us Japanese.

Korea and Japan have had long historical ties. In the first place, what my generation learned as the early history of Japan (now considered mythology) seems to be based on the arrival of Korean, and to some extent Chinese, civilians in Japan. Some scholars assume that the story about the god and goddess sending their son to rule symbolizes a tribal chief arriving from Korea. From around the 14th century on, a significant number of Korean craftsmen such as weavers, potters and toolmakers were invited to Japan by imperial and feudal rulers. They vitalized Japanese arts and civilization. Later, in 1592, after subjugating most of the local feudal lords in Japan, Hideyoshi Toyotomi invaded Korea but was beaten back. In more modern times, Japan continued to harbor ambitions towards Korea, and after the victorious Sino-Japanese (1894-95) and Russo-Japanese (1904-05) Wars, it colonized Korea under the pretense that it needed protection against aggression by China and Russia. This took place in 1910. The colonization was terminated, of course, at the end of World War II.

Wonsan is on the eastern coast of what is now North Korean territory, facing the Sea of Japan. I seem to remember the air base being on a piece of land that jutted out into the bay, which seemed like a landfill between the mainland and an island. More than anything else, the sight of rows of real Zero fighters excited us. We could hardly wait till the training began.

We didn't have much time left for training. The situation at the fronts was worsening. The Allied forces were taking island after island in the Pacific. American carrier-based planes occasionally came in to bomb and strafe Japanese mainland cities. The Japanese Army and Navy were losing front line pilots at a rapid rate. We were running short of high octane fuel. The authorities were anxious to send us out to the front as soon as we were able to fly well enough.

The Zero was a marvelous plane. Its engine had something like 1,000 horsepower, almost double that of the Model 96 fighter engine. It responded very sharply to the movements of the control stick. For the first time, we had a canopy over our heads. We were able to see ahead and all around us much better than we could in the old models.

As soon as we acquired the feel for the plane, we went right into training for formation flights and dogfights. We had night flights, night formation flights and target shooting. Accidents continued. We had strict orders not to turn around after takeoff and come back landing with a tail wind, even if the engine sputtered. Yet, one of my classmates panicked when his engine sputtered and burped right after takeoff, and went against the order. We could see him struggling to bring his plane down, but it kept gliding forward. Finally, his landing gears caught on a pile of gravel near the end of the runway and the plane turned over and skidded on the ground. He was badly injured but was lucky enough to live. Not so lucky was Ensign Narabayashi who, on August 5, had a mid-air collision during a formation flight, was ejected out but somehow got hit by his own propeller after his parachute got tangled with his tail wing.

Since the base was low on fuel, we were usually able to make the 15 to 30 minute training flights only once a day. Records show that our class had a total of only 70 hours of flight training by graduation, including the intermediate flight training.

While the outlook of the war and civilian living conditions were grim indeed, the remoteness of Wonsan from the heat of things enabled us to lead a more or less normal life. The Navy fed us well. For night flights, they supplied us with special pills, probably vitamins, to better our eyesight. On days off, they gave us *sake* to take out with us or to drink in our barracks.

On Sundays, we took a local bus into town. We got off the bus wherever we felt like, looked for a place to eat and drink, and generally had a good time. On one such Sunday, some of us decided to go out and take a look at the town's swimming beach. It was mid-summer and we swam a little but didn't want to tire ourselves out because of the next day's flight training. After drying off, we went into a small restaurant on the beach, where we had some food and drinks. There was a cute little waitress there who seemed to take a liking to me. So, the next Sunday, I went there all by myself. After I talked to the girl for a while, she disappeared briefly, came back to tell me that she had asked her boss to give her the rest of the day off and got it, so why don't we go to visit her home. I happily obliged. After she introduced me to her whole family, which was a large one, she and I sat in the living room chatting and sipping tea. We talked about life in the Navy, how some of the Navy men got drunk and misbehaved in town, compared life in Korea and Japan, and indulged in other mundane small talk. After about an hour, I began to get the feeling that she wanted to make love with me. I suddenly noticed that there was no one else in the house, or at least it seemed that way. I had to control myself very hard and I was glad I did. It was no use getting romantically involved with her, because I knew our stay in Wonsan would not be for very much longer. She looked 17 or 18 then. I wonder what she looks like now.

On another Sunday, I thought I saw a stable from the bus window. Being curious and not having any particular plans for the day, I got off the bus at the next stop and walked back. Sure enough, there was a stable with a beautiful horse in it. Since there was no one around, I just stood at the doorway and kept admiring the beauty. Then a man appeared, looked a bit startled to see a naval officer standing there, but collected himself and asked, "Are you interested in horses?" I told him how I got to be the captain of our riding club in college. He then smiled and invited me into the stable. We introduced ourselves to each other, and I found out that besides being the owner of the horse, he was the president of the only bus company in the city. I am fairly sure that his name was Mr. Kim. He said that the horse was the same breed as the ones used by the Russian Cossacks. No wonder the horse was taller and slimmer than the average Japanese horse.

As I started to bid him farewell, Mr. Kim asked me if I had plans for the evening. I didn't. All I had to do was to be back in the barracks by ten P.M. Mr. Kim then invited me to dinner. After spending the afternoon in town, I arrived at the Kim residence at six P.M. as I was told. The house was near the stable. It was a full course Korean dinner, all served on silver dinnerware. I love pepper-hot food, and Korean food is generally pepper-hot. I enjoyed the dinner immensely. I found Mr. Kim to be a very open-minded person. He told me that not all Korean people hated and were angry at the Japanese. Although the number was small, depending on how they or the members of their families and friends had been treated by the Japanese, some had no animosity toward the Japanese. Mrs. Kim was a beautiful lady. Her

Japanese was a bit halting, but with help from her husband, we were able to have pleasant exchanges. Mr. Kim appeared to be in his late forties, so he would be close to 100 years of age if he is still around. It is a pity that I did not keep up my correspondence with him after leaving Wonsan.

Today, we hear and read of anti-Japanese sentiments among the Koreans, Chinese and other peoples of Asia. Barbaric and brutal acts by the Japanese are being revealed. It is very unfortunate. As far as I am concerned, I have nothing but pleasant memories of my relationships with Korean citizens. It seems there is much left for us to learn about how to act with civility toward people of other countries — as well as toward our own countrymen.

In early October 1944, we completed our fighter training and were considered graduated from all training courses. There was no time for ceremonial functions. As we finished our last day of training, a group photo was taken in front of one of the hangars. In the evening, we were assembled in a hall to be given our transfer orders. This was a big event for us, since where we went next determined how much longer we were likely to survive. If we were sent to Okinawa or further south, it almost certainly meant that we would be sent out on *kamikaze* missions and die within a few months, or maybe a few weeks. I think we all half-anticipated meeting such a fate.

It turned out that my next assignment was at the Tokyo Detachment of Kasumigaura Naval Air Corps. I had never even heard of such a unit, and, upon inquiry, found out that it was a small training corps for *yokaren* flight cadets. I was also told that the airfield was commonly known as Haneda and that it was a civilian airfield used by a commercial airline. Strange. The Navy training its cadets at a civilian airfield? I really didn't know what to think. Obviously, my next assignment was as a flight instructor. That meant that I might be alive for some time yet. Unless I got into an accident, as quite a number of my classmates had by then, a flight instructor would have a better chance of survival than a front line fighter pilot. But then, going from a Zero fighter back to an intermediate trainer plane didn't seem much fun. Ensigns Utsumi, Yamamoto and Watanabe who came through Mie, Izumi, Oita and Wonsan with me, and Kawamura, who went to a different intermediate training corps and joined us at

Wonsan, were given the same transfer orders to the Tokyo Detachment. Others were assigned to either training corps or fighter corps around the country, but a few were sent directly to the front lines. And an even smaller number was ordered to remain at Wonsan to become instructors for the next class of reserve officers. Kobayashi, with whom I shared the lunch Father brought to Mie and with whom I enjoyed the hospitality of the Tanaka family while at Izumi, was among them.

About 50 of us boarded the train and traveled all the way back to Shimonoseki via Seoul and Pusan. From Shimonoseki, some went south to bases on Kyushu. How I envied the few who boarded the ferry for Matsuyama Naval Air Base! The five of us going to the Tokyo Detachment got together to make plans. We were to arrive at the Detachment by five P.M. the next day. If we took the train from Shimonoseki straight to Tokyo, we would arrive half a day too early. There was nothing wrong in arriving early, but we decided to make better use of our time. Yamamoto was the luckiest. His home was just outside of the Tokyo city limits. He could take the train straight to Tokyo, take a streetcar and go home and backtrack to join us in front of the Detachment gate shortly before five P.M. Kawamura and Watanabe were the next luckiest. Their homes were in Numazu and Shizuoka, about an hour's train ride this side of Tokyo. They could get off the train, go home for a few hours and get back on the train. Poor Utsumi. His home was in Sendai, way north of Tokyo. He decided to visit his uncle in Tokyo. And poor me: there was not enough time to cross the Inland Sea just to say hello to my folks. On the spur of the moment, I decided to stop off at Kure to say hello and thank you to Michiko, the girl who gave me the *senninbari*. She had written to me that she was with her girls' high schoolmates working at the Naval Arsenal in Kure.

I was the first one to get off the train. Finding my way to the Arsenal, I told the gate guard the purpose of my visit. He said it was still working hours, and workers, even volunteer workers like Michiko, were not allowed to leave their posts. But then, he said, since the visitor was a naval officer, maybe Michiko could get special permission to come to the visitors' room. She did. We chatted about our families, our friends and about Matsuyama. I thanked her for the *senninbari*, which had worked fine so far in keeping me alive and well. I could have stayed longer, but I didn't want to keep her away from work, so in about an hour I left. Getting back on the train and changing trains in Osaka, I arrived in Tokyo a bit too early, or so I thought.

Changing to an electric train at Tokyo Station and going to Kamata Station, then getting on a bus to Haneda took much longer than I had thought. Tokyo was a big city, unlike Matsuyama, where you can get on the electric train at Matsuyama City Station in the heart of the city and get to the port of Takahama at the edge of the city in 20 minutes. I got to the Detachment gate perhaps about ten minutes to five o'clock. Yamamoto and Utsumi were already there. Just before five o'clock, Kawamura and Watanabe showed up in a taxi.

Chapter 9

The Instructor

HANEDA
Tokyo Naval Air Corps

Haneda

Twice, in 1274 and 1281, Imperial Mongolia attempted to invade Japan. In the 1274 conflict, the invading forces came over by ships and landed near present-day Hakata in Northern Kyushu. They overpowered the defending army, but due to their own heavy losses, they decided to return to their fleet to regroup. That night, a gale storm hit the area and forced the damaged fleet to retreat. And again in 1281, the Mongolians made another attempt. Obviously, the Japanese warlords had learned how to deal with the invaders better. They succeeded in chasing the landing forces back to the fleet and kept them there for two months. Then another big wind-and-rain storm hit, forcing the fleet to flee back to the Continent. The storms were what we know today as typhoons. But ever since the attempted Mongolian invasions, the Japanese had come to believe that their country is protected by God against foreign invasions, that the winds that drove the Mongolians away were "Divine Wind," a direct translation of the Japanese word "Kamikaze." In this war, we pilots were the divine wind.

Returning to the mid-20th century, it became fairly widely known after World War II that the Japanese Navy was initially reluctant to begin a war with the United States. Many of the high-ranking officers *had lived abroad as naval attaches or academy and college students in their younger years. They knew the depth of the industrial and military strength of the West. In contrast, the Army brass had narrower visions. And the succession of minor victories against the Chinese inflated their egos. By a series of historical accidents, it was the Army that took over the leadership of the central government. The Navy was forced to go along with the aggressive war policies of the Army. It is said that Admiral Isoroku Yamamoto, who eventually led the Combined Fleet to attack Pearl Harbor, insisted that a war with the United States must be swift and decisive and that a prolonged war would lead Japan to a defeat. Unfortunately for Japan, the war did go on and the war tide turned against it, despite the victorious initial offensive. As the situation worsened, military leaders were forced to come up with new tactics and new weapons. One of them was the suicide missions, which they named "tokubetsu kogeki," meaning "special attacks."*

The scene is in October 1944, at the Japanese advanced naval air base at Mabalacat Air Field in the Philippines, just outside of the now former U.S. Clark Air Base. With a dwindling number of aircraft and experienced pilots, the senior officers, headed by Admiral Takijiro Onishi, had been fretting over the reality of the need to commence special attack tactics, otherwise known as the "body crash" tactic. The pilot would fly his plane with a bomb attached to the underside of the fuselage and crash into the target. On October 20, Admiral Onishi called Lt. Senior Grade Yuko Seki into his office and told him of the special attack plan. Lt. Seki was from Ehime Prefecture, my home state, and a Naval Academy graduate. Admiral Onishi asked Seki to lead a squad of suicide planes. It took some time for Seki to come back with a positive answer. The fact that he had married not long before may have had something to do with his hesitation. Lt. Seki and his squad took off after a few days, couldn't find their targets and returned to the base. After several attempts, he finally crashed into an American ship. This was the beginning of the kamikaze missions. Originally, the suicide mission was thought up as a voluntary service. However, in reality it became an enforced tactic.

It may have been in February or March of 1945 that Admiral Onishi paid a visit to the Tokyo Detachment. He seemed to be on a mission of talking to potential kamikaze pilots to relate how pilots willingly took off on their last missions for the sake of their country and fellow countrymen. I remember very well how sincere, almost apologetic, he sounded. Several times during his brief talk to us on the grass of the airfield, he seemed to have a hard time holding his tears back. When Lt. Seki's squad took off on its last mission, the unit was given the name "Shimpu-tai." Shimpu is written with the same Chinese characters as kamikaze and means exactly the same thing, divine wind, only pronounced differently. Later, the expression kamikaze came to be used for all suicide or body crashing tactics.

When we told the gate guards that we were new flight instructors just arrived from Wonsan Naval Air Corps, one of them led us to a one-story wooden building. It looked like it had been hastily built not much earlier. There were several rows of two-story structures, which were obviously barracks, but also wooden and shabby. Beyond those we saw at least one four-story concrete building. One of us asked the guard if that was a part of the corps. "Oh, no, sir. That is Japan Air Lines, sir," was the answer. Then we noticed a structure with windows on top of the roof. That must be the control tower, I thought. None of the airfields we had been at up till then had control towers. All takeoffs and landings were done subject only to ground observation.

Entering the commanding officer's office, we found a small, old man sitting behind a small desk. His hair was gray. His insignia showed that he was a Commander, but he didn't quite have the dignity of such a high ranking naval officer. He looked more like a kind, old grandpa than anything else. But he had a strong voice. "Where is your five-minute-before spirit?" was the first thing he said to us. Of course, when we were told to report at five o'clock, we were supposed to be standing in front of the Commander's door at five minutes to five, according to the Navy's tradition. All we could do was to apologize and promise not to repeat the error. We half-anticipated a punch on the cheek, but that did not happen. Since the room had no table or chairs for visitors, the Commander took us to the Gun Room (room for junior officers) to sit down and talk. Commander Fujimura told us that the Tokyo Detachment of Kasumigaura NAC was very new and that it would be renamed Tokyo NAC in the near future. He said about 200 *yokaren* cadets were in training and that we were to be their flight instructors. We were to use Model 93 Intermediate Trainers, sharing the use of the airfield with Japan Air Lines, which flew only infrequent, irregular service. Then he went on to talk about himself. In his younger days as a Lt. Commander, he commanded a destroyer, which collided with another destroyer in a night maneuver. As a result, he took early retirement, but was recalled to active duty due to the Navy's manpower shortage. Having been a fleet man, he knew very little about flying, and left all flight operations to Lt. Commander Shimizu, his flight commander. That explained his age and his grandpa-like appearance and manners. The meeting lasted for almost an hour and dinnertime was approaching.

We were pleasantly surprised to find that a seaman was assigned to each of us to take care of our personal needs. They wouldn't clothe us. No, that would be below an officer's dignity. But they made our beds after we got up in the morning, did our laundry, served our meals, fetched tidbits to go with our drinks in the evening, etc. The man assigned to me was Seaman 2nd Class Hashimoto. He was in his mid- to-late-forties. While Commander Fujimura could have been my grandfather, Hashimoto could have been my father. Hashimoto was one of those who were drafted into service when far past the peace-time draft age. He was rather effeminate, and, I learned a few days later, in civilian life he was a choreographer and director of traditional Japanese dancing. With all of this combined, our first impression of the Tokyo Detachment was, "What a shabby place we've ended up in!"

Our attitude toward the Detachment began to change at dinnertime. Rather than the mass-cooked meals served by ourselves, and rather than eating out of metal bowls and plates and rather than sitting at rows and rows of long tables in the barracks as we did for about a year, we were seated at a regular dinner table using chinaware. The food was cooked in the Officers' Kitchen, separate from the huge kitchen for the men. It tasted good enough. The assigned seamen did all the serving. Their supervisor, a non-commissioned officer, was there throughout the meal, making sure that everything was done right. About 20 junior officers, including eight pilots and four navigators, were eligible to eat in that room.

After dinner, the five of us from Wonsan were told to assemble in the Gun Room. Lt. Commander Shimizu, who served as vice commander of the Detachment, was in charge of the meeting. He first introduced himself as a former dive-bomber pilot, wounded in a crash landing and now doing mainly deskwork. He was a Naval Academy graduate, of course, around age 40. He appeared to be very sharp and well informed of the war situation. He introduced us to three officers with whom we would be working very closely. They were Lt. SG Yamauchi, Lt. SG Suga and Lt. JG Ota. Lt. Yamauchi was a Naval Academy graduate, but the other two were college-graduate reserve officers like us, Lt. Suga being six years our senior and Lt. Ota one year. Lt. Yamauchi took over the meeting from Commander Shimizu to explain to us in detail what our daily routine would be from the following day on. He also told us who the other junior officers we had dinner with were. Eleven of them were members of the 13th Class Reserve Officers. Of them, seven were pilots and four navigators.

The meeting was over around nine o'clock. The five of us were sitting around talking about our new environment, when Seaman Hashimoto appeared and asked if we would like *sake* or wine. Another pleasant surprise. We all preferred *sake* and got it. We were privileged to ignore taps but decided to heed it in view of the hard work that waited for us in the morning.

The first full day in Tokyo began with the "Five minutes before Reveille," Reveille and the morning assembly routine. Since the Detachment was small and there was no space for a parade ground, the morning assembly took place on the airfield apron. Standing at the head of the rows and facing the men was another new experience for us. It sort of gave us a feeling of self-importance. Going back to the Officers' Quarters after the assembly, we found our seamen making our beds and cleaning our bedrooms. For breakfast, we had a choice between Japanese style and Western style.

The training of the cadets was to start at eight A.M. as usual, but the five of us were told to assemble on the apron at 7:30. Each of us was to take a plane up to get the feeling of flying the Model 93 again. I got into the front cockpit of one of the planes and revved up the engine. The rpm was much lower than that of the Zero. I put it in full throttle and wondered if the plane would really get off the ground. But by the time I taxied out to the end of the runway, I got the feeling back for the Model 93. I took off to the south and made a left turn. I was flying over Tokyo Bay toward the Boso Peninsula across the Bay from Tokyo. Another left turn, to the north. Now, the range of Mt. Nokogiri (Saw) on the Peninsula was clearly visible to the right. Seeing the rugged edges of the peaks of the mountain, I knew how it got its name. To the left spread the city of Tokyo. It looked vast but somewhat smaller than I felt it was when I had traveled overland from Tokyo Station to Haneda. Left turn again toward the big city. Lo and behold, Mt. Fuji was clearly visible. I hadn't realized that Fuji was so close. Now, when was the last time I saw it? That's right, it was through the train window, going down to Matsuyama with Mother in 1932. Twelve years earlier! How time flies and how changed I was from then! The last left turn toward the north end of the runway, descending. The runway approached. Bingo, a three-point landing. Say, that was easy. Maybe I can be a good instructor.

Back on the apron, I parked the plane where it was before I taxied it out. I saw Lt. Suga and some of the instructors for Squad 2 and walked over to them. I saluted Lt. Suga and reported that the test flight went well. He introduced me to the four non-commissioned officer instructors for Squad 2, with whom I was to train the cadets. They all had front line combat experience. Kawamura, Utsumi, Watanabe and Yamamoto soon joined us. After a short wait, the cadets came running in formation from the direction of the barracks. The five new instructors were introduced to them and Lt. Suga added, "These officers are Zero fighter pilots. They are full of the Navy Spirit. Learn well from them." "Being full of the Navy Spirit" meant only one thing. We are going to be tough on them. At least that is what Lt. Suga expected of us.

After giving the instructions for the day at the ground command post, Lt. Suga ordered the training to begin. Which cadets were going to fly in what order on which planes was all prearranged. My first cadet was Cadet Y. He and I saluted Lt. Suga and ran toward our plane.

Cadet Y got in the front cockpit and I in the rear. Come to think of it, this was the first time for me to sit in the rear cockpit. It felt a little uncomfortable. I felt closer to the ground than in the front cockpit. The wings blocked the view ahead. I told Cadet Y to keep his hands on the throttle and the control stick very lightly. And we started to taxi out. I slightly zigzagged our way to the north end of the runway so we were able to see where we were going. "Takeoff!" We followed the same route I had flown alone a little while before. After reaching the designated 300-meter altitude, I let go of my hands. The plane started to turn its nose to the left and banked to the left. As the turn and the bank kept increasing, Cadet Y suddenly overreacted. The plane banked to the right and started to turn right. I took the controls and set the plane back on course. After a few seconds, I took my hands off again. And again, the plane started to bank and turn. It seemed that the cadet either didn't have the feeling for flying yet or he didn't have any talent for flying at all. I let my hands go several more times during the flight and each time I had to take over again. We came to a bumpy landing because the cadet gripped the control stick so tightly out of excitement at coming in for a landing that I couldn't pull the nose up in time. It goes without saying that Cadet Y got a whack on the cheek for that.

The next cadet, S, did much better. He had a little trouble maintaining altitude. He tended to dip a bit and I had to pull the plane back up a couple of times, but he seemed to have a good sense of balance. I flew with eight or nine cadets in the morning. More training after lunch. As it was mid-October and the days were getting shorter, we had to stop training around 4:30 P.M.

We were free on weekends, from after lunch on Saturday till six P.M. on Sunday. Yamamoto, whose home was very close to Tokyo, and who had gone to college in Tokyo, knew his way around the big city. He could have enjoyed the luxury of being with his family on weekends but he didn't. He stuck with the Wonsan group. We got on a bus near the compound gate for the trip to Kamata Station. From there we took a train and then changed trains at Shinagawa Station. After four stops, we were in Shibuya, one of the entertainment districts of Tokyo. We walked to the Dogenzaka area, where there were many Japanese inns. Up to that point, Yamamoto had no trouble leading us. He had heard a lot about the Dogenzaka inns, but he had never been in one. We had plenty of time till sundown, so we strolled up and down the streets, looking for a nice place. We found one and went in. The lady owner and the young maids went wild in excitement. Business was down for them those days, because people were busy, many in war industries, tired and had little money to spend. Cities were blacked out because of possible air raids. To spend the night at other than their own homes was not safe either. So, seeing five young men, neat in their uniforms and seemingly with plenty of spending money, they were excited. Each of us was given a small *tatami*-mat room upstairs, we all took a bath together and got together in a large room on the same floor, also *tatami*-matted. We all looked refreshed and happy.

Alcoholic drinks of any kind were scarce for civilians. Places of entertainment such as restaurants and hotels received meager monthly rations. I have no knowledge of how Army officers fared, but we Navy officers, especially pilots, were very lucky. We got a ration of 1 *sho* (1. 8 liters) of *sake* and one bottle of sweet wine a week. To make a sly guess, the *sake* was meant for us and the wine for our female companions. Three of us brought our week's ration with us, so there was plenty for all of us to drink. We asked that the *sake* be warmed and served, and told the girls they could have all the wine. The party began. The food was simple and modest. The inn didn't know we were coming, and even if they did they probably couldn't have bought much fish and other things anyway. We ate, drank and talked about the cadets, our senior officers, the good (?) old days at Wonsan, Oita, Izumi and Mie. We talked about the Sunday evening in Wonsan when one of us, Watanabe, came back to the barracks drunk and started chasing a fellow with whom he had an argument, with a drawn sword. We all got pretty high and started thinking about going to bed. It was obvious by that time, however, that the maids were willing, even anxious, to go to bed with us. It had to be decided which one of us was going to couple with which maid. We were all sitting in a circle on the *tatami* and the girl sitting across from me was very pretty. She occasionally looked at me as though to say that she wanted to go to bed with me. But I didn't have the courage to say that I wanted her. We finally decided to let the girls do the *janken* (scissors, paper and stone) and choose us. The second winner, a pretty, tiny girl, chose me. She and I went to my room, where the bedding was laid out with two pillows. The rest was the usual story.

The next morning, Sunday, we all got up rather late with slight hangovers. The breakfast was not as good or as plentiful as was our breakfast back at the Detachment, of course, but that was not important. We had a very good time at the inn. Yamamoto suggested that we go to the famous Ueno Park, where there were an art museum and a zoo. So we did that for the rest of the day. We often went back to the same Dogenzaka inn on weekends. Sometimes Yamamoto or Watanabe or Kawamura wanted to spend the weekends with their families back home. On such occasions, we invited some other young officers, mostly our classmates, from the Detachment. On some weekends the food at the inn was good, because the proprietor told merchants that she was entertaining Navy officers and they had better get good materials. My feelings against buying sex with money? Well, this time it was a bit different. We were not charged for sex as such. The girls not only entertained us at parties and in bed but also did laundry for us, ran errands for us and did many other small things. The charge for all this was put on the bill for the group as a service charge, very modest sums. We split the bill evenly. It was up to each of us to tip the girl if we felt like it. I often did. Besides, I think I was almost in love with her. She was my girl, not just another prostitute.

According to records, it was on November 1, 1944. Around noon it was, I think, as we came close to concluding the morning training, that we suddenly noticed a silvery plane flying north over our heads. At first, we could not tell how large the plane was or how high it was flying. Then, someone watching it through binoculars shouted, "Huge plane, not ours. Altitude 10,000 meters or more!" About five minutes after we first sighted the plane and it was almost out of our sight, the air raid siren sounded and the corps PA system announced, "Enemy B-17 raiding Tokyo!" This was repeated several times. We were simply stunned. An enemy aircraft flying right over our heads? In broad daylight like this? Why, it was even beautiful, the silvery body against the deep blue sky. We stopped all takeoffs but had no way to call down those in flight. Model 93 had no ground-to-air communication system. As the planes landed, we kept them on the ground. We didn't even have plans for hiding our planes from air raids.

Then, after 20 minutes or so, we saw the plane again, this time flying south on a course a bit to the east of its northern flight. Again, it was a beautiful sight. There was no sign of bombing. Fear sort of disappeared from our minds. We just watched it in awe. That evening in the Gun Room, that was all we talked about. It must have been a reconnaissance plane. It must have taken a lot of good pictures of the ground since the weather was so good. Air raids of Tokyo would begin soon. We've got to get ready for them! Of course, after the war, we were to learn that the plane was a modified B-29, not a B-17.

About three weeks passed without any air raids. Our training continued. Some of the cadets came close to soloing. Some of us learned new punishment techniques from the veteran non-commissioned flight instructors. For example, when the cadet did not follow our instructions or did something stupid in flight, we would unfasten the seat belt and stand up in the rear cockpit. Scolding the cadet on the voice tube, we would hit him on the head with our fists or with the Navy Spirit Injection Stick. With a 75 knot wind blowing against you, you must put a lot of strength in your arm to bring the fist or the stick down on the head. Consequently, the cadet's head hurt quite a bit, even hit through the thick, lined headgear. Once this punishment was administered, the cadet remembered not to repeat the mistake, as long as he could help it.

One day during training, we heard the air raid siren go off again. We grounded the planes one after another and ushered the cadets toward the air raid shelters. We waited to see what was going to happen. Nothing happened. Then we were told by the Communications Officer that an area west of Tokyo was being bombarded. Soon after, we heard planes flying eastward, a lot of planes. They were too distant for our naked eyes, but by the sound of their engines now more or less familiar to us, we had no doubt that they were B-29s. We later learned that an aircraft plant was bombed that day. Then, nighttime air raids on Tokyo city proper, mainly residential areas, started in late November. Night after night, air raid sirens went off. Early on, these raids on Tokyo took place only at the rate of about twice a month. One night, either in late 1944 or early 1945, we had a close call. The southern part of Tokyo was bombarded and incendiary bombs fell all around the Detachment. Some fell right on our grounds. One of them made a direct hit on the roof of the shelter we were in. The shelter had a thick dirt cover, not concrete, so it shook a bit and dirt came flying down. If it explodes we will be blown to pieces, we thought. So we jumped out of the shelter and saw that the hit was an incendiary bomb. We saw several other long can-like objects lying around nearby, bursting into flames. We wanted to do something to extinguish them but were helpless until some men came running with fire extinguishers. One cadet tried to stamp out the fire and got his flight boots burning. There was nothing else for him to do but to kick off his boots and run. Fortunately, none of the Detachment buildings caught fire.

Early the next morning, I was ordered by the Commanding Officer to take a patrol out to the neighborhood residential area to see how the area had withstood the raid. Much of the area was burnt to the ground, and here and there we saw scorched bodies on the streets. There were a few dazed people just standing around. I talked to one such man, and sure enough he had lost his home. His family was safe and had just been evacuated to a relative's home in another part of the city. He just didn't know what to do. I decided to hurry back to the Detachment with the patrol and made a verbal report to the Commander, with a recommendation that the Detachment provide food and shelter for these helpless people. The Commander sent several cables, presumably to Navy Headquarters, and got some answers. He then called in Vice Commander Shimizu and ordered him to load some of the Detachment trucks with emergency food and dispatch the trucks to transport civilian victims to wherever they needed to go within the city limits. Evidently, there was no space in the barracks to accommodate them. That was when all of us felt that the war had finally come to Mainland Japan.

The 13th Class had been promoted to ensign back on July 1, 1944. We therefore were not expecting our next promotion to take place until about a year from then. On December 1, I was called into Commander Fujimura's office. I kept wondering why he wanted to see me. Did I do something wrong? When? As I stood in front of the Commander and bowed to him, he smiled and said, "Congratulations." I didn't understand. I thought he might be kidding me, suddenly blow his stack and scold me for something. "May I ask what this is about, sir?" I asked. "As of this date, you are promoted to Lieutenant Junior Grade, Imamura," he said with another smile. "What about my classmates, sir?" I asked. I had thought that members of a class all got promoted at the same time. That usually was the tradition. To my surprise, the Commander said, "No, you are the only one among your classmates promoted at this Detachment this time. Here, put these on, Lt. Imamura." He handed me two small silver cherry blossoms to add to the emblems on my collar. I was overjoyed. I thanked the Commander and hurried back to our quarters. I felt like running down the hall, but naval officers didn't run while in uniform. I called for Seaman Hashimoto, my assigned seaman, and asked him if he would have the silver cherry blossoms added to the emblems. He said that would be no problem at all. Needlework was part of his profession. It would have taken me at least half an hour to cut the threads to remove the emblems from the collar, punch a hole in each emblem to push the stems of the blossoms through and then sew the emblems back on the collars again. By the time Hashimoto came back with the jacket, it was close to dinnertime.

I went to the dining room. Most of the junior officers were there already. I acted nonchalant and did not say a word about the added cherry blossoms. Nobody seemed to take notice until we sat down at the dinner table. I think it was Ensign Okajima sitting across the table from me who said something like, "Hey, Imamura. Are you sure you are wearing your own jacket?" Everybody in the room looked at me in disbelief, so I had to tell them what happened. They all congratulated me but obviously with some mixed feelings. Sure enough, after dinner, Kawamura came up to me and said loudly enough for all to hear, "Imamura, you're now one rank ahead of us but we're still classmates. Don't you dare pull seniority on us, you hear?" I was sure he intended to intimidate me, but, as I told everyone there, I wasn't scared or anything because I had nothing to do with the promotion. I didn't think I was that much better than the others in flying and I didn't think I worked any harder than the others either. Even to this day, I do not know why I was promoted ahead of my classmates. I later learned that only about 10% of my classmates were promoted at that time.

During the last two or three days of December, the average Japanese family is very busy. Under the direction of the mother, the father and children help clean up the house and throw out things that have accumulated during the year but are no longer useful. Mother devotes herself to preparing special dishes for New Year's Day and the following two days so that she doesn't have to cook during that period. The foods are well cooked so that, with the help of the low air temperature, they won't spoil. None of this applied to us. We just kept on training till dusk on December 31st. Then New Year's Day came. At the morning assembly, Commander Fujimura reminded us of the grave situation our country was in on all fronts. The menace from the B-29s was also certain to increase. Casualties would rise, among the civilians as well as in the military. "Yet," he said, "I have confidence in you men. It is your generation that will restore the glories of the Japanese Empire. *Kamikaze* is with us. Let us see to it that the 20th year of Showa (1945) will be the beginning of a new era for our divine nation." Of course, in using the word *"kamikaze,"* Commander Fujimura very deliberately intended a double meaning.

The first three days of January are sacred holidays for the Japanese, based on the Shinto (religious) tradition. There was no training. However, we were ordered not to leave the Detachment compound. We assumed that this was not to irritate the civilians who were beginning to harbor resentment toward us for not flying up to intercept the B-29s. They had no way of knowing the difference in the capability between a training corps and a combat corps. So, on January 1, 1945, after the New Year breakfast specially prepared for us by the Officers' Kitchen, we had photo sessions and generally took it easy. I have no memory of what we did on the second. On the third, a group of professional entertainers came to the Detachment. There were comic storytellers, dancers and singers. When I was promoted to Lt. JG the previous year, I was also appointed Deck Officer. One of the deck officer's duties was the maintenance of morale. Being in charge of entertainment was a part of that duty. So I met the group at the Detachment gate, had them served tea in the Gun Room, watched over their performance and led them back to the gate when their performance was finished. Officers and men all enjoyed the group, especially the comic story telling done by Mikimatsu Yanagiya, a nationally known professional.

There was a well-known *samurai* actor by the name of Ito enlisted in our corps. He was a seaman 2nd class, drafted into service. As Deck Officer, I often sent him out to movie distributors to borrow movie films. We offered to pay the distributors and rent out the films, but they would not accept payment. They preferred to have the service men entertained free of charge. At first we borrowed mostly *samurai* movies, some with Seaman Ito playing in them, because those were what the men enjoyed the most. One day, Seaman Ito came back to say that American films were available too if we wanted to watch them. We had thought American films were either locked up or destroyed as enemy propaganda materials. Movie theaters were prohibited from showing them. We officers wanted to see them very much, so the next time I sent Ito out, I asked him to bring back a couple of them. These American movies had Japanese subtitles, so many of the men liked them too, but not as much as they enjoyed *samurai* movies. After all, most of them had never studied English.

Jutting out into Tokyo Bay, the Detachment airfield was rather often fogged in. More often than not, there would be heavy fog in the morning, which slowly cleared up in mid-morning. On such days, or on days when the clouds were too low for us to fly, we had the cadets engage in several different activities on the ground. The most popular was volleyball. The squadron would be split into several teams and compete against one another. Another activity, not so popular, was singing. The cadets formed several large circles and marched around as they sang. On some warm spring mornings, we had them take their trousers off, wade into the shallow waters surrounding the airfield and dig for clams. Since the area was off limits to civilians and hardly anyone went after the clams, our catch was plentiful. The cadets had a good time doing this but had no way of cooking them. They willingly gave all the clams to us. On such evenings, we would haul a *hibachi* into the Gun Room, bake the clams over the charcoal fire and have a feast. It goes without saying that much *sake* went down with the clams.

Through these activities, incidentally, I discovered something. Good pilots were good volleyball players. I think the connection here is the sense of balance, or equilibrium. Good volleyball players were generally good singers. They carried the tune well. To what extent this observation can be substantiated, I don't know. Perhaps someone can make a Ph.D. thesis out of this.

Chapter 10

The Kamikaze

HANEDA
Tokyo Naval Air Corps

Special Attack Unit

Until the end of World War II, Japan's February 11 national holiday was called Empire Day. It was the day to celebrate the birth of the nation that took place some 2,600 years earlier, according to the divine myth. At the morning assembly on that morning in 1945, something special happened. At a little after six A.M., it was still dark. After the usual morning pep talk, Commander Fujimura solemnly announced that he had received orders from the Naval General Staff Office to form a Special Attack Unit at the Tokyo Detachment. By then, we all knew what that meant. Avoiding mentioning the suicidal aspect of the mission, the Commander said, "The time has come when you can serve your country in the best way possible. However, I want to organize the special attack unit with volunteers only. If you are the first son or the only son in your family, or if you are married, you need not volunteer. I am going to ask those who wish to volunteer to come one step forward." After a few seconds of silence, which seemed like long minutes, he ordered, "Volunteers, one step forward!" There was a big thud. It seemed like just about everyone stepped forward, cadets as well as instructors. I was among them. It seemed that I gave no consideration to the fact that I was the first son of the Imamura family. As a matter of fact, I don't think I gave consideration to anything. At the command, my body moved forward automatically. To volunteer to die for the country seemed to me the only right thing to do. Was I scared? No, not at all. At least not at the time. Did I regret my action afterward? Absolutely not. Seeing what happened, the Commander said, "I praise you for your courageous decision. However, I see that we have too many volunteers for the limited number of aircraft available to us. The squadron commanders will take down the names of those who stepped forward. Later, the senior officers will select the number of pilots and navigators needed for the unit."

Since the day was a national holiday, there was no flight training. We young officers were told to assemble in the Gun Room. An announcement was made. Lt. Commander Shimizu, appointed as the unit training commander, was to command two special attack unit squadrons. Each squadron consisted of three squads of four planes each. Squadron 1 was to be commanded by Lt. SG Yamauchi and Squadron 2 led by Lt. JG Imamura. The lead plane of each squad was to be piloted by an instructor, who could be either a commissioned or non-commissioned officer. A navigator was assigned to each squad lead plane. Since the Tokyo Detachment Special Attack Unit consisted of 24 planes, there were only about a dozen planes left for the rest of the instructors and trainees to use for the continuation of regular flight training.

Training for the Special Attack Unit began the very next day. Since the cadets were already able to fly solo, the training began with formation flights. The idea was for the unit to leave the base and approach the target area in formation, then break up so that each pilot could look for his own target and dive into it. Or, if the formation was attacked by enemy fighters on its way to the target area, we were to scatter in different directions to flee, then, if we survived, fall back into formation after the attack was over. The prospect of flying those bi-wing intermediate trainers against the much faster enemy fighters gave us a rather helpless feeling. Yet, we were determined to succeed in our mission. We put everything we had into our training.

The squad leader took off first and the other three in the squad followed one by one. There was only one runway, so we were not able to take off all at once. The squad leader had the difficult task of trying to gain altitude and at the same time flying slowly enough for the rest of the squad to catch up with him to form the formation. At first, we flew in a loose formation so as to make sure we didn't crash into each other. As the days wore on, the formation got tighter and tighter, to the point where the four pilots could see each other's facial expressions quite clearly. We cruised at the altitude of 2,000 meters to pre-planned destinations such as Odawara to the south and Choshi to the east, turned around and returned to the airfield.

As of March 1, 1945, our Detachment was renamed Tokyo Naval Air Corps and was placed under the 11th Combined Air Fleet. This was a change in name only, with the same commanding officer and the same men. It was about this time that we began night flight training. Since our slow-flying planes could easily become sitting ducks for enemy fighters, it was planned for us to take off and approach our target area in the dark and dive into our targets at the crack of dawn, as soon as the targets became visible. It was not too bad when the moon was bright. We gradually got used to judging distances in dim light. But when it was pitch dark, the only thing we were able to go by was the size of the exhaust flames from the engines of the other planes. From the flames, we judged how far or close we were from the plane next to us. We were not able to fly in formation as tightly as in daylight.

There was another kind of danger. In the dark, it was difficult to tell whether you were flying right-side up or not. To guard against sudden air raids, it had become customary by that point in the war for families to turn on only absolutely necessary lights. So, not many lights were visible on the ground. Between these few lights and some stars in the sky, it was difficult to tell in the air which side was the sky and which was the ground. Flying along the coastline or over water was easier in that respect. One very dark evening, I was following a squad flying ahead of us, when I noticed the plane at the tail end of that formation gradually banking to the right. It eventually banked 90 degrees, with its wings at a right angle against the ground below. Then, suddenly, it flipped over and went down. At that point, the squad turned around and headed back to the airfield. I did the same. Back at the airfield, Petty Officer Sato, the leader of that squad, was in a huddle with other officers. He didn't know what caused the cadet's plane to stall, but he was almost sure that the plane crashed and the cadet was killed. The next morning, Tokyo Naval Air Corps received a call from Kisarazu Naval Air Station across Tokyo Bay, saying that one of our planes had made an emergency landing there the night before and that the pilot was alive and well. We couldn't be happier. I flew Petty Officer Sato to Kisarazu. And there he was, Cadet M, grinning but looking terribly embarrassed. Sato checked the plane and found it undamaged. He flew it back with Cadet M in the rear cockpit and I followed them, practicing formation flight with myself being the rear plane for a change. Back home, Cadet M explained that at one point during the night flight, he became unsure which side was up. He kept watching the exhaust flames of the plane ahead of him, kept feeling that his plane was banked to the left, and kept trying to correct the position of his plane by banking it to the right. Then the plane stalled. He got into a spin but was able to pull out of it. He flew around to look for a place to land and found a runway. He didn't know where he was but decided to land anyway. That happened to be Kisarazu.

I believe it was the evening of March 9. All the officers and men were outdoors watching an American movie. If my memory serves me right, it was *Robin Hood*, starring Olivia De Havilland. Halfway through the movie, the air raid siren sounded. The movie was stopped, we all ran to the airfield, helped put the airplanes parked out on the apron into the hangars and closed the hangar doors. We then scrambled to the air raid shelters and hid ourselves. We didn't wait long to hear the roar of the B-29 engines. There seemed to be hundreds of them. They flew in from the southwest to the northeast, dropping bombs along the way — incendiary bombs. The bombing seemed to be concentrated on the central and northern parts of Tokyo. The great fires were so widely and clearly visible from the airfield that we risked our lives and came out of the shelter to watch. It seemed that the whole city of Tokyo was going up in flames. Tens of thousands of lives must have been lost in those fires. The silvery bodies and wings of the B-29s flying overhead turned red from the flames below.

We saw one B-29 slowing down and falling behind its formation. It was probably hit by anti-aircraft gunfire. We never saw it crash, but a little later received reports that several American airmen parachuted into Tokyo Bay. As Deck Officer, I was asked if we should dispatch one of our cutters to try to capture them. Since the report said that the Americans came down off the coast of Harumi or somewhere around there, my judgment was, "No, it's too far away. Men from other units closer to the scene, such as the Navy Paymaster School, have probably taken care of them anyway." Had the Americans come down closer to us and had we gone out to capture them, I, as Deck Officer, probably was in a position to imprison and interrogate them. And had I gone beyond just questioning them, such as beating them to get the answers I wanted from them, I most likely would have ended up as a war criminal at the post-war International Military Tribunal and, at worst, hanged.

The next morning, Commander Fujimura told me to fly around the city to assess the extent of damage done to Tokyo by the bombing. "Fly close to the Imperial Palace and make sure no damage has been done there," he said. I first flew directly toward the Imperial Palace and was relieved to see that there was no visible damage. As I turned northeast, it was a totally different picture. The central, northern and eastern divisions of the city were practically in total ruins. Most of those areas were burnt up and flattened to the ground. Only concrete buildings were standing, but they were all burnt out. I remember seeing the original Kokugikan Building still billowing smoke from its many windows on the roundish walls. That was where Japanese professional wrestling (*sumo)* took place. I flew around for about an hour, returned to the Corps and reported to Commander Fujimura. I told him what I saw and he was very much relieved to hear about the Imperial Palace. Among the various communications he had received, there was a brief report that the Palace was partially damaged, which had him worried. Later, we learned that that report was correct, that a small portion of the Palace grounds was hit, most likely by mistake.

Spring came. There was one very young cherry tree in front of the Officers' Quarters. It was the only cherry tree on the compound. The young tree must have been planted there only a year or two before. Just a few blossoms bloomed on it. As I looked at them, I thought rather sentimentally, "I'm lucky to be seeing these flowers. These are probably the last cherry blossoms I will be seeing in my life." Every spring since the end of the war, when the cherry blossoms come out, I remember that scrawny cherry tree.

The rather frequent visits by the B-29s were bad enough, but something more frightening began: raids by fighters and dive-bombers that came in from the American aircraft carriers cruising off our coasts. When this started, someone in the Gun Room said, "If we added up all the number of American aircraft carriers the Imperial Headquarters announced we have sunk, there shouldn't be any of them left. Now, tell me where the hell all these planes are coming from." B-29s flew way up there. They weren't very frightening. They even looked beautiful. But the carrier planes — they were scary because they came right at you. These were the feelings we had. We fighter pilots especially feared enemy fighters because we knew what they were capable of doing.

In one such raid, three or four Grumman fighters came swooshing down on our airfield. One of them hit a Japan Air Lines DC-3 transport plane and blew it up. Fortunately that was the only real damage done in that sweep. Or so we thought until we later learned that one of our men pulling a cart on the road outside the compound was strafed. We had to go out and retrieve his torn body from the river into which he was blasted. It was the most mutilated body I had ever seen or have seen since.

By mid-April, the Special Attack Unit at Tokyo Naval Air Corps was on to instrument flight training. As mentioned before, each squad leader had a navigator in the rear cockpit. This was so that if the squadron had to break up for strategic reasons, each squad would be able to fly on its own. Since we were to fly at night on our one, only and last mission, the navigator had to be able to guide the pilot by instruments only. We started out this training by flying during the daytime, with the rear cockpit for the navigator covered up so the navigator couldn't look out and see where the plane was or where it was going. Things went smoothly until one day I had Cadet B as the navigator. Taking off from Haneda, we first flew due east, crossing over Tokyo Bay and the Boso Peninsula to the Pacific Ocean. The coastline was cloud covered. A certain number of minutes after takeoff, we were to change course to 315 degrees (north-northeast), hit the coastline, fly over Katori Naval Air Base, change course to southwest and get home. I, the pilot, simply steered the plane as the navigator told me to. We made the north-northeast turn. We flew and flew but no coastline. After flying for quite a while, I knew there was something wrong. Since we had a fairly strong westerly wind, I figured that when we made the 315 degree left turn, from due east to north-northwest, the plane drifted to the right and we were flying northward, parallel to the coastline. I decided to climb down to below the clouds and change the flight course to due west. Sure enough, we hit the coast right away.

I told Cadet B to fold down the cover and look below. I asked him where he thought we were. He compared the ground topography with his map and said, "Sir, I think we are way up north." That made me chuckle, but I wasn't so sure where we were either. I had never flown over the terrain below us. So, I decided to follow the coastline south. Finally I sighted an airfield, but wait, there were two of them, not far from each other. I asked Cadet B through the voice tube which one was Katori, over which we were supposed to fly. The cadet must have studied the map closely. It took a while for him to come back with the answer, which was, "It's the one on the right, sir." For quite awhile up to that point, I was concerned about the fuel gauge, which showed we were getting low on gas. Because of the long flight north, we consumed more gas than originally anticipated. I decided that we should land at Katori to get some fuel. I took the plane down.

As we landed and I looked around, a strange feeling came to me. Things looked rather unfamiliar. Then I noticed. The ground crew's work uniforms were a different color and the aircraft were of different types from ours. Wow, this must be an army air base, I thought. I had the urge to turn right around, go back to the starting line and take off, but I knew that was against the rules. So, I made a big circle around the airfield, went back to the starting line and took off. Some people at the airfield, especially those at the control tower if they had one, must have noticed my action and thought it strange. Whether they recognized the big "To-14' mark on the vertical rudder as "Tokyo Naval Air Corps Plane No. 14" or not, I had no way of knowing. At least, they must have noticed that it was a Navy trainer plane. And they probably guessed correctly that it had made a wrong landing and took off hurriedly in embarrassment. It was not a warm day, but I was perspiring all over. After landing at Katori, I casually asked what the "other" airfield over there was. I don't remember what the name of it was, but it certainly was an Army unit.

As I was having a cup of tea while my plane was being refueled at Katori, an officer in a flight uniform kept looking at me. Finally he walked over and said, "Might you be Imamura from Matsuyama?" I told him I was and asked why he knew my name. He answered, "I am Norimasa Hayashi from Tokumaru outside of Matsuyama. My sister Nobue is married to your cousin Yukio Otani. It was at their wedding that I saw you. That was, let's see, about five years ago, wasn't it? We didn't talk to each other at that time, but I remembered your face." Norimasa was a Keio University graduate. I didn't know that he was a member of the 13th Class too. He was a dive-bomber pilot at Katori. Since I had to leave in a hurry, I just shook hands with him and wished him well. I was told after the war that Norimasa plunged into his target off the Pacific coast on August 9. Had he had the luck to survive for one more week until the end of the war, he probably would have lived on as I did.

The return trip to Haneda was a direct flight. Still, Cadet B got under the cover, read the gauges and tried to keep me on course. Having flown over the area for half a year now, I was quite familiar with the landscape and knew that we were heading in the right direction. As we approached Tokyo Bay from the northeast, however, things began to look unusual. First, I noticed puffs of smoke in the air, at about the altitude of 1,000 meters in the direction of Haneda. I couldn't hear any sound. Then, more smoke puffs, this time on the other side of the Bay, over around Kisarazu. Then came delayed action, "boom, boom, boom." Anti-aircraft guns! There must be an air raid going on. I told Cadet B to stop the instrument navigation, lower the cover and be on the lookout. We looked up to the clear blue sky but no sign of any B29s. It must be a raid by carrier-based planes, it hit me. Cadet B and I scoured the air below us and the ground surface. There they go! We saw a squad of small, camouflaged planes swooping over the Bay eastward. Kisarazu is being attacked, I thought. Boom, a big ball of fire erupted in the Bay.

I hesitated for a while to decide whether we should return to Haneda right away or take an evasion course. Without any armor, we were in no position to tangle with the raiders. My decision was not to go in for a landing just then. We could very well be shot down. So, I flew further south to see if areas of Yokohama and Yokosuka were under attack also. No, nothing was happening there. Giving ourselves the extra time of about half an hour, we turned north and went in for a landing.

The air attack by American fighters and dive-bombers was over by then. Cadet B and I were told that the raid seemed to go after the ships and boats sailing in the Bay. Maybe the American pilots were just having fun chasing after moving targets, but more seriously, they were probably out to destroy our marine transport system. Fortunately, no damage was done to our airfield. Upon landing, Lt. Suga asked me what took us so long to get back from the training flight and I had to tell him the whole story. I thought he might get mad at us for our stupidity in landing at an Army airfield, but he just laughed it off.

Around mid-May, rumors started to circulate that the Tokyo Naval Air Corps would be evacuated to another location. The American air raids had become too much of a threat for us to continue our training. With carpet bombings by B-29s with incendiary bombs, strafing and bombing by carrier planes, and even rumors of American submarines lurking in the waters of Tokyo Bay, we ourselves felt that we needed safer grounds to hone our skills for the success of our final mission. Toward the end of May, Commander Fujimura made the announcement that our Corps was to be absorbed by Kasumigaura Naval Air Corps as of June 1. Fujimura himself was to retire from the service and return to civilian life. "I am very saddened by the fact that I will not be with you when you depart on your last mission," he said.

We pilots who had planes to fly all flew to Kasumigaura on June 1. Pilot and navigator officers who had no planes led the cadets by train to get there. The ground crew had to scurry to get everything moveable ready to be transported in three days.

The author's birth certificate from San Jose

Shig on a tricycle in the
family's San Francisco
backyard

Shigeo Imamura at three months of age

Raphael Weill Elementary School in San Francisco. The author is pictured kneeling on the left in the second row

The Doll Exchange at Kimmon Gakuen School, San Francisco

Family portrait-father, mother, and the young Shig, 10 years old, just before the family's return to Japan

Matsuchu Music Club-Mr. Yamauchi seated in first row (third from the right) next to the author (second from the right) holding coronet

Shig's mother, pictured here on the left, during her service as an Army nurse

Kosho Riding Club

Five MIE Naval Cadets, 1943. Shig is seated on the right

Naval Cadet portrait,
November 1943

Author, at left rear of photo, a member of the Izumi Naval Air Corps, in 1944 with host family, the Tanakas, and his mother, seated in first row on the right

Izumi Naval Air Corps, graduation, May 1944. Shig is in second row, right of center

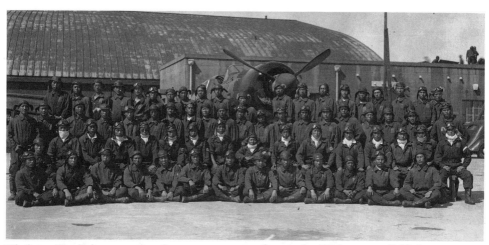

Fighter Training graduation ceremony after only 70 hours of flight training, September 1944, Korea. Shig is sixth from left in the last row

Four pilots at Tokyo Naval Air Station, 1944. Author pictured second from left

Formal portrait, Tokyo Naval Air Station, 1944. Author in first row on right

Shiego Imamura as a trained *kamikaze* pilot

Special Attack Unit, April 1945, Tokyo. Shig is on far left in the second row

Shig with GI pals, spring 1946

School visits, 1947, with Charles Boleske, CI&E officer

Yale University, Phelps Gate, 1951

Dr. C.C. Fries, pictured in center, with his class, 1951

Ehime Summer Seminar for English teachers, 1955

English Language Center, Michigan State University, Fall 1963

Shiego Imamura, 1997, at home in Himeji

Chapter 11

Aborted Mission

KASUMIGAURA
Naval Air Corps

Kasumigaura

K asumigaura is the name of the second largest land-locked lake in Japan. The name translates as Lake Mist. It is located about 30 miles northeast of Tokyo. On a plateau to its south, the Japanese navy built its first full-fledged airfield in 1922, the year of my birth. By the time of World War II, Kasumigaura Naval Air Corps had trained and sent off thousands of pilots, both commissioned and non-commissioned officers, and had come to be known as the "Young Eagles' Nest." It was a large airfield, a bit inland unlike most of the other naval airfields, which were right on the coastlines. There were several air squadrons in training when we got there.

One of them was the Shusui Corps. *Shusui*, Autumn Water in English, was the name of a prototype manned rocket plane. I ran into Lt. Tamotsu Chikazaki, a fellow who had gone through training with me from Mie through Wonsan in Kasumigaura's Gun Room. When I asked him if he was there as a flight instructor like myself, he said "No, I'm in the Shusui Corps." "Shusui Corps? What's that?" I asked. "It's top secret. Oh, well, I guess I can talk about it to a guy like you." According to Chikazaki, it was a rocket-propelled aircraft, small in size, its technology imported from Germany. "Rocket propelled? It must fly awfully fast. Can you stand the Gs (gravity)?" He then grinned and replied, "To tell you the truth, I haven't flown in it yet. We've yet to get a craft that really flies." I then asked what they meant when they said the Shusui Corps was in training at Kasumigaura. His explanation went like this.

The Japanese government had succeeded in persuading the German government to send over the blueprint of a rocket combat aircraft by submarine, but that sub was sunk by the Allies near Singapore. Mysteriously, only a drawing of the exterior of the aircraft survived. Based on the drawing, the Japanese Navy built several experimental bodies while the Army worked on the engine. The body of the rocket aircraft was 5.05 meters (16 ft.) from wingtip to wingtip, 9.5 meters (31 ft.) long and 2.7 meters (8.8 ft.) high. The fuel was known to the pilots only as Liquid C and Liquid T. The plane was designed to climb to a 10,000-meter altitude in three and a half minutes, mount aerial attacks on enemy heavy bombers, and glide back to the ground when it ran out of fuel. To make the craft lightweight, the landing gear was to drop off after takeoff. Landing was on sleighs attached to the bottom of the fuselage. Since we had heard that American jet planes were taking part in combat in Europe and elsewhere, I asked Chikazaki if the Shusui Corps' rocket plane was the same as a jet plane. His answer was no, a jet engine propels the plane by the air thrust created by the turbine, which is rotated by the combustion of the fuel, while the rocket plane is propelled by the thrust of the fuel combustion itself.

Chikazaki and his comrades first received training in flying gliders so that they would be able to land at the right spot without engine power. Since the speed ratio between the Shusui and the B-29 was approximately the same as that of the Zero fighter and the Model 93 Trainer, they moved from glider training to practice attacking the Model 93 with the Zero. They were in the midst of this training when I ran into Chikazaki. Early in July, an experimental Shusui flight took place at Yokosuka Naval Air Base. Lt. Inuzuka, a Naval Academy graduate, took a Shusui up about 300 meters. The engine exploded and pilot Inuzuka was killed. That was the first and the last Shusui flight ever.

Our squadron recommenced training the next day after we arrived in Kasumigaura. The orders were that we continue to train in special attack techniques with the volunteer unit and regular flight training for the other cadets. On July 4, Lieutenants Toru Sasakura and Jukichi Jinde of the regular training were in the front and rear cockpits of a trainer. Sasakura lived to tell that, as they were flying along, he suddenly felt the control stick jerk forward. He thought Jinde was either aiming the plane at something on the ground or was just having fun. But as they continued to descend, Sasakura became nervous and told Jinde through the voice tube to pull up. No answer. Sasakura looked back and saw nothing but a blood-splattered windshield. He tried to pull up but the stick was very heavy. He used both of his hands and a leg and finally got the plane to level off, just as it hit the ground. The plane disintegrated, but Sasakura survived the impact with minor injuries. Jinde was already dead, with his head blown off. They had been shot at by an American fighter raiding the area.

It was a few days after that incident that our airfield, along with Tsuchiura Naval Air Corps close by, came under attack by carrier-based American planes. First, we heard dull explosive sounds far to the west. Then the air raid warning went off. We turned and saw pillars of smoke rising. It's an air raid! It must be Yatabe (Naval Air Base), we guessed. We felt sorry for the poor guys there, but we were at a safe enough distance. With all of our planes hidden away in concrete hangars scattered all around the airfield, we kept sitting on the ground talking idly. Suddenly we heard planes approaching from the west. Not ours! I turned and saw five or six Mustang fighters, flying very low and coming right at us over the edge of the airfield. We fell flat on our stomachs but saw traces of bullets hit the ground past us in straight rows. The closest row was no more than ten feet away from the bunch of us. A flick of the pilot's hand or a slip of his foot could have gotten all of us. As the planes flew away eastward, one of them dropped what we thought was a bomb. We hit the dirt again, covering our ears with our hands. We waited and waited but no explosion. After the raid was over, some men went to retrieve the "thing." It was an auxiliary fuel tank. We smelled it and sighed, "Hey, they're still using the real stuff." We were using gasoline mixed with alcohol produced from sweet potatoes.

In the excitement of being narrowly missed by a squad of American fighters, we had failed to notice that other squads of planes had strafed and bombed other parts of our compound and the neighboring Tsuchiura Naval Air Corps. Soon, ambulances and trucks started to head toward the forest at the northern end of the airfield. We ran over to see what had happened. Casualties! Cadets who couldn't get to any air raid shelters had taken to the forest to hide from the enemy planes. Some of them didn't pay enough attention to the direction from which the planes were coming and got hit. Others were hiding behind trees away from the approaching planes but got hit by bullets ricocheting off other trees. A few had their limbs torn off. One was shot right through his heart. Tsuchiura had it worse. One of the barracks with dozens of cadets in it was destroyed. The next day, a joint funeral for both Kasumigaura and Tsuchiura was held at Tsuchiura. Since it was an indoor funeral, there was not enough space to properly line up the some 30 coffins on stands. The sight of them stacked up on the floor will never be forgotten. The bottom planks of some of the coffins were blood-soaked. The bodies were probably placed in the coffins without any embalming. The thought of avenging the cadets' deaths by eventually destroying the enemy did cross our minds. Tsuchiura's base commander made that statement in his farewell message. But considering the state of the war at that time, I was not so sure how much conviction we had in such a thought.

What happened on the evening of July 29, 1945 will be long remembered by those who were at air bases in the greater Tokyo region, including Kasumigaura. As we ate that evening, we heard the now-familiar roars of B-29s passing overhead. Mito City to the north of us was being bombed. Mito was far enough that we did not hear any sounds, but we watched till about midnight to see the whole city go up in flames. Then, very shortly after we went back to bed, the PA system blared out, "All hands, prepare for Operation Ketsu!" We couldn't believe our ears, because *Ketsu* was the code word for the operation for the entire Japanese military to defend the nation against the enemy invasion of the Japanese mainland. What's going on? Where's the enemy anyway? One question after another came to our minds as we ran towards the underground base headquarters. As most of the officers crowded into the headquarters conference room,

Base Commander Capt. Wada solemnly began to speak. An enemy fleet had been spotted off the coast of Boso Peninsula, east of Tokyo. From the large number of vessels involved, the top Navy headquarters judged it was an invasion force. All the Army and Navy air bases in the region were alerted for a dawn attack. "Even those of you flying slower planes will be able to reach your targets in about half an hour. We still have some time. Go back to your quarters, clean up your mess and return here for final orders by three zero zero," the Commander concluded.

Walking back, I told myself, "This is it. This is what we've been training for. Go at it!" But then, I began to have a strange sensation inside. Was I getting scared? Maybe. After dawn, no more cherry trees to see, no more friends to chat with, no more parents to look after, no more brother to care for. I was going to die! Back in the room, I first pulled out the desk drawer. There were letters from Mother, Father and Michiko, the girl who gave me the *senninbari*. I had read the letters over and over again. From the way the base commander described the enemy fleet, there must be tens of thousands of enemy troopers trying to land on Boso Peninsula. We will get most of them all right, but there is a chance some of them will slip through and come here. I mustn't let them read these letters, lest they might think there were sissies among the Navy fliers. I bundled up the letters and put them in my cloth shoe sack along with some other belongings, and wrote "Burn"on the sack with a marker. Then I opened the hamper and found some worn underwear. What am I going to do with these? I didn't want anyone, especially the enemy, to think that I was an untidy naval officer. Oh, well, there is nothing I can do with these now. I'll just leave them in the hamper. After tidying up the bed and the room, I suited up in my flight uniform and gave a salute, to no one or nothing in particular. I think it was an instinctive reaction as a farewell to the world.

Walking back to the headquarters, I found myself utterly calm. I looked up and saw the dark sky full of glittering stars. I saw the faces of Father, Mother, Takao, Michiko and many of my long-time friends in the sky. At least I thought so. There still was a reddish glow of Mito burning to the north. Hey, my mission is to crush the enemy. I'll hit the biggest transport ship I can find. That'll take the lives of a couple thousand of their men. Oh, I've got to lead my squad to the targets before Lt. Yamauchi gets his there. I can't let a Naval Academy guy beat me to it. As these thoughts came to me, excitement mounted in my mind. I felt not a speck of fear anymore.

As the pilots and navigators arrived back at headquarters, we were given the identification numbers of the planes we were to fly and where they could be located. As mentioned before, they were scattered throughout the airfield, in individual concrete hangars. Mine was way out on the other side of the runway. We would be given the signal for takeoff by telephone, we were told. As I walked toward my plane, I came across many men scurrying hither and thither. At one point, there was a group of men being addressed by an elderly officer who was saying, "Go out to nearby farm houses and confiscate all the foodstuff you can get — rice, vegetables, chicken, anything." "My gosh," I thought. "The farmers will have to be fighting alongside our men too. That is why they were trained to battle enemy foot soldiers with bamboo spears as well as with their plows and hoes. What are they going to do for food? Or are we going to feed them too?"

I arrived at my plane. The navigator was already there. Men were working on the plane. A 250 kilogram (approximately 500 lb.) bomb was about to be attached to the fuselage. The gas tanks were half filled because that was all that was needed to reach our targets, I was told. Now, what if the area is clouded and I can't find the target? I thought to myself. Well, we weren't supposed to have such thoughts at that point, I guessed. I was there for a few minutes when the field telephone rang. Takeoff already? No, it was an order for all the pilots and navigators to return to headquarters immediately. No reason was given. I hurried back and found that the operation had been called off. Even the top brass there did not know the reason for the cancellation. Several days later, we were informed that the red alert was called when our radar showed many blips on the screens and the top officers decided that an invasion was on. However, it was found that the blips were reflections of our radar beams on the tin foils dropped by the B-29s off the Boso Peninsula coast on their way home to their Tinian and Saipan bases from the Mito bombing. It was a false alarm. Anyway, it was a very mixed feeling of, on the one hand, relief at not having to die that dawn, and on the other hand, disappointment at not accomplishing our mission, which would have been one of the most significant had the invasion been a real one. Around that time of the year, every summer, I remember the series of events that happened that night and come to realize how lucky I am to be still alive and enjoying the many experiences I have had since that evening and dawn.

We moved from Haneda in Tokyo to Kasumigaura because it was assumed that Kasumigaura would be much safer from enemy air raids. But this was no longer true. Although Kasumigaura was never again directly attacked, air raid warnings were sounded almost every day, and other airfields and cities around us were attacked, by both B-29s and carrier-based planes. Early in August, we received orders that the entire training unit would be moved to Chitose Air Base on Hokkaido, the northernmost major island. What a fateful move. It began on August 14, my 23rd birthday.

Chapter 12

Bewildered Defeat

The War Ends

As when we moved from Haneda to Kasumigaura, the move to Hokkaido was made by air by pilots who had planes assigned to them; the rest traveled by train. Although I had an assigned plane, as the senior-ranking lieutenant I was ordered to lead a group of about 300 young cadets by train. Several officers came along. We were trucked to Tsuchiura Station and put on a train bound for Aomori, the northernmost major city on the main island of Honshu. In those days of steam locomotives, that was more than a half-day journey. As the train passed through the city of Sendai, about half way to Aomori, Lt. Utsumi, one of my classmates from our Mie days, became very sentimental. Sendai was his hometown. He very much wanted to stop off and see his parents, but he knew that was not possible. Realizing that his life would come to an end sooner or later, in one way or another, he wanted to be home just once more before that happened.

Servicemen traveling individually, whether on private trips or on military orders, had to compete with civilians for seats on the trains.

However, when groups of servicemen, especially large groups like the one I led, were on duty-bound moves, seat reservations were made ahead of time at the request of the military. Since most of the railways, especially the trunk lines, were owned and operated by the central government, it was an official request from one branch of the government to another, which was always acknowledged. For our travel to Aomori, a five-coach train arrived at Tsuchiura Station with two coaches jammed with passengers but three others fully reserved for us. Since all the cadets had seats for the long journey and nothing particular to do, it was like a school excursion for them. They chatted, played cards and generally had a good time.

Arriving at Aomori Station late in the afternoon, we found that the Seikan ferry, which we were to take to Hakodate Port in Hokkaido, was just a few minutes' walk from the railway platform. However, the ferry did not leave until ten P.M., so we whiled away some time in the waiting room inside the ferry building. I told the cadets to take little naps if they could, but no, they kept having fun. The ferry took about six hours to cross the Tsugaru Straits between Aomori and Hakodate. The cadets slept well after a day of frolicking, but, somehow, I couldn't sleep at all. Perhaps it was the sense of isolation that kept me awake, the feeling that I was being taken even farther away from my family, that I was heading for a strange place where my life would probably end in the near future. Or, it could have been the alertness of watching out over the youngsters, just in case of a torpedo attack by an American submarine. We had heard that American bombers mined the straits. The ferry could hit one of the mines. But we arrived safe and sound at Hakodate Port early in the morning. There was hardly any time to catch the next train for Sapporo, the capital city of Hokkaido. It was then August 15.

Thus far, we had seen, heard or felt nothing out of the ordinary. The shortage of food (and everything else) was obvious. People were scurrying around to secure food for their families. Many of them brought the vegetables and other items they had secured somehow onto the train to take home. The wrapping papers were without exception old newspapers. Very few automobiles of any kind were seen on the roads. But people seemed spirited. As we arrived in Sapporo and got down on the platform to change trains, however, a strange sensation hit me. It was shortly after noon. People should have been moving around looking for something to eat or catching trains. But no, aside from a few murmurs heard here and there, there was a strange silence, with many people hanging their heads down as though they were in mourning. I quickly led my group to the other platform and ordered the cadets to board the train right away and to stay there. I found an Army sergeant standing nearby and approached him. Noticing me, he saluted stiffly. Returning the salute, I asked him, "I sense something unusual. Was Sapporo bombed or something? Tell me what's going on." *"Sir, the war has ended."* "You're kidding, of course. How can the war end?" *"I just heard over the radio His Majesty announcing the acceptance of an unconditional surrender, sir."* "His Majesty on the radio? That's impossible. His Majesty doesn't go on the radio. An unconditional surrender? That's impossible too. We're still fighting. Are you trying to fool me? If you are, I'm going to hit you." *"Go ahead if you like, but I'm not fooling you. Look at all those people. Can't you tell?"* At that, I turned away from the poor sergeant and boarded the train.

On the train, I said nothing to the cadets, or to the officers. Proceeding from Sapporo to Chitose, the last leg of our long journey, I ignored all the goings-on around us and kept asking myself questions. Could any of what the sergeant said be true? Had the Emperor really spoken to the people on the radio? That had never been done before. He had spoken in public and his recorded voice had been broadcast in the past, but never directly over the radio. An unconditional surrender? That's even more impossible. Look at all the planes we have, the men we have. Sure, the Americans have new types of bombs. What did they call them? Atomic bombs? Yes, they dropped them on Hiroshima and Nagasaki, but it was reported that the damage was insignificant. Besides, those two bombs were probably the only ones they had. We've got the manpower and the spirit. If they ever tried to invade these islands, we'd be sure to overcome them. No, surrender is unthinkable. It must be a bad rumor someone is trying to spread, perhaps propaganda.

When we arrived at Chitose Station, it was already dark. We disembarked, transferred our baggage from the train to trucks, got into formation and marched to the base. Chitose Naval Air Base was one of the newest and the largest. As we passed through the gate, the guards saluted us as they always did. See, nothing is wrong. It's business as usual. Unconditional surrender, eh? Don't make me laugh, I told myself. After dismissing the cadets in front of their barracks, I urged Utsumi and the other officers to follow me to the Officers' Mess. Opening the door there and taking one step inside, we knew the war was over. There they were, all the officers in their uniforms, including the top-ranking officers, sitting with their heads bowed. It was as though if someone said a word, the ceiling would come tumbling down. I hesitated for a while but brought myself to do what I had to do. "Lt. JG Imamura, arriving from Kasumigaura Naval Air Corps with three officers and 300 cadets, sir." The commanding officer acknowledged my report only with his eyes, which then went right back to the table in front of him. The other officers seemed to pretend the new arrivals weren't even there.

Shortly after the war, it was revealed that the top Japanese military had consistently minimized news of the damage inflicted by the Allies, and maximized news of damage to the enemy. For example, after the Battle of Midway, the Battle of Coral Sea and other engagements, the Naval General Staff announced that some of our warships were "slightly damaged," when in actuality they were either put out of action or sunk. According to their announcements, U.S. carrier *Midway* was sunk at least twice. When Hiroshima was A-bombed, the initial announcement by the Army General Staff was, "A new type of bomb was dropped on Hiroshima at approximately 8:17 this morning but the damage was minimal."

In the 1930s and very early 1940s, the Japanese war machine was very powerful, relative to what it confronted. Not being a historian, I am reluctant to go into any further details on the military history of modern Japan. However, to believe what I was told repeatedly, the turning point in World War II came with our defeat at the Battle of Midway. The general tone of the official announcement made on the results of that battle was that, yes, there had been some damage on our side, but we had chased the Allies away. A few months after the battle, I was invited to a party by Mr. Yamauchi, the English teacher who put me on to the Gulick family in Matsuyama in 1932 so that I would not forget my English altogether. The party was to

---

welcome home Mr. Keisuke Mori, four years my senior at Matsuyama Middle School. Mori was among the crew on **Hiryu**, an aircraft carrier that took part in the Battle of Midway. Mori's revelation of what happened to the **Hiryu** and the Japanese fleet there as a whole was truly heartbreaking. The **Hiryu** was bombarded, went up in flames and eventually sank. The flames heated up the entire ship and most of those who abandoned ship suffered severe burns, he said. He himself had burn scars on his face and hands. As a college student, I listened to him intently. It seems to me now that I did believe him about the fate of the **Hiryu** and the casualties suffered by the crew. But when it came to the fate of the fleet, I listened with disbelief. It was impossible for the Imperial Navy to be defeated and run.

We are told that the Council in the Imperial Presence was held many times toward the close of the war, especially after the Soviet Union entered the war in the Far East. The Council was split between those who advocated the continuation of the war effort and those who sought peace. It is my understanding that Emperor Hirohito tended to side with the peace seekers, and after Hiroshima and Nagasaki definitely made up his mind to surrender to the Allies, mainly to prevent further sacrifices of his people. While there must have been people such as military leaders, top politicians and scholars who knew exactly what was really going on at home and on the fronts, the public was led to firmly believe that endurance and perseverance would eventually lead to total victory. Hardly any commoner thought that the end of the war would come so soon. When the war did come to a sudden end, we were numb. We didn't know what to do or what to think. Eat what you can, sleep well because there are no more air raids, and see what will happen tomorrow, seemed to be the general mood. The situation at Chitose was no different.

I don't remember whether or not we had dinner the evening we arrived at Chitose, nor how, when and where we went to bed. What I do remember is what the base commander said to us at the morning assembly. In effect, he said he had not received orders as to whether or not training should be continued and that we should use our judgment about what to do with the cadets. During breakfast, which was put on as usual, we young officers got together and decided that we should carry on as we had. Training would continue. There was confusion at the hangars. The mechanics, having received no orders from above, were hesitating to ready the planes for flight. Seeing us officers and cadets coming toward them, they scurried about to get the planes ready. That day and the next, the training went on schedule. On the third morning, we arrived at the hangars to find the mechanics just sitting around. "Get the planes ready!" I yelled at them. ""We can't. The carburetors have been taken away," was the response. "Who took them away? To where?" "The chief mechanic. We don't know where to, sir."

Before I was able to argue any further, the squadron commander came up. "Lt. Imamura, it's all over. We received orders last night to cease all flights." There was nothing I could say. Dead silence fell all around. After I was able to collect myself, I asked, "What are we to do now, Lt. Suga?" "I'm not so sure myself. Why don't you send the cadets back to their barracks and yourselves to the Gun Room. Wait till you hear further from me or somebody else." I did not feel like marching the cadets back to the barracks and broke up the group right there.

In the Gun Room, we talked and talked. For one thing, we seemed to have all the time we wanted. There was no sign that an order for us to do something was forthcoming. Most of us still found it hard to believe that Japan had surrendered unconditionally. What does "unconditionally" mean? Is the Imperial system going to be abolished? Is the military going to be totally dismantled? Are the Allies going to land here demanding our weapons and facilities? Allies? Who are they? Americans? The British, the Canadians, the Australians and lots of other forces were in it too, even the Russians. Are they going to come in too? When? Where? How many? Question after question came up but nobody had any answers. Questions closer to our own selves were also raised. What is going to happen to us? Are we going to be taken prisoner and sent overseas? If so, where to? Or are we going to be killed right here? An optimist thought we might be used as pilots in the American Navy. A pessimist bet that they would make us take off in our planes and then shoot us down for target practice.

Suddenly we realized it was dinner time. We had skipped lunch without realizing it. As we ate in the Junior Officers' Dining Room, the base commander made an appearance. He said, in effect, "I know how you feel, but there is nothing we can do at this point but wait for further orders. It is my understanding that we will be demobilized in a couple of weeks. That means you will be sent home. Until then, we must keep this base from disintegrating. I make it your responsibility to maintain order on the base. Ranks will be respected as always. You cannot fly anymore, but you are free to do anything to keep the men happy and in good order." The thought of going home gave us a very mixed feeling. I would be lying if I said it didn't make us happy on one hand. It would be good to see the families and friends we never expected to see again, alive. It would be wonderful to eat our mothers' cooking. But, on the other hand, what were we going to say to them when we got home? Would, "Sorry we lost the war," do? Were they really going to be happy to see us come home alive after we left them promising to die for the glory of the Empire?

We talked about these matters for a long time after the base commander left, but then we had to deal with the reality of what we were going to do with the cadets starting the next morning. Someone suggested that we engage the men in sports. "Yes, but we can't make them play softball and volleyball all day long. What about the evenings?" Finally, it was agreed that Lt. Utsumi and I would take turns reading novels to them in the morning and have them play softball and other games on a space-available basis in the afternoon. Now the question for Utsumi and me was which novels and how. It occurred to me that I immensely enjoyed listening to a radio series called, "Musashi Miyamoto." The radio series was based on a novel about a real *samurai* warrior who lived in the 17th century. The novel was written by Eiji Yoshikawa. As I remember, it was a 30-minute series from Monday to Friday and lasted for a year on radio. Utsumi agreed with me that it should last us long enough. Fortunately, we found the five-volume novel in the base library and started reading it to the cadets the next morning. That had to be about August 19.

The novel started out with tales of Musashi in his younger days when he was wild and unruly, and hated by everyone in his village, young and old, except for Otsu, his childhood girlfriend who always respected and liked his unusual talents, mental as well as physical. Otsu eventually fell in love with Musashi but never got to marry him because she died young. One day, Musashi runs into a Buddhist monk named Takuan, who manages to subdue him, tie him up and hang him from a tree. At Takuan's urging, Musashi changes his ways and trains himself as a swordsman, becoming a great one. Personalities such as Musashi and Takuan are real historical figures who lived in Western Japan. The novel involves a large number of characters, both men and women, warriors, feudal lords, merchants, villagers, etc. Therefore, Utsumi and I had to do a lot of impersonation of all kinds. I suppose we did a pretty good job, since the "performance" was highly popular and very well attended, even attracting listeners from other units. Utsumi and I enjoyed doing this too.

The sports went well too. The most popular was volleyball, as usual. About a week into this daily program, something unexpected developed. It is possible that the novel reading caused the young cadets to feel some intimacy toward us, something which they had not a speck of under our strict and harsh training. One morning after the reading session, some of them came up to Utsumi and me, asking if we would visit their barracks in the evening for chats. They had nothing in particular to do and were bored. We accepted the invitation that evening and went to chat with them. Upon returning to the Gun Room, Utsumi and I continued to talk a bit and agreed that it was a pleasant experience. It was good to get to know the cadets on a more personal basis, now that we didn't have to maintain the vertical relationship so strictly any more. I am not sure if it was Utsumi or me that came up with, "Wouldn't it be even nicer if we could have some drinks together too?" However, we had to remind ourselves of the strict rule the Japanese Navy had about not allowing officers and enlisted men to drink together.

The next afternoon, Utsumi and I went to see Capt. Wada to explain our situation and get special permission to take beer to the cadets' barracks. Capt. Wada thought deeply for a while. Then he said, "Well, under the circumstances, I guess you can go ahead, especially because I hear you two are doing a good job keeping the men in tow. Besides, the alcoholic beverages are the last thing we want to turn over to the Americans when they come. But remember, the cadets are still under age. Be sure not to let them go wild. Set a limit on how much beer you take with you." So the evening parties began. Other young officers began to join us. We made sure not to be loud enough to be heard outside of the barracks. And the evening became the highlight of the day.

Everything came to a sudden halt on September 5. It was announced that we would be officially demobilized as of September 7 and would be sent home that day. We spent all day the next day demolishing everything except buildings and furniture. Planes were dismantled, anything burnable was burnt, and the rest was either destroyed or dumped. We were ordered to destroy even photographs with aircraft in them. We thought this was a bit ridiculous in that we had lost the war and nothing could be considered classified information any more. So some of us, including myself, kept some pictures we particularly liked. It was one of these that was splashed on the page of the student newspaper at Michigan State University and picked up by papers everywhere after the UPI story, as mentioned in the Preface.

That same afternoon, I was in for a surprise. Capt. Wada called me into his office and told me that I had a promotion to Lieutenant Senior Grade as of September 1. I was not in for the promotion until December 1 that year. But those whose promotion dates were close enough were given early promotions as a part of severance awards. These early promotions later came to be known as Potsdam Promotions, taken from the Potsdam Declaration, by which Japan agreed upon surrender. At any rate, I couldn't have been happier. It was nice to have three cherry blossoms on my collar and to be addressed as *"Daii"* (Lt. SG) even just during the journey home. There was another real advantage. We were given severance pay equivalent to our six-month salaries. Mine was based on the Lt. SG rate, more than those of my classmates who remained Lt. JG. We were also given a month's supply of cigarettes. For civilians, cigarettes were rationed in limited amounts and not available for purchase, so we were very happy about that too.

It is hard to speak for others on how they felt about leaving the military and going home. As for myself, I was both eager and reluctant: eager because I wanted to see my family and friends again, reluctant because I didn't know what to say to them when I met them and because it was hard to say goodbye to the comrades with whom I had vowed to die.

Each officer was given a group of men to take with him. Generally, they were men whose homes were on the way to or near where the officer was headed. I had a group of about 20 cadets. We were told to keep our uniforms on with the rank emblems showing and to keep the daggers at our sides until we got home. In other words, we were to travel as full-fledged military personnel. Several of our groups got together and marched to Chitose Station. We got on the coach and took the seats reserved for us at the request of the base commander. We took a different route from Chitose to Hakodate from the one we took coming north from Kasumigaura, and the cadets were much more subdued. There was no problem taking the ferry across the straits. However, once we arrived in Aomori and went to the railway station to get tickets for reserved seats, we ran into trouble.

"All trains are just jammed. All the military and civilian personnel from the nearby regiments and bases want to go home. It's impossible to get you on," said the station master.

"But we can't be stranded here. We've got to hurry home too," I retorted.

"I understand. But what is not possible is not possible," he replied. I tried to calm down and negotiate for the best way out of this situation. After talking with his staff and making several phone calls, the station master came back to say, "All right. We will dispatch a special train around midnight tonight. Remember two things. First, there will be no reserved seats on this train, not even for officers. Second, there are hundreds of others who will try to get on this train." From his tone of voice, it was clear that the military was no longer held in high esteem by civilians. Before the end of the war, a Lt. SG emblem would have spoken fairly loudly in a situation like this. No more.

There was no space for us in the station waiting room, so we gathered around outside to kill time. After a while, it dawned on me that the station master had never mentioned how far that special train was going or by which route. There are two major railway routes going south from Aomori, one to Tokyo along the Pacific coast, and the other via the Japan Sea coast. We had planned to take the latter, change trains along the way, and reach Western Japan. It took quite a while to get the attention of the station master, who was besieged by irritated passengers, and when I did, his answer was, "Well, that one isn't a scheduled passenger train, but it is supposed to connect with an Osaka-bound train somewhere. At least it will start out on the Ou Line." The Ou Line runs along the Japan Sea coast.

"At least we're starting out in the right direction," I told my group.

As night approached, we saw a train pulling into the station. As soon as it shifted tracks and it became obvious which platform it was headed for, my men dashed toward it before anyone else was even aware that a train was entering the station. When the train came to a stop along the platform, the cadets rushed into one coach and secured enough seats for all of us in one section of that coach. Thus my group was able to be seated all the way. I had never expected our strict training and discipline to pay off this way, and I admired my men for their good sense and their quick move. Many other passengers, mostly soldiers, were not so lucky. Most of those without seats sat in the aisle. There were also some who appeared to be high-ranking non-commissioned officers who at first stood in the aisle in an "at ease" position, but after several hours passed, they too were crouching or sitting on the floor. There was no room for anyone to lie down. Evidently, the Army men had orders different from ours. They had stripped themselves of all rank emblems. I got to talking to a man sitting on the floor next to my seat, obviously a draftee in his forties. He said he had waited at Aomori Station since early that morning. He was luckier than most since his destination was Akita, less than half a day's trip. He would be getting off the train before dawn.

It probably was hunger that woke us up the next morning. We were all so exhausted that we dozed off soon after the train left Aomori and then fell into deep sleep. When I opened my eyes, the sun was already up. I think it was about eight a.m. The man sitting on the floor next to me was still there, wide awake. "Weren't you supposed to have gotten off a long time ago?" I asked.

"Yes, sir, but we still have quite a bit to go before Akita."

I looked out and saw that the train was moving at a speed normal for trains those days. Then it came to a stop on the sidetrack at a very small station. It didn't move for quite a while. Then another passenger train passed us, some minutes after which our train started to move again.

"That is what we have been doing all along, sir," the man on the floor said. So, our train must be on a freight train schedule, I thought. Sure enough, it made frequent stops, always on the sidetracks. We reached Akita close to noon and the man got off, along with some others. There was more space in the aisle, or so we thought. Then a whole horde of new passengers came on, making it even tighter for those in the aisle. This scene was repeated at most major stations. It was that evening or the next that the train was stopped at a small station. When we woke up the next morning, we noticed to our surprise that we had moved only one station during the whole night.

It was very hard to get anything to eat. Only at major stations were there any box lunches, but they sold out fast. When the train stopped, the men ran off the train to drink water from the faucets on the platform. Dropping one or two cadets at stations along the way, my group was down to six by the time we reached Osaka on the third day out of Aomori. We changed trains in Osaka and reached Okayama to change trains again for the port of Uno. There we took a ferry across the Seto Inland Sea to Takamatsu on Shikoku, where the first of the last two in my group left for home. It was on the fourth day that we finally reached Kita-Iyo Station, where I was to get off. When I got off, the only cadet left in the group, heading for home further down the line, carried my luggage, a wicker trunk, down to the platform for me. We shook hands and saluted each other, and he got back on the train. Today, we can probably cover the Chitose to Kita-Iyo distance in one day.

The street in front of our Yanai-machi house was a fairly wide one. Still, when the chances of Matsuyama's being air raided by B-29s became great in early 1945, the city decided to broaden some of the streets, including ours, making them wide enough to serve as firebreaks. Houses lining one side of the street—our side—were torn down. Thus, my family had been forced to move out, and since the project was in the name of national defense, there was no room for protest. The only place the family could think of moving into was the small detached house on my uncle's estate in Ishii Village. It was there that I went "home" to. As mentioned much earlier, I used to go to my uncle's estate rather often during my childhood, so the outside of the detached house was quite familiar when I reached there on the afternoon of September 11, 1945, after a four-day train ride. I had called ahead from Osaka as I changed trains to let the family know approximately when I would be reaching home, but I had to do it through my uncle since there was no phone in the detached house.

Father and Mother must have heard my footsteps. When I opened the front door, they were sitting on the floor right inside. I took my hat off, bowed, and said, "I'm home. I'm sorry I…"

That was all I was able to utter. Father then said, "You must be disappointed that we didn't win the war." He was immediately followed by Mother, who said, "It's good that you're home safe." Father started to cry and so did Mother. I cried too, standing inside the open door. I noticed Takao sobbing, sitting behind our parents. At age 11, I wasn't sure how much he understood the meaning of what was happening in front of his eyes.

Chapter 13

Ronin Again

MATSUYAMA

Now What?

Once back home, I was in total despair. I didn't know what to do. I didn't want to do anything. It seemed that I had lost my purpose for living. Occasionally, I would try to tell myself, "Hey, you're still alive. People are still out there for you to be useful to. Do something worthwhile." Then my inner self would raise its head and say, "Go to Hell. I've done my share. Leave me alone." For a couple of days, I stayed home, not wanting to go out or see anyone. As a matter of fact, I think I was afraid to see people. "They might think I am a coward, coming home alive without accomplishing my mission." Hundreds of thousands, perhaps millions, of people died for their country as they said they would.

As days passed, my 23-year-old body commanded me to take some exercise. I wasn't used to sitting around doing nothing. So I took a walk to a nearby riverbank, walking through the narrow dirt paths between rice paddies where I knew few passed. On the bank of Shigenobu River, I sat and thought. The first thing that came to my mind was "What's-his-name" at Izumi, whose plane flipped up and crashed in front of the visiting dignitaries. Then Narabayashi at Wonsan, whose parachute got tangled on the tail wing of his own plane and who was slashed by his propeller, and Jinde, who got shot over Tokyo Bay. What about all my classmates from whom I parted at Mie, Izumi and Wonsan? Many of them must have died as *kamikazes.*

Later, of course, as days and months passed, I heard about many, many others, those who were with me in school and those who were in the 13th Class. Why did they have to die? Why them? Why Kobayashi, for example? He and I went from Mie to Wonsan together. He was one of the nicest persons I had ever known. He was handsome, intelligent and congenial. We shared many things: the fried chicken Father brought all the way from Matsuyama to Mie; the Tanakas, our host family in Komenotsu; and some of the outings in Wonsan. Why did he have to die and not me? Oh, I wouldn't say I would have asked to die in his place, but there were others who weren't as nice as he was and who were still alive. Was God being fair?

Speaking of God, what was that "divinity" thing before and during the war all about anyway? To begin with, was the Emperor really divine? Did we really believe that? Well, perhaps we only half believed. We knew he ate and slept like anyone else. "Do you still think of him as a demi-god? No, not any more, but if the Allies allow him to remain as the ruler of this country, I think he deserves our due respect as the direct descendant of the creator of this country," I began asking and answering myself. "Why did you so eagerly and voluntarily bow to the *Hoanden* (the small shrine where the portraits of the Emperor and the Empress were kept at school), even when you knew no one was watching? I don't know. I guess it was because that was the rule. I was brought up to always obey rules, you know. What about always praying for the eternity and prosperity of the nation when you passed by shrines and temples? You never failed to do so. I'm not so sure on that either. I don't remember how it got started, but it just became a habit for me. Do you still believe in God? Well, give me time to think about that one too." In the minds of the Japanese people in those days, it was not very clear whether there were many gods or one god who appeared in many different forms. To an extent, this is true even today. It seems that, at least, there is no concept of one absolute, almighty God.

As I kept talking to myself, my gaze into the distance suddenly focused on the peak of Mt. Ishizuchi, the highest mountain on the island of Shikoku. "It's still there, unchanged from my younger days." Then a Chinese poem I learned in school crossed my mind. *"The nation is defeated, but the mountains and rivers are still there."* That's right. Japan was defeated but the country is the same, the people are the same. I've got to do something. I've got to keep serving the country! I remembered I was issued a license to teach English when I was graduated from college. But no school offered courses in English as far as I knew. The teaching of English was banned during the middle part of the war, because English was an enemy language. "Wait a minute," I thought, "I can drive. Maybe with a little training I can drive trucks or buses. I'd prefer taxis, but there don't seem to be any taxis around."

When I came to this thought, I went home and talked to Father and Mother about this idea. "Oh, no. Naval officers don't become truck or bus drivers," was their reaction.

This went on for several days. Many bits of memories and many questions, most of them without any answers, crossed my mind. One day, a motorcycle drove up as I was about to leave for the riverbank. It was Mr. Yamauchi, the middle school English and music teacher. "Welcome back, Imamura. I asked around your old neighborhood and heard you were living out here. I'm glad you're home alive. By the way, I came here to see if your family or some neighbors of yours might have some food to spare. Living in the city, it is awfully hard to get enough food these days." Mother came out to greet Mr. Yamauchi. She said she didn't have any food to share, but some of the neighborhood farmers might. She ran off, and while Mr. Yamauchi and I were catching up on what had happened to us during the past two years, she came back with her apron full of sweet potatoes. Mr. Yamauchi thanked her profusely, turned to me and said, "Have you been to the site where your house used to stand?" I said I hadn't. He then said, "Get on the back of this motorcycle. I'll take you there now."

It was scarcely a 15-minute ride on the back of the motorbike before we got to where our house used to stand. The street in front was widened indeed, about three or four times what it used to be. The new wide street slashed diagonally through the area where we had lived, and all the old neighbors were gone. Standing and looking around, I thought of the good eleven years we had lived there before I joined the naval air force. "Now everything is gone. I will have to start a really new life," I thought to myself. Then, Mr. Yamauchi said, "Have you had enough of this? Hop on. We're leaving." I thought he was taking me back to my Ishii Village home, but he started to head in the opposite direction. "Where are we going?" I asked. "You'll see," he said, and kept going in the direction of Bancho Elementary School. He stopped the motorcycle in front of the Prefectural Library building, across the street from the Bancho School. Mr. Yamauchi started to walk into the building. I was reluctant to follow him, because I noticed a big sign above the main entrance that read, "HEADQUARTERS, ADVANCED PARTY, 24TH INFANTRY DIVISION" in English. I had heard that there was a small party of American soldiers in Matsuyama already, although I had no idea what they were there for or what they were doing. "Come on, Imamura. They won't hurt you," said Mr. Yamauchi. Since I still considered him my teacher, I obeyed him.

Once inside, Mr. Yamauchi took me straight to an office with an open door. We walked right in to face a uniformed American sitting at the desk. I had no idea what his rank was. "Colonel, this young man was born in America and can speak English. His name is Shigeo Imamura." At that, the colonel looked up at me, sized me up and then said, "Say 'lollypop.'" Reflexively I said, "Lollypop." "Good. You speak English. Report to work here at eight in the morning." Again reflexively, I said, "Yes, sir." When Mr. Yamauchi called the man "Colonel," I knew that he was three ranks above me, and I think it was the military still in me that made me give that answer. A few days later, I found out that his real rank was Lieutenant Colonel, but that was still two ranks above me.

Suddenly, I was in a new job I did not seek for myself. In a sense, I was tricked into it. Of course, Mr. Yamauchi meant well. The Americans were having a hard time finding people who spoke both English and Japanese well enough to serve as translators and interpreters. And here was a kid who spoke both languages. Why not put them together? But I was reluctant, very reluctant. Why should I work for people I had been fighting against only a month before? It was with a very heavy heart that I reported to the headquarters at eight the next morning. As soon as the colonel saw me, he called in a man who I later learned to be a sergeant and said, "Take this gentleman to the Translation Section and put him on to Lt. Elmendorf." I doubted my ears for a moment. "Gentleman? Did he call me a gentleman?" This was the first surprise I encountered in my association with the post-war Americans. In the Translation Section, I found four or five Japanese working on translations. Lt. Elmendorf told me that we would occasionally be called upon to serve as interpreters, either at the headquarters or at Japanese offices, as needed. My main job was to translate Japanese newspaper articles into English so the American officers would know what was going on in Ehime Prefecture and in Matsuyama and how the Japanese public reacted to those events.

As the days passed, I learned many things. Lt. Elmendorf was a UC Berkeley graduate, had learned Japanese in the Army Special Training Program, and was able to read Japanese as well as speak it. There were a few other officers and about two dozen men in support. Among the translator interpreters were the Sawada sisters — Carol and Louise. They and most others were American born *nisei*. We Japanese worked full-time for the Americans but were paid by the prefectural government as its temporary employees. We were all amateurs at the kind of work we were doing and occasionally ran into problems. Translating Japanese into English was relatively easy. We often came across words we didn't know in English, but dictionaries were always available. The hardest were official documents, especially directives from the U.S. government to the Japanese government, because we were not familiar with bureaucratic jargon. Interpreting between American officers and Japanese officials, businessmen, etc., was relatively easy when the topics of discussion were of a general nature, but we found it difficult interpreting technical matters pertaining to topics such as civil engineering, plant pathology and medicine.

Early in this new career of mine, I was amazed at how rusty my English had become. I hardly had spoken a word of it or read anything in English during my two years in military service. So I really had to study up. Besides, the kind of English I had control of was mostly colloquial, not suitable for translating official documents. Doing translations at my desk was one thing, but human relations with the

Americans was another. It took me a couple of weeks to shake off the thought of "working for the former enemy." Particularly hard was taking orders from enlisted men, some of them younger than me. They didn't really order us around or anything, but a PFC would bring a document and say, "Here, translate this," which to me seemed like an order. "How dare an enlisted man give an order to an officer," was my feeling. But that too went away with time. Once I got to know them better, I found them to be treating us very fairly. As I got to even like most of them, I came to realize that all those talks about how devilish, beastly and barbarous all Westerners are were sheer propaganda by the Japanese government. While the Allies held absolute power over the Japanese government and people, I was able to regain the view of Americans as equal partners, something I had lost since returning to Japan as a child. I think it was in mid- or late-October that the whole 24th Infantry Division moved into Matsuyama. It was known as the Oak Leaf Division, home-based in Hawaii. They camped mostly on the grounds where Matsuyama Naval Air Base used to be. It seemed to me that there were hundreds of large tents put up there. The Division set up checkpoints on major roads leading into Matsuyama, and sent out road patrols to all parts of the island of Shikoku. One day when I got home to our Ishii Village house after work, Father laughed and told me what had happened that day. He was walking to our patch of vegetable farm with a hoe on his shoulder when he passed a GI standing sentry at a checkpoint. The GI said, "Hi there, old man. How are you today?" Father replied, "Fine, thank you. And how are you?" The GI did a double take and said to Father, "Did you just speak English?" So, Father felt he had to explain why he was able to speak English.

Shortly thereafter, however, all of us translator-interpreters had a new job. Small teams of American army personnel moved anew into the capital cities of the four prefectures on Shikoku: Matsuyama, Takamatsu,Tokushima and Kochi. Each of the teams was set up as a U.S. military government team and took over all civil administrative functions from the Division. The Division itself soon moved across the Inland Sea to the city of Okayama. The team in Takamatsu doubled as the military government for the whole island of Shikoku. Matsuyama was the capital of Ehime Prefecture, and the Ehime

Military Government Team (MGT) office was set up on the fourth floor of the Prefectural Government Building, in a room which had been used for ceremonial functions. It was ironic that the Americans were put to work in that room which had a raised platform on which the prefectural governor had stood and bowed to the Imperial portraits and read off the Imperial decrees.

The team was headed by a colonel, under whose command were the Civil Information and Education (CI&E) Section, the Economic and Labor Section, the Legal and Government Section and the Medical and Social Welfare Section, each headed by an Army officer. Of a dozen or so enlisted men, some worked in the offices as clerks and typists, and others manned the men's living quarters set up in the Prefectural Library Building they had taken over from the Division. There was a motor pool there too. The Japanese translator-interpreters were assigned to the various sections, one or two to an office. My assignment was to the CI&E Section, and my first boss there was a Captain Borish, a soft-spoken gentleman. It seemed he was there just to help set up the outfit, and he was soon replaced by a Captain Robert Rudolph. The job of the CI&E officer was to visit schools all over Ehime Prefecture to make sure that the schools were being administered in compliance with the various directives issued by the Allied Forces General Headquarters (GHQ) through the Ministry of Education. This included making sure that no weaponry was stored or hidden on school grounds, that the "right" textbooks were being used and that no imperialistic, ultra-nationalistic or militaristic teaching was going on. We translator-interpreters started out working for the Ehime MGT, as they were often called, with considerably more confidence than we had first done at the Division Headquarters.

Capt. Rudolph drove a jeep and I rode along. At first, we hit some of the larger schools in major cities. As time went on, we had to drive distances to get to schools in remote areas. Especially in those out-of-the-way places, way up in the mountain valleys and in small fishing villages way down the coast, our appearance caused quite a commotion. Most often, it was the very first time for the villagers to lay their eyes on a foreigner. Captain Rudolph, with his large body, big round eyes, and a high nose seemed scary to them. He more or less fit their image of the "foreign devil" they were told about so often during the war. Occasionally we would lose our way on the road, spot a few villagers way up the road and want to ask them directions. By the time we drove up to where they were, they were all gone, hiding. I sometimes had to ask Captain Rudolph to drive ahead out of sight, wait till people came out of hiding and ask them where the village school was. Once we got to the school, it was a different picture. As soon as children saw the jeep coming, they all came running out and surrounded us, whether classes were in session or not. The teachers came running after them, but not knowing how to react to the situation, they stood among the students in the crowd around the jeep. We asked them for the school principal and were led to his office. Captain Rudolph asked questions all prepared in advance and I did the interpreting. We hardly ever found anything out of line.

One day, the CI&E received an anonymous letter saying there were old army rifles buried in the sandbox at a certain junior high school in the suburbs of Matsuyama. Captain Rudolph and I went out there. When we met the principal, he was as pale as a ghost. I sensed that he knew why we were there before we said anything. The Captain told the principal about the letter and asked him to get the custodian to dig up the sandbox. Now the principal was trembling. He hesitantly interrupted the Captain to say, "Yes, there are some things buried in the sandbox but they are dummy rifles carved out of wood, used during the war to train civilians for bayonet fighting." What were dug up were exactly what he said they were.

There were other similar but smaller incidents. On such occasions, I felt caught between, or felt sorry for, both parties. For example in the above case, Captain Rudolph had to act rather sternly because of the possibly serious nature of the case. Yet, to him, he was simply carrying out his routine duty as a CI&E officer. On the other hand, for the principal, he had heard that some young men came and buried the dummy rifles right after the end of the war, but forgot all about it due to his busy daily schedule of reforming the school under the new directives. Yet, if the American officer had regarded the dug-up materials as weapons nonetheless, he could have been jailed. The fact that he appeared to be scared to death proved that such a thought did cross his mind.

Captain Rudolph's term of service was up in a couple of months, and he returned to the United States. In his place came Mr. Charles Boleske, a civilian who previously served as a high school principal in West Virginia. He and I did the same things Captain Rudolph and I used to do, except that, being a civilian, Mr. Boleske had much milder manners toward people, Japanese as well as Americans. He was actually in Matsuyama on temporary duty until a stateside man arrived to take the post of CI&E Officer. That stateside man was William Scott. Bill, as I started to call him, was a bit younger than I was. He had been a psychology major in college and went through the Japanese language program at the U.S. Navy Language School in Denver, Colorado. He was already fluent in Japanese when he arrived. That made my job easier and more difficult at the same time. For example, when Bill and I went to a school for a visit and talked to the principal, Bill would talk with the principal in Japanese and needed my help only once in a while. Yet, he never attempted to speak to groups of people in Japanese, because he did not want to make mistakes or give them wrong information. When I interpreted his speeches or lectures, occasionally he stopped me and said, "Hey, Shig, that's not what I said." That resulted in my need to really study up on educational terminology and philosophy. Thanks to Bill, I became pretty much of an expert in education and language teaching before ever getting formal training in those fields.

At this time, several important events were happening, locally as well as nationally. Nationally, perhaps what kept the people's attention was the Far East Military Tribunal, the result of which was the hanging death of General Tojo and others who were found guilty of war crimes. Most Japanese seemed to take that as an inevitable consequence. Some apparently felt that justice always sides with the victor. Purging from public offices of those looked upon as lesser war criminals was also taking place throughout the nation. Locally, a board of investigation was established to look into the wartime activities of local citizens and leaders. Those who were in leading positions to advocate the support of Imperial expansionism were purged. The Military Government was deeply involved in supervising the investigation board. Bill Scott and I attended some of their meetings. Near the conclusion of the screening process, the members of the investigation board themselves were screened. Mr. I, the chairman of the board, who was found to be a long-time local leader of the Imperial Rule Support Association, was banished from the board as well as from the Prefectural Board of Education on which he was serving.

Perhaps a more significant event was the restructuring of the public education system. The old system was not only very complicated but was also fundamentally based on elitist principles. GHQ, pushing for a democratization of Japan, did not like this and ordered a change to a six-year elementary, three-year lower secondary, three-year upper secondary and four-year higher education system, patterned after the system widely used in the United States at the time. If I remember correctly, the changeover took place in 1948. The change involved many things. First of all, educators needed to be well informed on the need and benefits of the transformation. Conference after conference was held, nationally and locally. Textbooks all needed to be rewritten. New school buildings had to be constructed, because compulsory education was extended from six or eight years to nine years. English was made an elective subject at the secondary level, but in fact just about everyone wanted to take it. There was a need for a much larger number of teachers to teach English, so inservice training was started all over the country. This was indeed a period of activism, and to a certain extent, confusion, in educational circles.

Parallel to this was the establishment of democratic civil organizations and trade unions. Before and during the war, there were women's organizations and youth organizations, but they were all hierarchical, with leadership tied to the central government and the military. New organizations were needed, formed on the bases of voluntary membership and democratic administration. Again, numerous meetings were held for lectures and discussions. Bill Scott participated in many of them.

Let us go back in time a little. In late 1945, after I began working for the Americans, some Ishii Village children started to come knocking on our door. They wanted me to teach them English. At first, I told them that I worked all day, often into the evening, and was too tired to do anything else. But they were very persistent and I broke down. I negotiated with the Village Office and got permission to use the Village Public Hall, free of charge since I did not charge any tuition. At first, a bunch of junior and senior high school students came and I taught them conversational English. Hearing about the class, student after student came, wanting to join the class. After I started to turn them away because the class was getting too large, parents began to pester me, trying to talk me into letting their children into the class. I decided to split the class and eventually found myself teaching two 45-minute sessions three evenings a week. Of course, when I was out of town on road trips, classes were canceled. Around early spring, 1946, these students started to ask me to teach them the American popular songs they heard on the radio, so I had to learn many songs, old and new. I taught most of them to the students. I say "most," because some of the songs I picked up from GIs I could not possibly teach to these young people.

When my family later moved to a new Yanai-machi house, I thought I was going to be relieved of the teaching. I did enjoy teaching English, but the burden was too heavy. But, no, many of the students wanted to continue learning from me, even if they had to commute to our new place in the evening, 20 to 25 minutes each way by bicycle. I told them that I would start charging them tuition, but that did not do much good. The two-sessions-an-evening, three-evenings-a-week classes continued. The Ishii Village English classes were the beginning of my English teaching career, but I had no idea then that it was going to last half a century. The tuition for each student was very nominal, but the extra income did help.

I think it was in the early summer of 1947 that Bill Scott left. He said he was going back to graduate school, either in Colorado or in Michigan. He was replaced by a WAC (Women's Army Corps) Captain Shirlie Snyder. Captain Snyder (I did not dare call her "Shirlie" because she was much older than me and, besides, she had a rather stern personality) was a high school principal in East St. Louis before she retired and joined the Army. She was an expert in school administration and contributed greatly to the betterment of post-war education in Ehime and neighboring prefectures. Thanks to Bill Scott's good training, my expertise in education, especially in the teaching of English as a Second Language, was fairly high and I had become just about equally fluent in Japanese and English. This,

I am sure, helped Captain Snyder's effectiveness on her job.

I might add that Captain Snyder was well received by the male officers but not by the young enlisted men. They seemed to feel ill at ease having her around and among them, and tended to shy away from her. Fortunately for Captain Snyder, she was not the only female officer around. At about the same time, the Team had a middle-aged officer nurse as Assistant Medical and Welfare Officer. Also, the CI&E Officer at the Kagawa MGT in Takamatsu was a female. She used to come down to Matsuyama quite often on official business and to socialize with the two ladies in Matsuyama.

Early in 1948, I was approached by the head of an educational institution called Nitta Gakuen in the suburbs of Matsuyama. They were setting up a new Matsuyama Junior College of Foreign Languages to be added to the Nitta Junior and Senior High Schools they had been running for several years. They wanted me on the faculty of the Junior College to teach English. I told the representative of Nitta Gakuen I didn't think the U.S. military would allow me to have another job, but that he could contact them directly and see what happened. He did, and to my surprise the Army agreed. I was told that the reason behind this decision was that I would become a better translator-interpreter in the field of education by gaining teaching experience in the classroom. In that case, I thought it would be better for me to gain teaching experience at all levels, so I successfully negotiated with Nitta Gakuen to allow me to teach at the Junior and Senior High Schools as well as at the Junior College. This meant three classes on one day each week. I had been reading quite a few books on education, especially in language teaching. For example, I had read a book written by Dr. Charles C. Fries of the University of Michigan. I found this book, ***The Teaching and Learning of English as a Foreign Language***, thrilling because the substance of the book backed up many of the thoughts I had developed myself teaching the Ishii Village students. The Fries book was later translated into Japanese and was very widely read among Japanese teachers of English. Therefore, it was with a certain amount of confidence that I started teaching at the Nitta Institute. I think I did a good enough job of teaching there. I was particularly popular at the Junior College, presumably because the students liked learning spoken

English, which they never had in the secondary schools.

The Allied occupation of Japan did not officially end until the signing of the peace treaty in 1951, but evidently the GHQ decided that the ultra-nationalism and militarism so prevalent during World War II were sufficiently dissipated and the local government now functioned well enough on democratic bases that a U.S. military government team in each prefecture was no longer necessary. In the spring of 1949, an announcement was made that all of the military government teams on Shikoku, except the one in Takamatsu, would be disbanded. We were told that a few of the translator-interpreters from the Ehime Team could be absorbed by the Takamatsu Team, but the rest of us would have to look for jobs elsewhere. Since the four years with the Americans had been rather strenuous for me, mentally as well as physically, I thought of moving on to an easier job, at least for a while. I was about to contact Mrs. Funada, the principal of Saibi Girls' High School, to see if she would hire me as an English teacher. Since Saibi wasn't an academically competitive school and hardly any of its graduates went on to college then, I thought it would be a fairly easy job. But before I was able to make that move, Colonel Searls, the commanding officer of the Ehime MGT, called me into his office and told me that he had arranged for me to be hired by the Prefectural Board of Education as their first English Teacher Consultant. It was a position rather high for a person of my age and background. I was grateful to the colonel for his kind consideration and did nothing to resist the fine arrangement he had made on my behalf.

On leaving the translator-interpreter job, I looked back on the 27 years of my life up to that point and became filled with emotion. I was born and brought up in America. Had my parents not decided to bring me back to Japan when they did, I could have lived on in America, and probably shared the sad experience of being sent to a relocation camp with other Japanese-Americans, and may even have been killed fighting for the United States, like many of the *nisei* GIs. Instead, at age ten, my parents placed me in an environment totally new to me. I gradually adjusted myself to the new surroundings, and before I knew it, I seemed to have become just another Japanese, or, in fact, more Japanese than an average Japanese youth of the day.

Ultimately, I came to regard the Americans as my enemies and voluntarily offered my life in the defense of Japan. Just by chance, I survived the war. I was then thrust into a position of having to work for the U.S. Army. As time went on, I came to realize that all of us, Japanese or Americans, have similar thoughts and emotions. In war, we fight for our country; in peace we all work together. Coming to realize that I was helping both Americans and Japanese, I took pride in my work. That career came to an end and now I was about to begin a new career as a full-fledged Japanese citizen. In a sense, I started my life as an American, metamorphosed into a Japanese, and reverted to a more-or-less neutral being. "Who am I now? What am I? Am I bilingual, bicultural or am I just a mixed-up person?" As happened to me after returning from the war, I was troubled by these and other questions about my identity. Perhaps these questions were inevitable for someone with my varied background. I would struggle with them throughout my life.

Epilogue

The
Teacher

HIMEJI

Atsugi •

Matsuyama

• Okinawa

Between Two Worlds

Written by the Editors

After serving in the Japanese military during the war and working as a translator-interpreter for the U.S. Allied Forces in Japan, Shigeo Imamura went on to be a leading force in English language education in Japan and in the United States. He did much to promote cultural understanding and to professionalize the teaching of English as a foreign/second language, serving as a teacher and mentor to many beginning teachers and graduate students.

Professor Imamura served as the English teacher supervisor for Ehime Prefectural Board of Education from 1949-1955. During that time, he introduced the first inservice training seminar for teachers of English in Matsuyama in March 1950. Due to the success of the first program, Professor Imamura was invited to organize similar seminars in other regions of Japan: Sendai, Hiroshima and Kyushu. In writing of the need for such seminars and the first one in Matsuyama, Professor Imamura wrote:

> *As the English teacher supervisor, I observed that many, if not most, of those teaching English in secondary schools were not quite equipped to do their jobs. Their ability to listen to and understand or speak English was rather limited. Some of them were never trained in the methods of teaching English as a second/ foreign language. In March 1950, I took upon myself a major operation: a two-week inservice training for teachers of English. We had the use of the wooden buildings of the former Ehime Normal School, then totally vacated because of the abolishment of the normal school system throughout the country. We laid tatami mats on the wooden floors of classrooms, and the participants, as we called them, slept on them curled up in blankets they brought with them. There were about 100 participants, so we made several classrooms into bedrooms. Other classrooms were used for instruction during the daytime. As instructors, there were about a dozen native speakers of English, educators, and military personnel from all over Western Japan. In March, it was fairly cold even in Matsuyama, which is in a temperate zone. Heating systems in school buildings were unheard of in those days. The participants were sturdy as well as enthusiastic. They came voluntarily and tolerated the hardships. The use of the Japanese language was prohibited throughout the program. It was the very first time for most of them to speak with native speakers of English, but they very actively took part in the drills, recitations, and lectures. It seemed that they went home happy with the thought that they got what they wanted, a bit better command of the English language.*

In 1950 Imamura was awarded a scholarship to study for one year at the University of Michigan. Learning of the scholarship one month before he needed to depart for the United States presented two obstacles:

getting permission from his superiors at Ehime Prefectural Board of Education for a year's leave of absence on such short notice and getting a student visa from the U.S. Consulate in Kobe. In describing the complications of getting a student visa, he wrote:

> *The Consul was a kind gentleman. He explained to me that I had Japanese/American dual citizenship but that my U.S. citizenship was revoked for three reasons: (1) that I volunteered to serve in a foreign (Japanese) military force; (2) that I had an official status in a foreign government, even though local; and (3) that there was evidence that I had voted in public elections in a foreign country. All three of these violated existing U.S. Immigration Acts. He said that I had a choice of either renouncing my U.S. citizenship or applying for a reinstatement of the citizenship and having it denied. He suggested that I take the latter step because that would leave me with the opportunity to apply for a reinstatement again in the future. Then I would be eligible to apply for a U.S. student visa as a Japanese citizen. That is what I did.*

So, 19 years after having left his hometown of San Francisco for Yokohama, Shigeo Imamura shipped out of Yokohama for San Francisco and the United States. In describing arriving in San Francisco, he wrote:

> *All of us were on deck watching the approaching land. I was full of emotion as the white houses and the streets of San Francisco became visible. Ah, my hometown! The ship slowed down and passed under the Golden Gate Bridge . . . . The ship docked at Fort Mason, we disembarked and were taken to Mills College in Oakland by army buses. As we passed through parts of San Francisco, I recognized some of the streets and landmarks . . . . As the buses began to climb the hill on the Mills campus, I smelled the scent*

> *of the eucalyptus trees, which triggered my memories*
> *of Golden Gate Park.*

After staying at Mills College for several days, during which time he visited family friends in San Francisco, Imamura and others on scholarships boarded trains for their destinations. Imamura had a month-long orientation at Yale before going to the University of Michigan.

At the University of Michigan, Imamura was able to study under Professor Charles Fries, one of the foremost linguists in the area of teaching English as a Foreign/Second Language. Professor Fries advised Imamura to enroll as a regular student and earn as many credits as possible towards a Bachelor's degree. After one year, Imamura was able to gather enough money, through translation work, savings, and scholarships, to be able to extend his stay for one year so that he could complete his degree in June 1953. Upon sailing back to Yokohama from San Francisco, Imamura noted, *"When we arrived in Yokohama, I thought the air smelled strange. It smelled like a mixture of takuan (pickled radish, a common side dish) and soy sauce. Anyway, it certainly smelled different from the air in America, which to me often smelled of Campbell soup."*

Back in Japan, Imamura returned to working for the Ehime Prefectural Board of Education and to organizing inservice teacher training seminars and later received funding from the Asia Foundation for the seminars. In 1955, he was invited to join the faculty at Ehime University as an assistant professor in the English Department, College of Education, and subsequently established the English Language Training Center there. Junior and senior high school English teachers came to the Ehime Training Center for three-month seminars in language use and teaching methodology. At this time, Imamura also began working closely with the Asia Foundation in Japan, headed by Dr. Robert Brown, who had employed Imamura as a translator at the University of Michigan.

In 1957, Imamura was sent to the University of the Ryukyus in Okinawa by the Asia Foundation to set up their first language laboratory, a rarity in those days. Through the advisory commission of the University of Ryukyus, Imamura met educators from Michigan

State University: Drs. David Mead and Robert Geist. Mead and Geist took an interest in Imamura's inservice teacher training seminars and the Training Center at Ehime, later inviting Imamura to come to Michigan State University to help set up the English Language Center in 1961-1962.

Imamura returned to Ehime University and taught for one year (1962-1963) before resigning from Ehime and returning to Michigan State University, where he directed the English Language Center (1964-1974) and taught for 18 years. He and his wife Isako made their home in East Lansing until 1981. While at Michigan State University, Imamura earned an M.A. in Linguistics from the University of Michigan (1964) and became involved in professional organizations, often serving in elected and appointed positions and frequently making conference presentations. In addition, he published widely in English and in Japanese, teaching materials and professional articles. The organizations included the Linguistic Society of America (LSA), NAFSA: Association of International Educators and its ATESL section (Administrators and Teachers of English as a Second Language), Teachers of English to Speakers of Other Languages (TESOL), and the Modern Language Association (MLA).

In the capacity of consultant for NAFSA: Association of International Educators, he visited universities, helping them organize and improve intensive English programs. On one such visit to the University of San Francisco, he was invited to set up an intensive program there and, thus, founded and directed the intensive program from 1974-1976 in San Francisco, his hometown.

In the late 1970s, Imamura was invited to join the faculty of a new college at Aoyama Gakuin University in Tokyo: the School for International Politics, Economics and Business (SIPEB) to be established in Spring 1982. Imamura would head the English program and all students in the college would have an emphasis in English. The challenge of starting a new program was too much to resist, so Imamura and his wife Isako left Michigan State University in 1981 and returned to Japan. In Japan he became actively involved in professional organizations such as Japanese Association of Teachers of English (JALT) and served as JALT president. After working at Aoyama Gakuin University for several years, Imamura was lured away to Dokkyo Institute by the offer of starting a new language institute and heading the English Department at a new university Himeji Dokkyo University. So, in 1986 he once again started a new program. He retired from Himeji Dokkyo in 1997 at the age of 75.

Imamura remained in Japan until his death in December 1998. At his request, on August 14, 1999, his 77th birthday, Imamura's ashes were scattered in the San Francisco Bay by his wife Isako along with relatives and close friends.

Throughout his life, people, curious about Imamura's World War II experiences, asked him to speak to community groups. He recounted one such evening from the 1950s in Ann Arbor, Michigan:

> *A silver-haired old gentleman came to me after my talk and held my hands gently without saying a word for a moment. I saw tears in his eyes. After a while he said, "Forgive me. I have hated you Japanese for killing my only son in the war. Listening to you, I came to realize that there are old fathers like me in Japan too, who lost their sons in the war. I was wrong. It wasn't the Japanese who killed my son. It was the war that did it. Forgive me." I was deeply moved but no words came to my mouth. All I could do was grip his hands firmly in return.*

Later in writing of his experiences, Shigeo Imamura wrote of his hope for more people to understand his story.

> *I am sometimes asked where I would prefer to live in retirement, in the United States or in Japan. I am always hard put to answer that question, because I know I can live as comfortably and pleasantly in either country. Besides, having visited some thirty countries around the world, I can think of several other places I might want to reside for the rest of my life. But such thoughts inevitably bring to my mind the sad fact that conflicts are still going on in various parts of the world, almost daily. The conflicts are brought on because of politics, economics, religion and race.*

Especially tragic are the ones that go way back in history.

As I look back on my wartime experience, I cannot help but wish that I had known then what I know now. It wasn't worth Japan and the United States fighting each other, not with the great losses of lives on both sides. Which leads me to wonder if there are any wars that are worth fighting, from an objective point of view. My experience and observation tell me that there aren't. I sincerely hope that this writing will help me to prove that point.

—Johnnie Johnson Hafernik

Pacific War Chronology

Primary source: John Keegan, The Second World War (Penguin 1989)
Imamura dates and story highlights appear in italic type

1894	Japan wins war against China
1895	Formosa (Taiwan) ceded to and occupied by Japan
1905	Japan wins war against Russia—this is when Japan established "rights" in Manchuria, *e.g.*, over the railway system
1910	Japan annexes Korea
1913-1918	Japan fights in World War I on the side of the Allies—fights against Germany in its Pacific colonies
1922	Washington Naval Treaty relegates Japan to a place in world naval hierarchy below U.S. and Britain
August 14, 1922	*First child Shigeo born in the "Japanese Hospital" in San Jose to Keijiro and Hisako Imamura, Japanese emigrants from Matsuyama, Shikoku living in San Francisco*
September 1928	*Imamura begins elementary education at Raphael Weill School in Japantown, San Francisco*

September 1929	*Imamura begins after-school studies at Kimmon Gakuen in Japantown*
1931	The Manchuria Incident: Japanese garrison in Manchuria takes possession of the whole of Manchuria
March 1932	*Imamura and his mother return to Matsuyama. Father follows a year later*
April 1932	*Imamura begins 4th grade at Bancho Elementary School in Matsuyama*
October 5, 1934	*Imamura's younger brother Takao born in Matsuyama*
April 1935	*Imamura enters Matsuyama Middle School (Matsuchu)*
February 26, 1936	Young, right-wing soldiers of the Tokyo Garrison attempt assassination of Prime Minister and a military coup. (Army actually strengthened because it quickly distanced itself from the mutineers.)
1937	The China Incident: Conflict between locals and Japanese garrison of the international embassy guard at Peking sparks widespread war in China
1938	Most of China under Japanese occupation
Fall 1939	*Imamura's mother called up for Nurse Reserve Corps*

February 1940	*Imamura fails entrance exam for Matsuyama High School*
July 1940	Prince Konoe becomes Prime Minister; General Tojo becomes Minister of War; and Yosuke Matsuoka becomes Foreign Minister
September 27, 1940	Japan forms Tripartite Pact with Germany and Italy
November 1940	*Imamura fails entrance exam for Naval Academy*
February 1941	*Imamura passes entrance exam for Matsuyama Commercial College ("Kosho")*
April 1941	*Imamura enters Matsuyama Commercial College*
July 24, 1941	Japan extracts permission from Vichy France to place troops in Indo-China
July 26, 1941	U.S. (supporting Britain and the Dutch) imposes additional embargoes on Western trade with Japan
September 6, 1941	Japanese cabinet meeting presents Emperor with three alternatives: begin war preparations; continue negotiating with the U.S.; accept U.S. restrictions on Japanese strategic activities, including a withdrawal from Indo-China
Early October 1941	Tojo, advocating war, increases pressure on Konoe

October 17, 1941	Konoe resigns and Tojo becomes Prime Minister
November 5, 1941	Final decision on war with U.S. taken
December 7, 1941	Japanese attack on Pearl Harbor (December 8th in Japan)
December 8, 1941	Japanese attacks Wake and Guam. Siege of Hong Kong begun. British ships sunk near Singapore. Guam falls
December 10, 1941	Japan begins amphibious assaults on Malaya and the Philippines
December 14, 1941	Northern Malaya falls
December 23, 1941	Wake falls
December 25, 1941	Hong Kong falls
December 1941	Japan invades Thailand, Burma, and the Philippines
January 7, 1942	Japan overruns Central Malaya. Pushes toward Singapore
February 15, 1942	Singapore surrenders
February 27, 1942	Battle of Java Sea
March 12, 1942	Formal surrender of Java. Japanese land on Sumatra. MacArthur's "I shall return" departure from Manila

April 1942	*Imamura begins second year at Kosho. Starts riding club*
April 8, 1942	Surrender in the Philippines; Bataan Death March
April 18, 1942	Doolittle raids on Tokyo, from U.S. carriers in the Pacific (13 aircraft; 80 fliers, 71 of whom survived) (no public acknowledgment to citizens of Tokyo from their government) – the carrier *Hornet* came within striking distance through the "Midway Hole"
May 6, 1942	Fall of Corregidor—all of Philippines in Japanese hands
May 1942	Japanese footholds established in New Guinea
	Interceptions of Japanese messages— "Magic" (intercepted Japanese messages about Midway)
May 1942	British expelled from Burma. By mid-1942, Japan controls all of Indo-China, the Indies and Malaya
May 7, 1942	Battle of Coral Sea, won by Allies, prevents planned Japanese landing at Port Moresby in southern Papua New Guinea
June 4-6, 1942	Battle of Midway. U.S. loses only the Yorktown carrier (struck by **Hiryu**, which is mentioned by Imamura); Japanese fleet devastated (**Akagi, Kaga** and **Soryu** carriers sunk)

	A few months later, Imamura hears an account of the battle from a member of the crew of **Hiryu**, *but, because of government press reports of the battle, disbelieves the eyewitness story of Japanese losses*
March 1943	*During school vacation, Imamura does a month of "voluntary labor service" packing powder into battleship gun shells*
May 29, 1943	*Japanese Navy announces large recruitment drive for college graduates, to supplement dwindling number of front-line pilots*
August 1943	*Imamura takes naval air reserve exam and is one of 5,000 out of 70,000 to pass*
September 7, 1943	*Graduation from Kosho moved up by half a year for Imamura and six classmates destined for the 13th Class of Naval Reserves*
September 13, 1943	*Naval Cadet Imamura reports to Mie Naval Air Station*
January 1944	*Imamura assigned to flight training at Izumi Naval Air Corps on Model 93*
Mar/Apr 1944	Japanese offenses in Burma (*U-Go*) and southern China (*Ichi-Go*). *U-Go* fails; *Ichi-Go* more successful

End of April, 1944	*Imamura assigned to Wonson Naval Air Corps in Korea, but sent to Oita first*
May 1944	*Fighter training at Oita on Model 96 fighters*
June 1944	Tojo resigns as Prime Minister; replaced by more moderate Kuniaki Koiso but military still controls cabinet
June 1, 1944	*Imamura promoted to ensign and becomes a full-fledged naval officer*
Mid June 1944	*Zero fighter pilot training at Wonson*
June-Aug 1944	Capture of Marianas
July 1944	Fall of Vogelkop Peninsula in New Guinea
Sept 15, 1944	Capture of Morotai, halfway between New Guinea and Mindanao (southern Philippines). Fall of Guam and Saipan and invasion of Peleliu, in the Palau islands
Early October 1944	*Graduation from training and assignment to Tokyo Detachment at Kasumigaura Naval Air Corps (Haneda) as flight instructor*
Oct 10-17, 1944	American Third Fleet destroys 500 Japanese carrier and land based aircraft
October 20, 1944	MacArthur begins landings on Leyte (Philippines)

Oct 23-25, 1944	Battle of Leyte Gulf. Japanese lose virtually all aircraft engaged (approximately 180), three battleships, six heavy cruisers, three light cruisers and ten destroyers (a quarter of the losses of the Japanese Navy losses since Pearl Harbor). The first *kamikaze* attacks made during this battle. (Imamura describes this in Chapter 9.)
Nov 24, 1944	Bombing of Japan begins with 111 B-29s based in the Marianas, 1500 miles south of Tokyo
December 1, 1944	*Imamura promoted to Lieutenant Junior Grade*
December, 1944	Americans win battle for Leyte (Japanese lost 70,000; Americans 15,500)
End of 1944	Half of Japan's merchant fleet and two-thirds of its tankers destroyed; flow of oil from East Indies almost stopped; imports to home islands down by 40%
January 9, 1945	Invasion of Luzon. In this period, Australians mop up Japanese resistance in New Guinea, New Britain and Bougainville. Offensive in Burma opens, and *Ichi-Go* offensive halted at Kweiyang by Chiang Kai-chek
January 27, 1945	Burma Road reopened (allowed direct supply by British from India of the Chinese). Japanese, however, still dominant in southern China

February 12, 1945	*Special Attack Unit volunteers solicited at Tokyo Detachment. Imamura volunteers. Lt. JG Imamura put in charge of one of two kamikaze squadrons*
Feb 19, 1945	Marines assault Iwo Jima (in the Bonin Island chain)
February 1945	Yalta Conference
March 1945	*Tokyo Detachment renamed Tokyo Naval Air Corps and placed under the 11th Combined Air Fleet. Night flight training begins*
March 9, 1945	(March 10th in Japan) 325 bombers attack Tokyo; incendiary bombing; 267,000 buildings destroyed; 89,000-100,000 dead and twice as many injured. By mid-June, Nagoya, Kobe, Osaka, Yokohama and Kawasaki also devastated. Total of 260,000 killed; 2 million buildings destroyed; 9-13 million made homeless. Campaign involves virtually no losses to bomber crews. By July, 60% of ground area of Japan's 60 largest cities burnt out
	Imamura witnesses bombers and inspects damage to Tokyo the next day from the air
March 16, 1945	Iwo Jima secured at the cost of 6,821 Americans killed and 20,000 wounded; 21,000 Japanese defenders died "almost to a man"

Spring 1945	Japanese formulate *Ten-Go* defense plan, with sub-plan *Ten-Ichigo* for the defense of the Ryukyus (the island chain that includes Okinawa). 4,800 aircraft in Taiwan and on home islands committed to these plans for *kamikaze* attacks
Mar 24-31, 1945	Bombardment of Okinawa
Early April 1945	Koiso replaced as Prime Minister by Admiral Kantaro Suzuki, a moderate figurehead. Tojo, however, due to his standing in the army, still retains a veto over cabinet action and is determined to fight to the end
	Food ration reduced below 1500 calories/day. One million people set to collecting pine roots for distillation into aviation fuel
April 1, 1945	Invasion of Okinawa. 120,000 Japanese forces on island. 50,000 Americans land the first day (eventually a total of 250,000 American troops on the island)
April 6, 1945	Dense waves of *kamikaze* attacks (300 of a total of 900 Japanese aircraft in the battle): 108 shot down, but 3 destroyers, 2 ammunition ships and an LST sunk by the Japanese. **Yamato**, Japan's last giant battleship sets sail for Okinawa, with only enough fuel for one way. On April 7 **Yamato** attacked and sunk with 2,300 on board.

Yamato's cruiser and 4 of her 7 destroyer escorts also sunk. Between April 6 and July 29, 1945, 14 American destroyers and many other ships sunk by *kamikaze*: 5,000 U.S. soldiers die as a result of the *kamikaze* campaign (greater than the loss of life at Pearl Harbor). The *kamikaze* attacks especially heavy between April 6 and June 10, and include ten mass attacks by 50-300 aircraft

Mid April

Instrument flight training for Imamura kamikaze squadron

May 29, 1945

Daylight raid of Yokohama by B-29s. The P-51 escorts of the B-29s shoot down 26 Japanese fighters

June 1, 1945

Tokyo Naval Air Corps absorbed by Kasumigaura Naval Air Corps, 30 miles northeast of Tokyo

End of June, 1945

Resistance in Okinawa finally ends: 4,000 Japanese surrendered in the last days. All senior officers committed ritual suicide. Final toll at Okinawa: U.S. army 4,000 killed; U.S. marines 2,938 killed; 763 U.S. aircraft destroyed; 38 U.S. ships sunk. Of 110,000 Japanese troops on the island, all die, except for 7,400 who were taken prisoner; 16 Japanese ships lost; 7,800 Japanese aircraft lost (1,000 in *kamikaze* missions)

June 18, 1945

Chairman of Joint Chiefs emphasizes to Roosevelt that the army and marines suffered 35% casualties in Okinawa and that a similar percentage could be expected in Kyushu. Plan as of end of May is to invade Kyushu in autumn 1945 and main island of Honshu in March 1946

July 16, 1945

First Atomic weapon successfully detonated at Alamagordo, New Mexico

July 21, 1945

Truman and Churchill agree in principle at Potsdam conference that atomic bomb to be used on Japan

July 26, 1945

Potsdam Proclamation broadcast to Japan, threatening "the utter destruction of the Japanese homeland" unless the imperial government offered its "unconditional surrender." Order given to commander of Strategic Air Forces to deliver first "special bomb" as soon as weather permitted after August 3, 1945 to Hiroshima, Kokura, Niigata or Nagasaki

July 29, 1945

Imamura prepares for kamikaze mission the next dawn, to attack invasion fleet off Tokyo coast. Mission canceled when radar reports of invasion fleet prove inaccurate

August 6, 1945

Enola Gay drops atomic bomb on Hiroshima. 78,000 killed. White House calls on Japan to surrender or expect "a rain of ruin from the air." No response

August 8, 1945	Soviet Union declares war on Japan and opens offensive to Manchuria. Japanese driven back across Yalu River into northern Korea; final Japanese collapse on August 20th
August 9, 1945	Nagasaki atom bombed. 25,000 killed
	Imamura in-law Norimasa Hayashi (mentioned in Chapter 10) killed in kamikaze mission
August 14, 1945	*Imamura's squadron begins move from Kasumigaura to Chitose in Hokkaido. Transfer by train and ferry*
August 15, 1945	Emperor Hirohito broadcasts to his people news of unconditional surrender
	Imamura hears news of surrender upon arrival at Sapporo Station, but does not believe it and keeps news from his men. He only accepts the news when he arrives at Chitose Naval Air Base
August 28, 1945	MacArthur arrives at Yokohama to begin Occupation
Sept 2, 1945	Instruments of surrender signed on board *Missouri* in Tokyo Bay
September 5, 1945	*Demobilization orders for Imamura and promotion to Lt. SG. Train trip home begins September 7th*

September 11, 1945

Imamura arrives home in Matsuyama. Greets parents with an apology

September 1945

After being home for a few days, Imamura is visited by his old English teacher, Mr. Yamauchi, who tricks him into visiting HEADQUARTERS, ADVANCED PARTY, 24TH INFANTRY DIVISION (Occupation Force) in Matsuyama, where Imamura is hired on the spot as a translator

Mid-October 1945

Imamura assigned to Civil Information and Education (CI&E) Section of Ehime Military Government Team, which is headquartered in Matsuyama

Editors' Notes

Notes to the Preface

Kamikaze literally means "divine wind." In the 13th century, two attempts by the Mongolians to invade Japan failed, thanks to storms of typhoon magnitude. The term *kamikaze* was used to describe the wind that saved the nation. According to the *Kodansha Encyclopedia of Japan* (Vol. 4, 1983), "the myth of the *kamikaze* was never forgotten by the Japanese, reinforcing their belief that their land was protected by the Shinto gods. During World War II the term *kamikaze* was applied to the pilots who attacked Allied ships in suicide dives in explosive-laden planes." (pp. 126-127). *Kamikaze* was the general name used to describe the units of specially trained pilots in the Special Attack Force, *Tokubetsu Kogekitai*, or *Tokkotai*. Appendix I is a report on *kamikaze* prepared by Mr. Lewis Gulick.

Notes to Chapter 1 The Native Son: Ten Years in San Francisco

p. 2-California's Alien Land Law went into effect in 1913, prohibiting aliens from owning land. A 1920 amendment tightened the restrictions. (Kikumura, 1992, pp. 42, 47; Ichioka, 1988, p. 227). A number of legal challenges failed. In addition, in 1922, the Supreme Court of the United States ruled that, under federal law, which limited naturalization to "free white persons, and to aliens of African nativity and to persons of African descent," Japanese residents of the U.S. could not become citizens. *Ozawa v. United States,* 260 U.S. 189 (1922). Takao Ozawa, who challenged the citizenship ban, had lived in the U.S. for twenty years, graduated from Berkeley High School and studied at the University of California for three years. The Supreme Court noted he "had educated his children in American schools, his family had attended American churches and he had maintained the use of the English language in his home," concluding, "[t]hat he was well qualified by character and education for citizenship is conceded." 260 U.S. at 189. The Court also stated that it had "no reason to disagree" with the "briefs filed on behalf of [Mr. Ozawa, which referred] in complimentary terms to the culture and enlightenment of the Japanese people." *Id.* at 198. Nevertheless, the Court ruled against Mr. Ozawa. *Id.* (See also, Kikumura, 1992, p. 84; Ichioka, 1988, pp. 210-26; Wilson and Hosokawa, 1980, p. 137, 247; Hosokawa, 1969, pp. 90-91.)

p. 3-Keijiro Imamura was typical of the Japanese immigrants who arrived in the U.S. during this period, in that he was from western Japan. The marriage of Shig's parents, Keijiro and Hisako, is a good illustration of the view that "marriage and the selection of a spouse was a serious matter that concerned the entire family….Marriage strictly for the sake of love was considered immoral because it placed individual interests and welfare above that of the *ie* [household]." (Kikumura, 1992, p. 55). However, as Professor Imamura explains, his parents' marriage was somewhat atypical in that it took place at home. At the time, few of the men who had emigrated to the U.S. could afford to return to Japan to fetch a bride. (Kikumura, 1992). According to Wilson and Hosokawa, "[m]en with the means could return to Japan to marry women chosen for them by the time-honored system of go-betweens. Others legally married picture-brides in matches made after an exchange of photographs." (Wilson and Hosokawa, 1980, p. 54). Wilson and Hosokawa (1980) speculate that approximately 5,000 Japanese women emigrated to the U.S. as picture brides in the early decades of the twentieth century. (pp. 54-56). The picture-bride practice Professor Imamura describes came to an end when the government of Japan stopped issuing passports to the would-be brides in 1921. (Wilson and Hosokawa, 1980, p. 136; Daniels, 1988, p. 147; Kikumura, 1992, pp. 55-58).

p. 5-The Japanese language schools of this era are described in Hosokawa (1969, pp. 158-160) and Daniels (1988, pp. 175-176).

Notes to Chapter 2 The Returnee: Bancho Elementary School

p. 11-Yasukuni Shrine *(Yasukuni Jinja)* is one of Japan's most famous. Because it honors those killed in battle, including famous Japanese military figures of World War II, it has long been a political flashpoint in Japan, both for those opposed to and those in favor of official government recognition or support for Yasukuni Shrine. The *Kodansha Encyclopedia of Japan* (Vol. 8, 1983) describes *Yasukuni Jinja* as follows:

Shinto shrine in the Kudan district of Chiyoda Ward,
Tokyo, dedicated to the spirits of the approximately
2,400,000 persons who died in Japan's various wars since
1853, both civil and foreign. The origins of the shrine go
back to 1868....

Before the end of World War II the shrine was used
by the military to promote patriotic and nationalistic
sentiments. After Japan's defeat in 1945, the government
was compelled, first by the Occupation authorities and
after 1947 by the new constitution, to terminate all support
for Yasukuni Shrine, which was converted into a private
religious organization. (p. 319).

p. 14-The official 1937 translation of the Imperial Rescript by
Japan's Department of Education reads as follows:

Know Ye, Our Subjects:
Our Imperial Ancestors have founded Our Empire on
a basis broad and everlasting and have deeply and firmly
planted virtue; Our subjects ever united in loyalty and
filial piety have from generation to generation illustrated
the beauty thereof. This is the glory of the fundamental
character of Our Empire and herein also lies the source
of Our Education. Ye, Our Subjects, be filial to your
parents, affectionate to your brothers and sisters; as
husbands and wives be harmonious; as friends be true;
bear yourselves in modesty and moderation; extend your
benevolence to all; pursue learning and cultivate arts,
and thereby develop intellectual faculties and perfect
moral powers; furthermore, advance public good and
promote common interests; always respect the
Constitution and observe the laws; should emergency
arise, offer yourselves courageously to the State; and thus
guard and maintain the prosperity of Our Imperial Throne
coeval with heaven and earth. So shall ye not only be Our
good and faithful subjects, but render illustrious the best
traditions of your forefathers.

The Way here set forth is indeed the teaching

bequeathed by Our Imperial Ancestors to be observed alike by the Descendants and the subjects, infallible for all ages and true in all places. It is Our wish to lay it to heart in all reverence in common with you, Our subjects, that we may all attain to the same virtue. (Borton, 1955, p. 205).

A photo of a copy of the Imperial Rescript, *Kyoiku chokugo,* appears in Kikumura (1992, p. 65).

p. 19-The *Kodansha Encyclopedia of Japan* contains a lengthy account of the Japanese creation myths, including the stories related here of *Amaterasu, Susano* and *Amenouzume.* (Vol. 5, 1983, pp. 292-297).

Notes to Chapter 3 Botchan: Matsuyama Middle School

p. 30-*Botchan* is generally regarded as Soseki's most popular work. First published in the first decade of the twentieth century, it remains in print. *Botchan* is a compendium of the views of a young, self-proclaimed Tokyo sophisticate exiled to Matsuyama, which he considers hopelessly countrified, even though it is the largest city of Shikoku. In the narrator's words, *"Their castle town is so small an affair that an hour's sight seeing will bring you to an end of everything it contains...."* (Soseki, 1968, p. 47). According to Donald Keene, Soseki himself, unlike the "uncomplicated, not overly bright Botchan, ... was well treated in Matsuyama and left without rancor." (Keene *(Fiction)*, 1984, p. 315). During his stay in Matsuyama, Soseki "profited by his isolation to devote himself to composing poetry," especially *haiku*, "under the influence of Masaoka Shiki, who was a native of Matsuyama," (Keene *(Fiction)*, 1984, p. 309), and who is considered both the creator and popularizer of modern *haiku*. (Foreign Press Center, 1997, p. 326). Soseki's association with Shiki is commemorated in what Keene *(Poetry)*, 1984, p. 106) refers to as "[p]erhaps Soseki's most affecting haiku, at least in translation," which "bears the title, 'Hearing in London the News of Shiki's Death'":

kiri ki naru	See how it hovers
ichi ni ugoku ya	In these streets of yellow fog
kageboshi	A human shadow

Notes to Chapter 4 Ronin: The Perplexing Years

p. 41-*Ronin* literally means "floating man." According to the *Kodansha Encyclopedia of Japan* (Vol. 6, 1983), the term is "most familiar as a label for the masterless samurai of the Edo period (1600-1868), but in early Japan it referred to peasants who left their land to work elsewhere....Today it refers to high school graduates unable to enter the university of their choice on their first attempt, who live 'masterless' until successful in later attempts." (pp. 336-337).

p. 41-Cram Schools (*yobiko*) are specialized private tutoring schools (*juku*): "Most cram school enrollees are recent high school graduates who are seeking admission to the nation's top-flight colleges and universities and who failed in their first sitting for the entrance examination." (*Kodansha Encyclopedia of Japan,* Vol. 2, 1983, p. 41; see also Vol. 4, pp. 83-84).

Notes to Chapter 5 Prelude to Glory: College Life

p. 46-Although Professor Takahashi's penchant for *haiku* was notable, he was part of a strong Matsuyama tradition. As the notes to Chapter Three indicate, Matsuyama has a strong tradition of haiku, and works to preserve that tradition. According to the Foreign Press Center, "Traditionally, Ehime [Prefecture]'s capital, Matsuyama City, has been famous for citizens' active practice and enjoyment of haiku. One poet in particular, Shiki Masaoka, was active at the end of the 19th century and revolutionized both the haiku and tanka (31-syllable) poetic forms. He inspired a multitude of followers, which led to the city's reputation as a mecca for haiku enthusiasts. Today, haiku collection boxes are located all over the city, and many residents continue to compose poems in their spare time. Since haiku is well-known throughout the world, the prefecture is working to boost international recognition of the city's role in promoting haiku. Ehime has set up an international haiku salon, regularly publishes poetry compilations, and conducts haiku seminars under the auspices of the Ehime Prefecture International Center." (Foreign Press Center, 1997, p. 331).

p. 46-Mr. Hoshino's comments were probably necessarily oblique. A March 1941 defense security law, passed at about the time Shigeo Imamura entered *Matsuchu,* according to Havens (1978), resulted in further "darkening the clouded climate of public assembly and discussion." (p. 53). Dower (1993) reports on the "Home Ministry's notorious Thought Police (*Tokkotai,* literally Special Higher Police)" (p. 103), and according to the *Kodansha Encyclopedia of Japan* (Vol. 2, 1983) despite the guarantee of free speech in the Meiji Constitution of 1889,"[b]y the beginning of World War II, such extreme restrictions had been imposed on freedom of speech that it could scarcely be said to have existed at all." (p. 338).

Notes to Chapter 6 The Cadet: Basic Training

p. 52-Japanese inns, *ryokan*, are repositories of tradition. According to Japan National Tourist Organization (1999), "A room in a Ryokan is usually a single large, undivided room with traditional rice-straw Tatami matting, with only a single low table as furniture. Doors are Shoji screens, and decoration will usually be one or two simple ink brush drawings or scrolls. Guests sleep on Futon bedding laid out in the evening by maids." Most *ryokan* have a communal bath, often a hot spring, and meals, which feature local delicacies, are served in the guests' rooms. (p. 29).

p. 52-Food shortages. This is the first of several mentions of the wartime food shortages in Japan. Havens (1978) reports that the first rice controls were imposed on Christmas Day, 1940, and that formal rations in the six largest cities began the next April, with a "network of distribution centers" throughout the country by the end of 1941. Shortages and privations of all types grew worse as the war progressed. (pp. 114-132). The food shortages of the war and the rationing systems are also described in Terasaki's *Bridge to the Sun* (1957, pp. 101-123).

p. 54-*Yokaren.* According to the *Kodansha Encyclopedia of Japan* (Vol. 8, 1983), *yokaren,* the nickname for the Junior Pilot Training Corps, was an "[a]bbreviation for Kaigun Hiko Yoka Renshusei (Aviation Cadets of the Imperial Japanese Navy). The cadets, ranging in age from 14 to 23, took a three-to-four-year course at a school, established in 1930, at Kasumigaura, Ibaraki Prefecture. They played an active role in the Sino-Japanese War of 1937-45 and the Pacific War." (p. 329).

Notes to Chapter 7 13th Class: Intermediate Flight Training

p. 64-The Model 93 Intermediate Trainer "was the basic flight trainer for the Japanese Navy from 1934 through the end of the war." Mikesh records its full name as "Kugisho Navy Type 93 Intermediate Trainer (K5Y)." Its Allied Code name was "Willow." (Mikesh, 1993, p. 146).

Notes to Chapter 8 The Warrior: Flight Training

p. 73-The Model 96 Fighter (Mitsubishi Navy Type 96 Carrier Fighter (A5M)) was nicknamed "Claude" by the Allies. The Model 96 Fighter was the "backbone" of the Japanese Navy's fighter force, "and over 1,000 were built in several models," one of which remained in production until 1940. The "Claude" was "the fifth generation of Navy carrier-based fighters that preceded the Zero." Although "[m]ost of these open-cockpit, fixed-landing gear fighters were retained in Japan by second-line and training units," this plane was what "designers and the Navy would use as a measure when creating fighter design qualities that would evolve into the Zero fighter." (Mikesh, 1994, p. 15). According to Mikesh (1993), the Model 96 Fighter "was well known over China and at the beginning of the Pacific War," and before the Zero "entered combat over China, ... was the most feared fighter of the Japanese forces." However, "[f]ew saw combat in the Pacific War, for by this time most were relegated to the training-role." (p. 41). A Japanese military writer provides additional detail: "The second Shanghai Incident of 1937 (the start of navy involvement in the China war) marked a new era in the development of Japanese naval aviation. Up to this time, the naval air force had been considered only an auxiliary of the fleet. Consequently, it was expected to perform the minor roles of reconnaissance, gunnery observation, aerial attack, and cover in the decisive battle. However, the remarkable achievement that Type 96 medium bombers and Zero fighters accomplished in China tremendously encouraged the self-confidence and pride of Japanese naval aviators. They began to feel that Japan's main naval strength was shifting from battleships to aircraft." (Yoki, 1986, p. 508).

p. 74-Japanese hot springs, *onsen*, are a traditional get-away, where guests enjoy relaxing at *ryokan*, Japanese inns. Japan has more than 1,800 hot springs to accommodate the "Japanese love of a good, hot bath." *Onsen* resorts "offer a mind-boggling array of variations on the seemingly simple act of soaking in hot mineral waters." (Japan National Tourist Organization, 1999, p. 30). Beppu is one of Japan's largest and most famous *onsen* resort towns.

p. 79-The Zero (Mitsubishi Navy Type 0 Carrier Fighter (A6M)), nicknamed "Zeke" by the Allies, "appeared to be invincible" at "the onset of the war" (Mikesh, 1993, p. 147). The Japanese name of the Zero was *Rei Shiki Sentoki* (Type Zero Fighter), usually shortened to *Reisen.* (Mikesh, 1994, p. 8).

Notes to Chapter 9 The Instructor: Haneda

p. 85-*See* Notes to the Preface and Appendix I on the Special Attack Forces. General histories of the *kamikazes* are listed in the Editors' References and Resources, and Shigeo Imamura's story is recounted in *The Sacred Warriors: Japan's Suicide Legions* by Dennis and Peggy Warner (with Commander Sadao Seno, JMSDF (Ret.)). See also the contemporary assessment of Russell Brines (1994), a Japanese-speaking Associated Press correspondent who had lived in Japan before the war:

> *"We will fight," the Japanese say, "until we eat stones!" The phrase is old; now revived and ground deeply into Japanese consciousness by propagandists ....they will continue the war until every man – perhaps every woman and child – lies face downward on the battlefield. Thousands of Japanese, maybe hundreds of thousands, accepted it literally. To ignore this suicide complex would be as dangerous as our pre-war oversight of Japanese determination and cunning which made Pearl Harbor possible. ...*
>
> *American fighting men back from the front have been trying to tell America this is a war of extermination. They have seen it from foxholes and barren strips of bullet-strafed sand. I have seen it from behind enemy lines. Our picture coincides. This is a war of extermination. The Japanese militarists have made it that way. (p. 9, 11).*

pp. 96-97-New Year (*Oshogatsu*) is Japan's biggest holiday: "New Year observances are the most important and most elaborate of Japan's annual events. Though customs differ by locality, at this time homes are decorated, and the holidays are celebrated by family gatherings, visits to shrines or temples, and formal calls on relatives and friends." *Kodansha Encyclopedia of Japan,* (Vol. 5, 1983, p. 371).

Notes to Chapter 10 The Kamikaze: Special Attack Unit

p. 102-103-The devastation and horror of the March 9, 1945 (March 10 in Japan)fire-bombing of Tokyo is described in Richard Rhodes, *The Making of the Atomic Bomb* (1986, pp. 595-600) and in Richard Frank, *Downfall: The End of the Imperial Japanese Empire* (1999, pp. 3-19). The *Kodansha Encyclopedia of Japan* (Vol. 8, 1983) reports that on "10 March 1945, American B-29 Superfortress bombers from Saipan and Tinian began massive incendiary raids on Japan's major cities. The bombers – three, four, or five hundred to a raid – would fly in low over a selected portion of the defenseless city and cover it with clusters of napalm sticks. Jellied gasoline quickly ignited wooden housing. Perhaps as many as 100,000 died in the first fire-bombing raid on Tokyo. Successive raids destroyed half the city, including government buildings, and damaged the Imperial Palace. By the end of May, most of Yokohama, Nagoya, Osaka, and Kobe had been incinerated." (p. 276). A Western eyewitness in Tokyo described "a kind of flaming dew that skittered along the roofs, setting fire to everything it splashed and spreading a wash of dancing flames everywhere." (Guillain, 1981, p. 184). Watching from his roof, Guillain said, "All the Japanese in the gardens near mine were out of doors or peering up out of their holes, uttering cries of admiration – this was typically Japanese – at this grandiose, almost theatrical spectacle." (p. 182).

pp. 103-104-Cherry Blossoms (*sakura*) hold a special place in the Japanese imagination: "The *sakura* is foremost among plants mentioned in Japanese literature.…The traditional Japanese values of purity and simplicity are thought to be reflected in the form and color of the blossoms.… The cherry is one of the oldest flowers known in Japan. The word appears in the *Kojiki*, a book of history completed in 712, and the *Man'yoshu*, an anthology of poems compiled in the late 8th century, contains about 40 poems which mention the tree and praise its blossoms…. During the Heian period (794-1185), popular enthusiasm for cherry blossoms was such that the word *hana* (flower) was simply taken as a synonym for *sakura.*" (*Kodansha Encyclopedia of Japan,* Vol. 1, 1983, p. 269). During World War II, the *sakura* was linked to the *kamikaze* and "[t]he falling cherry blossom became the best known symbol of the young flyers, appearing in their poems, their songs, their farewell letters, and in the hands of the virgin schoolgirls who assembled to see them off on their final missions in the spring of 1945." (Dower, 1986, p. 232).

Notes to Chapter 11 Aborted Mission: Kasumigaura

pp. 109-110-Some information on the *shusui* rocket project is available electronically. The Imperial Japanese Navy Page website, in words very similar to those of Professor Imamura, announces that it is "dedicated to promoting a greater understanding of what went on during the war, so that such conflicts do not occur again." (Parshall, www.combinedfleet.com/disclaim.htm). The website features extensive information on the Imperial Japanese Navy, and a portion on naval aviation provides details on all aircraft of the Japanese Navy, including the *shusui*. (Matsuura, www.combinedfleet.com/ijna/j8m.htm).

p. 112-Frank (1999) describes Operation *Ketsu* as having three distinct features: the aim of destroying the enemy beachhead; the reliance on *tokko* (special attack) tactics; and incorporation of the civilian population into the plan. (pp. 85-86).

Notes to Chapter 12 Bewildered Defeat: The War Ends

pp. 123-124-Eiji Yoshikawa lived from 1892 to 1962. According to the Edwin O. Reischauer's Forward to the American edition of *Musashi* (1981), Yoshikawa was one of Japan's "most prolific and best-loved popular writers." (p. ix). *Musashi* "is a long historical novel, which first appeared in serialized form between 1935 and 1939 in the *Asahi Shimbun,* Japan's largest and most prestigious newspaper."(p. ix). Donald Keene (*Fiction,* 1984) notes that historical fiction was tremendously popular in Japan in the 1920s and 1930s.

(p. 760). The *Kodansha Encyclopedia of Japan* (Vol. 8, 1983) makes the point that in Yoshikawa's hands, "Japanese popular fiction, hitherto written primarily for entertainment, was elevated to something approaching a true people's literature." (p. 347). Ambassador Reischauer, who labeled *Musashi* the *Gone With the Wind* of Japan, wrote that "Miyamoto Musashi was an actual historical person, but through Yoshikawa's novel he and the other main characters of the book have become part of Japan's living folklore. They are so familiar to the public that people will frequently be compared to them as personalities everyone knows....[T]he novel ... [p]rovides a romanticized slice of Japanese history, [and] gives a view of how the Japanese see their past and themselves.... [It is] "a dashing tale of swashbuckling adventure and a subdued story of love, Japanese style." (Yoshikawa, 1981, p. ix).

Notes to Chapter 13 Ronin Again: Now What?

p. 134-The *Kodansha Encyclopedia of Japan* (Vol. 6, 1983) notes that the initial 500,000 American Occupation troops under the command of General Douglas McArthur, SCAP (Supreme Commander of Allied Powers) "was quickly reduced to about 150,000 in the absence of any security problems." (p. 51). According to the *Kodansha Encyclopedia*, "[m]ore important were the roughly 5,500 bureaucrats who made up the SCAP government." (p.51). Education reform was a major goal of the Occupation:

> *The reform of the Japanese school system, education administration, school curriculum, and course content was a high priority of the post-World War II Allied Occupation. The prewar education system was thought to have been a significant source of nationalism and militarism, and thus education reform was a key element in the effort to "democratize" Japan. Early reform directives in 1945 were followed by the establishment of an American education mission and of the Japanese Education Reform Council in 1946; their recommendations were incorporated in basic legislation enacted in 1947 and 1948. This legislation established the essential framework of the postwar*

educational system, which has undergone some modification in the ensuing years.

The first reform effort was initiated during the early months of the Occupation in late 1945. The headquarters of the Supreme Commander for the Allied Powers (SCAP) issued four directives that were intended to put an end to the teaching of ultranationalism and militarism; many educators were purged, history and geography texts were revised, and the teaching of Shushin (moral education) was suspended. In March 1946 the first of two United States Education Missions to Japan arrived, composed of 27 American educators headed by George D. Stoddard. The report of the mission, which formed the basis for later SCAP reform directives, recommended the decentralization of educational administration, the adoption of coeducation and equal access to educational opportunity, the establishment of an American style elementary-middle-high school system, an emphasis on learning through experience, and the revision of textbooks to emphasize principles of democracy and peace.

Working with the Japanese Education Reform Council, SCAP formed these recommendations into the Fundamental Law of Education (Kyoiku Kihon Ho) and the School Education Law (Gakko Kyoiku Ho), both of which were enacted in 1947. The Fundamental Law, popularly referred to as the "education constitution," stated the basic aims of the education system: contributing to the peace and welfare of humanity, the full development of personality, and the creation of a love for truth and justice among students. The law also contains a commitment to academic freedom, equal opportunity, and coeducation. The School Education Law outlined the new system of six-year elementary schools, three-year middle schools, three-year high schools, and four-year universities. Compulsory Education was extended from six to nine years, and provision was made for the education of the handicapped. (Kodansha Encyclopedia of Japan, Vol. 2, p. 180).

The post-war reforms to the educational system are also described in John W. Dower, *Embracing Defeat: Japan in the Wake of World War II* (1999, pp. 244-251).

Notes to Epilogue: Between Two Worlds and Chapter 14 (Appendix II)

p. 148-Professor Fries' landmark book, *Teaching and Learning English As A Foreign Language,* was first published in 1945.

—Constance O'Keefe

EDITORS' REFERENCES AND RESOURCES

Includes books cited in Appendix I, prepared by Mr. Lewis Gulick.
*Indicates books that mention Shigeo Imamura.

Ambrose, S. E. (1994). *D-Day: The Climatic Battle Of World War II.* New York: Simon & Schuster.

Borton, H. (1970). *Japan's Modern Century.* (2nd ed.). New York: Ronald Press.

Brines, R. (1944). *Until They Eat Stones.* New York: Lippincott.

*Crewe, Q. (1962). *Japan: Portrait of Paradox.* New York: Thomas Nelson & Sons.

Daniels, R. (1988). *Asian America: Chinese and Japanese in the United States since 1850.* Seattle: University of Washington Press.

Dower, J. W. (1999). *Embracing Defeat: Japan In The Wake Of World War II.* New York: Norton/New Press.

Dower, J.W. (1993). *Japan In War & Peace: Selected Essays.* New York: New Press.

Dower, J.W. (1986). *War Without Mercy: Race And Power In The Pacific War.* New York: Pantheon.

Duus, P. (1988) (Ed.) *Cambridge History of Japan.* (Vol. 6) (J. W. Hall, M. B. Jansen, M. Kanai and D. Twitchett, General Eds.). Cambridge: Cambridge University Press.

Evans, D. C. (Ed.) (1986). *The Japanese Navy in World War II: In The Words Of Former Japanese Naval Officers.* (2nd ed.). Annapolis: Naval Institute Press.

Foreign Press Center. (1994). *Japan: Eyes on the Country: Views of the 47 Prefectures.* Tokyo: Foreign Press Center.

Frank, R. B. (1999). *Downfall: The End of the Imperial Japanese Empire.* New York: Random House.

Fries, C. C. (1945). *Teaching And Learning English As A Foreign Language.* Ann Arbor: University of Michigan Press.

Guillain, R. (1981). *I Saw Tokyo Burning.* New York: Doubleday.

Havens, T. R. H. (1978). *Valley Of Darkness: The Japanese People And World War Two*. New York: Norton.

Hosokawa, B. (1969). *The Quiet Americans*. New York: Morrow.

Hoyt, E. P. (1983). *The Kamikazes*. New York: Arbor House.

Ichioka, Y. (1988). *The Issei: The World Of The First Generation Japanese Immigrants 1885-1924*. New York: Free Press.

Iriye, A. (1981). *Power and Culture: The Japanese-American War, 1941-1945*. Cambridge: Harvard University Press.

Japan National Tourist Organization. (1999). *Your Guide To Japan*. Tokyo: Japan National Tourist Organization.

Johnson, S. (1975). *American Attitudes Toward Japan, 1941-1975*. Washington, D.C.: AEI-Hoover.

Keegan, J. (1989). *The Second World War*. New York: Penguin.

Keene, D. (1984). *Dawn To The West: Japanese Literature In The Modern Era (Fiction)*. New York: Holt.

Keene, D. (1984). *Dawn To The West: Japanese Literature In The Modern Era (Poetry, Drama, Criticism)*. New York: Holt.

Kikumura, A. (Exhibit Curator). (1992). *Issei Pioneers*. Los Angeles: Japanese American National Museum.

Kodansha Encyclopedia of Japan (Vols. 1 - 8). (1983). Tokyo: Kodansha.

LaFeber, W. (1997). *The Clash: U.S.-Japanese Relations Throughout History*. New York: Norton.

Matsuura, J. P. J. (No date). Imperial Japanese Naval Aviation. In Parshall, J. (Managing Ed.) *Imperial Japanese Navy*. [Online] Available: www.combinedfleet.com/ijna/ijnaf.htm [2000, December 1].

McCullough, D. (1992). *Truman*. New York: Simon & Schuster.

Mikesh, R. C. (1993). *Japanese Aircraft: Code Names And Designations*. Atglen, Pennsylvania: Schiffen.

Mikesh, R. C. (1994). *Zero: Combat & Development History Of Japan's Legendary Mitsubishi A6M Zero Fighter*. Oseola, Wisconsin: Motorbooks.

Morris, I. (1975). *The Nobility Of Failure: Tragic Heroes In The History Of Japan*. London: Secker & Warburg.

Nagatsuka, R. (1972). *I Was a Kamikaze*. (N. Rootes, Trans; R. Leckie, Introduction). New York: Macmillan.

Naito, H. (1989). *Thunder Gods: The Kamikaze Pilots Tell Their Story.* Tokyo: Kodansha International.

Parshall, J. (Managing Ed.) (No date). *Imperial Japanese Navy.* [Online]. Available: www.combinedfleet.com/kaigun.htm [2000, December 1].

Rhodes, R. (1986). *The Making Of The Atomic Bomb.* New York: Simon & Schuster.

Sakai, S. with Caidin, M. and Saito, F. (1991). *Samurai!* Annapolis: Naval Institute Press.

Sansom, G. B. (1978). *Japan: A Short Cultural History.* Stanford: Stanford University Press.

Seward, J. (1999). *Strange But True: Stories From Japan.* Boston: Tuttle.

Soseki, N. (1968). (U. Sasaki, Trans.) *Botchan.* Rutland, VT & Tokyo: Tuttle.

Spector, R. H. (1985). *Eagle Against The Sun: The American War With Japan.* New York: Free Press.

Terasaki, G. (1957). *Bridge To The Sun.* Chapel Hill: University of North Carolina Press.

Toland, J. (1970). *The Rising Sun.* New York: Random House.

U.S. Naval Institute. (1952). *The Japanese Navy In World War II.* Annapolis: Naval Institute Press.

*Warner, D. and Warner, P. with Seno, S. (1982). *The Sacred Warriors: Japan's Suicide Legions.* New York: Van Nostrand Reinhold.

Wilson, R. A. and Hosokawa, B. (1980). *East to America: A History Of The Japanese In The United States.* New York: Morrow.

Yoki, T. (1986). Thoughts on Japan's Naval Defeat. In Evans, D. C. (Ed.) *The Japanese Navy in World War II: In the Words of Former Japanese Naval Officers* (2nd ed.). Annapolis: Naval Institute Press, pp. 499-515.

Yoshikawa, E. (1981). *Musashi.* (C. S. Terry, Trans; E. O. Reischauer, Forward). Tokyo: Kodansha International. (Original work published 1935 – 1939).

Appendix I

Kamikazes in World War II

Prepared by Mr. Lewis Gulick

The word *kami* in Japanese means "God." The word *kaze* means "wind." Japanese historians record that in the twelfth century a Mongolian horde of superior force was poised to invade Japan when a great typhoon arose unexpectedly, dispatching the raiders and saving the country. The heavenly intervention was called *kamikaze* - the Divine Wind.

Centuries later the term gained currency in the latter stages of World War II. As American forces advanced ever closer to the homeland and Japan's military situation grew desperate, the Japanese resorted increasingly to suicide missions against the enemy, particularly by air. Proponents of targeted suicide attacks hoped to turn the tide of war against a militarily superior foe. With its historic symbolism, the appellation *kamikaze* gained wide use even though the specific military units and weapons involved in the no-return missions carried other names.

That suicide attacks became a notable feature of Japanese combat performance in World War II is hardly surprising. Although Americans too knowingly and heroically fought to the death in some actions, their culture and military doctrine placed far more value on the saving of lives than did Japan's. In feudal Japan suicide was accepted, indeed it was required, in certain circumstances for those under the samurai code. A ritual developed for performance of *hara-kiri* ("stomach-cutting"). To die by one's own hand was deemed to be an act of honor.

The concept of loyalty to the death extended to civilian followers as well in various episodes throughout Japanese history. A famous early example was the mass *hara-kiri* at Kamakura in 1333 of Japan's then-ruler, Takatoki Hojo, and his entourage. Faced with certain defeat by rebellious forces, Takatoki shunned an escape opportunity and retreated instead to a cave, accompanied by more than 870 liegemen and 283 relatives, courtiers and assorted retainers. There they committed suicide to the last individual, more than 1,150 in all. Thousands of others faithful to the Hojo cause elsewhere disappeared by unknown means.[1] In the early days of World War II Japanese civilians on Pacific islands committed suicide as their soldiers were defeated, spurred by warnings by their leaders of a dire fate awaiting them should they be captured by the Americans.

The ethic of honorable suicide fit well with the structure of Japanese society. The emperor was atop the society and he was divine. He embodied the concept of the nation. Loyalty to the emperor (and to the nation) was expected of all subjects. Along with loyalty to the family and respect for elders, obedience to the emperor's wishes was a central fabric of the Japanese way. Military leaders operating in the emperor's name thus were assured of widespread compliance by civilians in defense measures.

In the latter days of World War II mobilization for the anticipated enemy invasion of the homeland included integration of civilians with military in a virtually seamless web. All men from age 15 to 60 and women 17 to 40 were subject to duty in local fighting units controlled by area military commands. Villages and towns were to organize support groups. Citizens along the coasts were to help in fortifications. School classes above 6th grade were suspended so students and teachers could help produce food and in defense tasks.[2] They were instructed on how to kill American soldiers. Dying for the emperor in the country's defense was an honor.

Fight-to-death suicides by Japanese soldiers were commonplace during the island stepping-stone advances by American forces in the earlier stages of World War II. No Japanese combat units surrendered. A few Japanese soldiers surrendered as individuals, mostly when wounds prevented them from avoiding capture. The number of Japanese prisoners-of-war increased as the war went on but never was large. One estimate places the number of Japanese troops facing Gen. Douglas MacArthur's forces in the southwest Pacific at more than 600,000, of which 19,000 were taken prisoner. Even including the extensive Philippines ground campaign, the Japanese surrender/capture rate thus was only around 3 per cent.[3]

In the air war the first suicide attack was at Pearl Harbor when a Japanese pilot aimed his damaged plane at an American warship. Other such incidents happened from time to time as the war went on, but did not become a planned element of Japanese strategy until 1944. By then the U.S. forces had achieved air superiority over the Pacific waters generally, and locally in each island invasion.

Although they still had a large number of planes, the Japanese suffered serious and increasing pilot losses in the attrition from the aerial contests as the war continued. On the American side, the warplanes were improving in combat effectiveness, the fliers were becoming more experienced, and surface defenses growing more adept. On the Japanese side airmen were going into combat with less training and experience. Aircraft repair and maintenance were deteriorating. Fuel supplies were diminishing.

Meanwhile word of the results of crash bombing spread. With a pilot guiding a plane right to the point of impact, prospects for serious damage to the specific target were far greater than from explosives launched at a distance.

In March 1944 Prime Minister Hideki Tojo ordered the Army Air Corps to prepare for special suicide missions. *Kamikaze* tactics were included in the army's training of bomber pilots and of fighter pilots as well. The first officially planned suicide attack against an American ship was carried out on May 27, 1944, when a Japanese army flier crash-dived into U.S. Subchaser 699 off West New Guinea.[4] On August 20, 1944, a Japanese army pilot rammed a B-29 bomber during a bombing raid on the Yawata Iron and Steel Works. The suicide missions were called "special attacks" and in due course became commonplace.[5]

Meanwhile the Japanese navy was assiduously developing its own version of a *Tokubetsu Kogekitai* (Special Attack Corps), as the *kamikaze* forces were officially named,[6] with airborne suicide tactics, weaponry and units. The first navy *kamikaze* unit was formed by Vice Admiral Takijiro Onishi, commander of the First Air Fleet, with 24 Zero fighter pilots. The first organized sortie of 18 planes went out October 25 in the Battle of Leyte Gulf. Six of the attackers returned without finding their target, but the other twelve scored heavily, sinking one ship and damaging two escort carriers.

Suicide sorties in the Philippines mounted thereafter, averaging around 200 a month until the end of the campaign in early 1945. Up to the beginning of the Okinawa invasion, at least 2,200 Americans died from *kamikaze* attacks.[7]

The rate of *kamikaze* attacks climaxed at Okinawa. With 1,900 sorties over a few weeks' period Japanese suicide fliers wreaked extensive damage to the American fleet. They sank 15 American ships, damaged 59 others, and killed around 3,000 American sailors.[8]

The last American vessel to be sunk by *kamikaze* attack went down on July 29, 1945. The last official *kamikaze* sortie was launched on August 13, two days before the emperor announced Japan's surrender. Onishi committed suicide by *hara-kiri* on August 15, leaving a farewell note of appreciation to his special-attack pilots and apologies to them and their bereaved families for not achieving the victory he had expected.[9]

All told, *kamikaze* planes flew nearly four thousand "special attack" missions against American and allied forces during World War II. Of the 3,913 suicide pilots 2,525 were navy fliers, mostly between ages 18 and 20. The army lost 1,388 pilots on these missions, most in ages 18-24.[10] These numbers do not include those who died in unplanned, spontaneous suicide attacks.

Ships being the most vulnerable category of targets for *kamikazes*, the American navy bore the brunt of casualties and damage from the "special attacks." Defenses were improved though none of them guaranteed success. The most effective was air interception of the attacker before he could begin his suicide run. U. S. carriers increased their ratio of fighters aboard, compared with attack planes, to stiffen their airborne protection against *kamikazes*. Another response was to increase anti-aircraft ordnance and to gather in formations to concentrate the fire. However this caused a problem of "friendly fire" when *kamikaze* pilots flew in among the ships in heading directly to their targets. Ship maneuvering also was less effective against *kamikazes* than against conventional bombing runs because the suicide pilot steered to his target on a one-on-one basis.

Early warning nets including land, sea and airborne radar pickets helped against surprise approaches. Bombing of Japanese airbases inflicted only peripheral damage on the numbers of planes available for "special attacks" and did not reduce the supply of suicide pilots.

Notwithstanding enhanced defenses, the special attacks continued to score impressively against American ships compared with strikes by aviators whose missions allowed for return after combat. The Japanese too were learning from *kamikaze* experience and were improving their weaponry and tactics. With expectation of survival removed, the pilots could focus completely on the target without attention to escape options.

The Okinawa results were particularly instructive as a presage to the expected invasion of Japan proper. *Kamikaze* sorties rose to unprecedented levels during the assault on the island and continued thereafter on American forces marshaling for an advance on the homeland. *Kamikazes* sank 15 American ships and damaged 59 others during the campaign.[11] Of 4,907 American sailors killed at Okinawa, 3,389 (69%) died from "special attacks" by air.[12] Starting with the preinvasion period March 3 and ending August 16, 1945, upon Japan's surrender, a Japanese summary records 1,637 suicide sorties in the battle of Okinawa by navy airmen and 934 by the Army, for a total of 2,571. The results were 13 smaller warships sunk (including 9 destroyers), and 174 vessels damaged. Damaged by *kamikaze* hits were 9 American battleships, 10 aircraft carriers, 4 cruisers, 58 destroyers, and 93 various other craft.[13]

Okinawa was 350 miles from Kyushu, the southernmost of the four main Japanese islands. MacArthur's invasion plan called for an initial largescale amphibious landing in southern Kyushu. The invasion date was tentatively set for November 1. The U.S. Navy would have a major role. Most of the ground forces would be brought in by ship.

On the Japanese side, the leadership correctly assumed that Kyushu would be a logical locale for the first American invasion of Japan proper, and they prepared accordingly. Their strategy involved a heavy buildup on Kyushu and forces nearby so as to force a decisive battle early in the invasion. The landings were to be met with an avalanche of destruction before the Americans could solidify a foothold on the island. Any further advances on the ground would face well-prepared defensive positions and counter-attacks.

Under the Japanese plan the initial defense would be spearheaded by waves of suicide attacks on troop-laden vessels and their accompanying naval support. Virtually all of Japan's available *kamikaze* resources would be committed against the landings. Several hundred sorties an hour would assault troop transports, which had been largely spared in the Okinawa "special attacks." The downpour of "special attacks" on the amphibious invaders would continue for days.[14]

Prospective effectiveness of *kamikazes* increased as the Americans approached the Japanese homeland. The distances from base to target grew shorter. Aircraft of limited range could be used, including several thousand training planes converted for "special attack" duty. Potentials for surprise attacks were greater because of shorter flight times. The Kyushu land mass and hills helped radar evasion in approaching nearby targets.

Richard B. Frank, in his deeply researched book *Downfall*, speculates on the toll of American navy personnel from *kamikaze* attacks in event of an attempted invasion of Kyushu. Citing statistics from the postwar U.S. Strategic Bombing Survey reporting an 18.6% hit rate by *kamikazes* at Okinawa and 5,350 planes designated for "special attacks" in a Kyushu invasion, and a Japanese estimate that 60% of the planes would be operational, Frank calculated that the suicide waves would sink about 95 American ships and damage about 995, or around one third of the invasion fleet. Using the Okinawa ratio of 1.78 Americans killed per suicide hit, he estimated American naval fatalities from the ship attacks at 5,714. Another 1,514 U.S. navy personnel deaths could be expected, according to the Okinawa experience, from other causes such as mines, submarines, shore batteries, conventional air attacks, other suicide vehicles, Navy medical personnel in Marine units, and air crew losses, putting the total at 7,228.

However, if the Japanese committed up to 7,500 or more planes to suicide duty in the actual event, as they appeared prepared to do, the U.S. casualties would have been correspondingly greater. With a 7,500 *kamikaze* plane commitment by the Japanese, Frank projected American naval fatalities from the Kyushu combat would have been 8,010 under the Okinawa ratio plus 1,514 deaths from other causes, for a total of 9,524, about double the Okinawa number.[15] This heavy toll expected for the U.S. Navy and the more than 25,000 anticipated fatalities among the U.S. landing forces in the first 90 days, plus well more than 100,000 expected to be wounded, would have made the Kyushu invasion one of the most costly military operations of World War II.[16] (Allied casualties on D-Day in Normandy totaled some 4,900.[17])

While the potential *kamikaze* torrent at Kyushu may not have been decisive, it was intended by the Japanese military at a minimum to be a significant aid in raising the cost of an invasion to a point at which the Americans would negotiate for an end to the war instead of pursuing unconditional surrender. On the American side the Navy in particular took the *kamikaze* threat seriously. With U.S. decision-makers the expectation of heavy casualties from the invasion helped to solidify plans to use the atomic bomb. President Truman later wrote that his commander-in-chief, General George C. Marshall, had estimated American casualties from the invasion would be at least a quarter million.[18]

In sum, in the larger war picture the damage to American ships from *kamikazes* was only marginal. American naval and air superiority became and would remain overwhelming. Still, the margin counted in the estimates of leaders on both sides as they prepared for what they expected would be the climactic battle of the war.

How about the cost to Japan in lives and resources of the nearly 4,000 good pilots lost in deliberate suicide attacks? During the war there was some reluctance in the Japanese leadership to embrace a strategy of sending young men to pre-planned death, and more criticism was voiced after the war. Two former Japanese naval officers, in a history of the *kamikaze* campaign, called it "the most diabolical tactic of war the world has ever seen."[19] The Chief of Staff of the navy's Fifth Air Fleet at the Okinawa campaign, Rear Admiral Toshiyuki Yokoi, denounced the "murder attacks" as "sheer lunacy" in which the leadership had lost sight of humanity while exhausting naval resources.[20]

Yet the strategy was widely accepted in the Japanese armed forces, and understandably so. Sacrifice of one's life in certain circumstances had been part of the warrior code for centuries. Dying for the emperor and nation was portrayed as an honorable act. There was no lack of heroic volunteers among youthful aviators. The closer Japan came to defeat the more pressing became measures to stave it off. Partly because of exaggerated reports of *kamikaze* successes, commanders viewed suicide missions as an effective tool. Lives were being lost in combat anyway; why not direct the deaths purposefully to inflict the most damage on the enemy?

It could be said that adoption of *kamikaze* as official policy by the Japanese military leadership as the war went on was just as inevitable as the U.S. atomic bombing of Hiroshima and Nagasaki. Both sides were determined to do whatever they could to win. While some critics argued differently after the war, the leaderships did what they perceived to be necessary at the time.

The Japanese *kamikaze* effort included also the building of manned missiles to be launched from airplanes. A small rocket plane with a nose packed with explosives was suspended under a carrying plane. When the time came for attack, a suicide pilot from the mother plane would crawl through a hatch into the rocket craft and head for the target.

The manned bombs were called *ohka*s (Exploding Cherry Blossoms) by the Japanese and *baka* (stupid) bombs by the Americans. In theory they would have devastating effect, being guided at high, near-unstoppable speed with high explosive payload directly to target by a trained pilot. A special naval unit, *Jinrai Butai* (divine thunderbolt unit), was organized for *ohka* operation.

The first sortie by *ohka*s was launched on March 21, 1945, after the Japanese sighted an American task force with three carriers 320 miles off Kyushu. A flight of 18 bombers, 16 with *baka* bombs, headed for the quarry but was intercepted by U.S. fighters 50 miles before reaching it. All 18 were shot down.[21]

Planes carrying *ohka*s were vulnerable to attack because the increased load and air resistance lowered their speed and maneuverability. The *ohka*s themselves had technical deficiencies. Development work on the suicide bombs continued but the war ended before they saw much use in combat.

While *kamikaze* is commonly used in referring to airborne suicide operations, the Japanese also had nautical *kamikaze* devices. These included midget submarines, swimmers with explosive charges, and small suicide surface boats.

Acknowledgments

The preceding summary was prepared by Lewis Gulick, who wishes to express deep appreciation for the help of others although he retains responsibility for the contents of the manuscript. Among those to whom he is indebted are Katherine Dillon, an outstanding writer with professional expertise on Japan in the World War II period; Dr. William S. Dudley, Director, U.S. Naval Historical Center; Mark L. Evans, Historian, Naval Aviation History Branch; Richard B. Frank, author of *DOWNFALL: The End of the Imperial Japanese Empire;* Fred S. Hoffman, former Associated Press military correspondent and senior Department of Defense official; and Arthur E. Klauser, whose close experience in and knowledge of Japanese affairs dates back to World War II.

Endnotes to Appendix I

1. Seward, Jack. *STRANGE BUT TRUE. Stories from Japan.* Tuttle Publishing, Boston, 1999, Chapt. 4, p. 37.

2. Frank, Richard B. *DOWNFALL. The End of the Japanese Imperial Empire.* Random House, Inc., New York, NY, 1999, pp. 188-9.

3. *Ibid.*, pp. 71-72.

4. Naito, Hatsuho, *Thunder Gods. The Kamikaze Pilots Tell Their Story.* Kodansha International Ltd., Tokyo, 1989, p. 22.

5. *Ibid.*, pp. 22-24.

6. Nagatsuka, Ryuji. *I Was A Kamikaze.* Macmillan Publishing Co., Inc., New York, NY, 1974, p. 141.

7. *DOWNFALL, op. cit.*, p. 180.

8. *Ibid.*, pp. 180-2.

9. *Thunder Gods, op. cit.*, pp. 196-7.

10. *Ibid.*, p. 25.

11. *Ibid.*, p. 25.

12. *DOWNFALL, op. cit.*, p. 182.

13. *I Was A Kamikaze, op. cit.*, p. 175, quoting Takushio Hattori's *General History of the Battle of the Pacific.*

14. *DOWNFALL, op. cit.*, pp. 184-5.

15. *DOWNFALL, op. cit.*, p. 187.

16. *Ibid.*, pp. 194-5.

17. Ambrose, Stephen. E. *D-DAY June 6, 1944: The Climactic Battle of World War II.* Simon & Schuster, New York, NY, 1994, p. 576.

18. McCullough, David. *Truman.* Simon & Schuster, New York, NY, 1992, p. 437.

19. *The Japanese Navy In World War II*, U.S. Naval Institute, Annapolis, Md., 1952, Chapt. 10, "The Kamikaze Attack Corps," by Rikihei Inoguchi and Tadashi Nakajima, p. 127.

20. *Ibid.*, Chapt. 11, "Kamikazes in the Okinawa Campaign," by Toshiyuki Yokoi.

21. *Ibid.*, "The Kamikaze Attack Corps," p. 126.

Appendix II

A TRIBUTE TO SHIG FROM EAST LANSING

Prepared by Mr. Lewis Gulick

Shig in his *Memoir* writes rather briefly and matter-of-factly about his civilian career after World War II and the immediate post-war period. We as friends and colleagues of Shig's during his service at Michigan State University wish to say more about his outstanding contributions during his years at East Lansing.

It is no exaggeration to describe Shig as a major player in developing MSU's stature in English language teaching and in particular the University's relationships involving Japan, which since have flowered in many ways. He personally achieved national prominence in the field of teaching English as a second language both in the United States and in Japan. He pioneered educational methods and programs that have continued to evolve since his departure.

Shig is still remembered by old-timers from MSU's English Language Center, which he assisted in setting up in 1961. He had already proven his administrative skill in Japan and Okinawa in organizing English language instructional programs. He was brought back to East Lansing in 1963 to help put the MSU program on its feet. He served as an assistant to Edward Erasmus, Director of the Center, and succeeded to the Directorship when Erasmus left in 1964. As the *Memoir* notes, the Center flourished, from a beginning of around 45 students to nearly 300 in the early 1970s before he left for San Francisco. And clearly, he was well known and well liked on campus.

Shig's successor as Center Director, Dr. Ralph Pat Barrett, recalls that Shig brought in his own materials in developing the curriculum. One of Shig's most admired innovations was the Tripod Drill materials. This exercise involved three steps for the foreign student learning English pronunciation: first, work on pronunciation of the word; second, use the word within a common intonation pattern; third, employ the word in full sentences. The technique was very effective and proved to be an enjoyable exercise for both students and instructors.

Shig did not specialize in textbook writing for students or for other teachers, although he did publish some materials primarily in Japan. Rather than immersing himself in academic research, he preferred a hands-on "real world" approach to instruction. The Center's students received not only language teaching at school but also enjoyed field trips to interesting sites such as the Kellogg Center Cereal Company in Battle Creek, Greenfield Village and the Ford Museum in Dearborn, and a local Oldsmobile factory. There were outdoor picnics. Firsthand impressions from these experiences expanded the sense of the students about things American by exposing them to the U.S. culture beyond the classroom.

Dr. Iwao Ishino, a former Chairman of the Anthropology Department at MSU, describes information imparted aside from direct instruction as "tacit knowledge." Shig, he says, was a master at achieving this in introducing students to a second culture. And serendipitously, he came to MSU at the right time in the University's development as it began to expand its involvement in international programs.

Shig impressed not only his colleagues at MSU but also others in his field, both in the United States and in Japan. He got along well with his peers. He was active in national organizations and often traveled to professional meetings. Again, his innovative and organizational abilities came into play. He was an important figure in NAFSA, the National Association for Foreign Student Affairs. One of NAFSA's components was ATESL, the Association of Teachers of English as a Second Language. He rose in national prominence as a chairman of ATESL and as a founding father of CIEP, the Consortium of Intensive English Programs. CIEP has now evolved into UCIEP, a consortium of University and College Intensive English Programs, which has grown to include more than sixty university members.

Dr. August G. Benson, an MSU colleague and longtime friend, recalls appointing Shig to a team organized by an AID-NAFSA committee. Benson was committee chairman at the time. He said he assigned Shig to represent the English as a Second Language function on the team because of his leadership in ATESL and other ESL programs. Funded by the Agency for International Development (AID), the team prepared an inclusive document, *A Guide for the Education of Foreign Students-Human Resources Department*. Shig was an important contributor to this special document, which portrayed the variety of functions performed or offered by the Admissions Office, the English Language Center, the Foreign Student Advising Office and volunteer community programs.

Dr. Charles Gliozzo recalls that as MSU's Director of Study Abroad in the 1970s, he admired Shig's administrative prowess and precision in getting tasks accomplished. He regarded Shig as a mentor who was tactful and who could easily relate to others, and as a multiculturalist who understood people since he understood the importance of their cultures to them.

Shig of course was active in promoting visits of students and others between Japan and the United States. His bilingualism and familiarity with both cultures made him a natural choice as a liaison official when the State of Michigan was looking for assistance in proceeding with a sister-state relationship with Shiga Prefecture in Japan. His understanding and fluency in both worlds enabled him to be influential in getting the program off to a good start. The emphasis of the exchanges is in the environmental field, since Shiga is the site of Japan's largest lake (Biwa) and Michigan is bordered by the American Great Lakes. Many projects have ensued from this relationship.

Mrs. Lillian Kumata, then an Assistant Administrator at MSU's Asian Studies Center, succeeded Shig in the Shiga project assignment. Having lived in both countries herself, she recalls how well Shig performed in the job because of his ease in operating in both cultures. She found too that Shig was well known in his field in Japan.

Close associates at MSU regarded Shig as Japanese, but completely comfortable in either Japanese or American surroundings. When in America, he was not one to operate in the Japanese mode.

He is remembered by friends as fun to be with, a good joke teller, a considerate colleague. He was known for driving around in late model Buicks, obtained from a Buick dealer/friend. He was proud of his *kamikaze* service and, upon occasion, would show a visitor at his home his old *kamikaze* jacket, which was tucked in a closet.

We who knew Shig at MSU personally will forever value his friendship. We take this opportunity to pay tribute to him and to his many accomplishments.

Joining in this tribute were Dr. Ralph Pat Barrett, Dr. August G. Benson, Dr. Charles A. Gliozzo, Dr. Iwao Ishino, Mary Ishino, and Mrs. Lillian Kumata.

A TRIBUTE FROM SAN FRANCISCO

Shigeo Imamura was a tremendous influence on my life, as he was on the lives of generations of ESL/EFL teachers who worked under and with him. Many of us who began teaching ESL at Michigan State University, where he directed the ESL program for so many years, learned much of what we know about teaching from him. He was an exemplary guide, model, teacher, and mentor. He was always generous with his time and expertise, and helpful and encouraging in so many ways. Besides working under Shig's tutelage at MSU, I had the further good fortune to work for and with him when he was invited by the University of San Francisco to set up an ESL program. There I had the opportunity to watch him, and to assist him, as he set up a program from the ground up, a complex process which he handled with great competence, diplomacy, and grace.

Shig not only guided and assisted new (and not-so-new) teachers, at MSU and USF and elsewhere, but also watched over us, encouraging us and inspiring us to try new things and go new places. He was always warm and hospitable as well; he and his wife Isako, whom we graduate students and teachers were all very fond of, often welcomed us to their home for delicious meals and good conversation.

It was a particular pleasure to be working with Shig during his two years in San Francisco, as he so much enjoyed living once again in the city where he was born and lived for much of his childhood. He revisited the scenes of his childhood, and he told us, his colleagues, many stories about those days. During part of his stay in San Francisco, he lived in the Japan Center area, very near to where he had lived as a child. He and Isako thoroughly enjoyed the Japanese stores, restaurants, and community events at the Japan Center, and they often shared these experiences with us, his colleagues and friends.

One restaurant expedition stands out in my memory: the evening of my initiation into the mysteries of *sashimi* and *sushi*. Long before *sushi* became as popular, even ubiquitous, as it is in the United States today, several colleagues and I went to a *sushi* restaurant with Shig, where he announced that he would order a selection of *sushi* and *sashimi* for all of us. He ordered in Japanese, and didn't tell us what each morsel was until after we had eaten it. He then announced with great glee that we had just eaten, for one example, eel! Back in 1975, before we all became accustomed to eating international food routinely, eating eel was considered quite adventurous! That evening epitomized Shig's pleasure in introducing elements of and people from his dual cultural backgrounds to each other; his way of treating us and also surprising us was also typical of his hospitality, his conviviality, and his sometimes mischievous sense of humor.

Although Mr. Imamura left the University of San Francisco (to return to MSU) after two years, I kept in touch with him over the years and followed his career. He continued to be a mentor figure to me and to so many of the other teachers who worked with him at MSU and at USF. For example, he helped some former USF instructors set up an ESL program for women at Mills College, and he served on the Board of that program and advised its administrators for many years. I know he stayed in touch with, and gave assistance to, many others who had worked with him in the past. He always showed a genuine interest in his faculty and his students, past and present.

I must note here that Shig always treated his female colleagues as complete equals, never in any way showing any sense of superiority or condescension. This was quite unusual for a man of his generation. With Shig, one felt that he saw people for themselves, and didn't judge them based on their gender or race or any other such characteristics.

Mr. Imamura, in his unassuming way, had a great influence on the field of ESL/EFL and on those who work with university students in the United States, Japan, and around the world. The fact that he worked in the USA and in Japan, and had roots in both countries and cultures, greatly enhanced his ability and understanding. In addition, his long and productive career in this field gave him a perspective that few others could claim. In a sense, he represented the confluence of many of the influential historical and cultural streams that made twentieth century international education what it was.

Despite Shig's achievements and stature in the field of education, he was always down to earth, realistic, honest, and scrupulously fair in his interactions with colleagues, students, and others. He also had a great sense of humor, and often employed that humor to put things in perspective. He was a genuinely good man, one whom I trusted completely, and a dear friend. I will always remember him with gratitude and affection. He is greatly missed. And yet I cannot feel he is really gone, as the power of his personality and his influence lives on.

—Stephanie Vandrick
Associate Professor
University of San Francisco

Original Full Text of Chapter 14

The Teacher

Between Two Worlds

I served as the English teacher supervisor for Ehime Prefectural Board of Education from 1949 to 1955, but between 1951 and 1953 I was a student at the University of Michigan. In 1955, I was appointed assistant professor of English at the College of Education, Ehime University, in Matsuyama. That was interrupted between 1961 and 1962, because I was invited by Michigan State University to help set up their English Language Center and teach English to foreign students. Michigan State University wanted me to extend my stay, but I was obligated to return to Ehime University because I was on leave with pay from there. After returning to Ehime and teaching there for a year, I decided to go back to Michigan State with a long stay in mind. It did turn out to be a long stay, 18 years until 1981. But that period was also interrupted, twice. Once I served as a visiting professor at the University of San Francisco from 1974 to 1976, and then as director of a program called Konan-Illinois Center at Konan University in Kobe, Japan, from 1978 to 1979. Aoyama Gakuin University in Tokyo planned to open a new college called the School of International Politics, Economics and Business (SIPEB) and wanted me to head its English language program, so I left Michigan and returned to Japan in 1981. Then, Dokkyo Institute, which was administering Dokkyo University, Dokkyo Medical University and two high schools, all located in and around Tokyo, was going to open a new university in Himeji in Western Japan and asked me to join its faculty and head the English Department. So I moved there in 1987.

Including the fact that I was born in the United States and lived there for ten years before being brought to Japan in 1932, these moves back and forth between the two countries add up to approximately

30 years of residence in the U.S. and 40 years in Japan. Of course, I made a number of short visits to Japan while living in the U.S., on business and on vacations, and went to the U.S. almost yearly while residing in Japan. It is therefore difficult to determine exactly how much of my life I have spent in each of the two countries. To be honest, I am not sure if I am more American or more Japanese in my ways of thinking and acting. However, I would like to summarize here some of the highlights of the span of my life between 1949 and the present for you to see how American or how Japanese I am.

As the English teacher supervisor, I observed that many, if not most, of those teaching English in the secondary schools were not quite equipped to do their jobs. Their ability to listen to and understand or speak English was rather limited. Some of them were never trained in the methods of teaching English as a second/foreign language. In March 1950 I took upon myself a major operation: a two-week long inservice training for teachers of English. We had the use of the wooden buildings of the former Ehime Normal School, then totally vacated because of the abolishment of the normal school system throughout the country. We laid *tatami* mats on the wooden floors of classrooms, and the participants, as we called them, slept on them curled up in blankets they brought with them. There were about 100 participants, so we made several classrooms into bedrooms. Other classrooms were used for instruction during the daytime. As instructors, there were about a dozen native speakers of English, educators and military personnel from all over Western Japan. In March, it was fairly cold even in Matsuyama, which is in a temperate zone. Heating systems in school buildings were unheard of in those days. The participants were sturdy as well as enthusiastic. They came voluntarily and tolerated the hardships. The use of the Japanese language was prohibited throughout the program. It was their very first time for most of them to speak with native speakers of English, but they very actively took part in the drills, recitations and lectures. It seemed that they went home happy with the thought that they got what they wanted, a bit better command of the English language. Incidentally, this program was the first of its kind in Japan and later spread to other regions of the country. I was invited to places like Sendai in Northern Japan, Hiroshima, and Kyushu to show how to run such programs.

Late in 1950, there was a competitive examination for scholarships to study in the United States for one year. This was the third year that the GARIOA (Grant in Aid and Relief in Occupied Areas) scholarships were to be offered. In the spring of 1951, I went to Tokyo to take the exam. There was a written test and an oral interview. I was surprised to see the large number of people who came from all over the country for the exam, perhaps thousands of them. I did not think the exam was very difficult, but seeing that the competition was very keen, I was not at all sure that I would be accepted. A few weeks later, I got a telephone call from the States, from Capt. Snyder, the WAC officer I worked for at the Military Government Team. She told me that she had retired from the army as a major, was working at the Washington, D.C. office of the Institute for International Education, and that she accidentally found my name on the list of GARIOA examinees in Tokyo. "If you pass the exam, which university would you like to go to?" she said. Without any hesitation I answered, "The University of Michigan, please." Among the books on language teaching I had read, I was most impressed by those by Dr. Charles C. Fries, who was then one of the most distinguished professors at the University of Michigan. I wanted to study under him.

In late June, I received a letter from the U.S. Educational Commission in Tokyo, notifying me that I had won a scholarship for a year's study at the University of Michigan, and that I was to participate in a month-long orientation program at Yale University first. The letter instructed me to appear at their office by ten A.M. on July 9, ready to leave for the United States by ship. I did not have much time. First of all, I had a hard time getting permission from my superiors at Ehime Prefectural Board of Education for a year's leave of absence on such a short notice. Then I had to make a quick trip to Kobe to obtain a student visa at the U.S. Consulate there. I was surprised that they already had a file on me. The Consul was a kind gentleman. He explained to me that I had Japanese/American dual citizenship but that my U.S. citizenship was revoked for three reasons: (1) that I volunteered to serve in a foreign (Japanese) military force; (2) that I had an official status in a foreign government, even though local; and (3) that there was evidence that I had voted in public elections in a foreign country — all three violated existing U.S. Immigration Acts. He said that I had a choice of either renouncing my U.S. citizenship or applying for a reinstatement of the citizenship and having it denied. He suggested that I take the latter step because that would leave me with the opportunity to apply for a reinstatement again in the future. Then I would be eligible to apply for a U.S. student visa as a Japanese citizen. That is what I did. Once back in Matsuyama, I had to make last-minute preparations to leave. One problem was that there was no one around who could tell me what the climate was like in Michigan and I was at a loss as to what kind of clothes I should take with me.

We were shipped out of the port of Yokohama on July 13. The ship was the **General Gordon Collins**, an 8,000-ton troop transport. We were initially told that we would be accommodated in the officers' quarters above deck, but once we boarded we found ourselves in dimly lit large compartments below deck. Only the females on GARIOA scholarships were given officers' quarters. Besides some 470 individuals on GARIOA scholarships, the ship was packed with GIs going home from the Korean battlefront. We slept in three-tier canvas bunk beds that were folded up on steel poles when not in use. There wasn't much to do on the ship. It seemed like long hours between meals, until we heard the call over the PA system, "Compartments E and F, line up on starboard side for chow."

On the day we approached the mouth of the Golden Gate, all of us were on deck watching the approaching land. I was full of emotion as the white houses and the streets of San Francisco became visible. Ah, my hometown! The ship slowed down and passed under the Golden Gate Bridge. It hadn't been complete when Mother and I sailed out in the opposite direction 19 years before. The ship docked at Fort Mason, we disembarked and were taken to Mills College in Oakland by army buses. As we passed through parts of San Francisco, I recognized some of the streets and landmarks. "This is Market Street, one of the main streets of the city, and that's the Ferry Building over there," I pointed out to those sitting around me. As the buses began to climb the hill on the Mills College campus, I smelled the scent of the eucalyptus trees, which triggered my memories of Golden Gate Park.

We lived in the Mills College dormitories for a few days, during a brief orientation period. We had a lot of free time, but were told not to leave the campus because we were unfamiliar with the area. I decided to sneak out. I called Mr. Nishikage, an old friend of my father. Father had written ahead about me, so Mr. Nishikage agreed right away to come and pick me up. He drove me into San Francisco and took me to all the places I wanted to see again. We drove past our old Cedar Avenue house, then on to Fillmore Street, to Golden Gate Park, the beach, the Cliff House, North Beach, Fishermen's Wharf and Chinatown. It was when we stopped off at Mr. Nishikage's house before returning to Mills that I saw a television for the first time in my life.

After our short stay in Oakland, we were put on a train specially arranged for our group. Those who were to enter their orientation programs at Mills and UC Berkeley stayed behind. The train made several stops on its trip to Chicago, letting a few off at each stop. The group got smaller and smaller as we went on. Those of us going toward the East Coast changed trains in Chicago and proceeded to our destinations. At Yale University, we stayed in a dormitory with other GARIOA scholarship students from other countries such as Finland, Greece, Poland and Turkey. Each of us had a roommate from a country different from our own. My roommate was from Finland. Directed by Professor David D. Denken, otherwise known as Dr. Triple D, our orientation program consisted of lectures on American history, American architecture and other things American. We were taken on tours to places of interest. All the participants had a good command of English and did not need any language training.

We were matched with host families to stay with over the weekends. The host family for my roommate and me was the Weber family in nearby Westport. Mr. Weber was a member of the school board for the town of Westport, and through his work he knew the famous Ms. Helen Keller well. He asked us if we would like to meet Ms. Keller. Of course we did. So, one Sunday, the Webers took us to Ms. Keller's home, which was also in Westport. Ms. Keller could not see or hear, of course, but her assistant scribbled what we said on her palm, very rapidly, and she understood all of what was said. While her intonation was off a bit, at least I understood just about everything she said. The most impressive part of that visit came when we left her house. The house was built on a small hill, and as we left we drove on a curved road leading downhill. We saw that Ms. Keller kept waving at us exactly in the direction of the moving car. Mrs. Weber told us that Ms. Keller sensed the air vibration coming from the car and knew exactly where the car was going.

There was about a week between the end of the Yale orientation program and the date that I had to be in Ann Arbor, Michigan. I spent the first couple of days in New York City, sightseeing. Then I went on to Washington, D.C., where I stayed with Major Snyder. She took two days off from her work and on the first day took me to all the major landmarks in and around the city. On the second day, something that I shall never forget happened. We watched the signing of the World War II Peace Treaty on television. There I was, alive and well, sitting in a room in the capital city of the country I once considered my enemy, watching the Prime Minister of Japan, Mr. Shigeru Yoshida, signing the treaty in San Francisco. It was at that moment that I realized completely that I was happy that I had not died in the war.

From Washington, D.C., I backtracked to New York, changed trains and arrived in Ann Arbor. The first thing I did was to seek out Dr. Fries and ask him to be my academic adviser. He agreed and advised me to enroll as a regular student and to earn as many credits as I could carry. Some individuals on GARIOA scholarships were registering as special students without credits to make the going easier for themselves. I, however, followed Dr. Fries' advice.

Toward the end of that academic year, Dr. Fries strongly suggested that I extend my stay for a year and get a bachelor's degree. There were some problems. For one, I did not have enough money to pay for the costs for another year. I went to see Dr. Fred Kerlinger, the foreign student adviser in the International Center. He called the Institute for International Education and found out that the scholarship could not be extended, although if I stayed for another year on my own they would pay for my return trip to Japan. Dr. Kerlinger then called some local sources and got a few hundred-dollar donations for me. Adding that to the several hundred dollar savings I had from the first year was still not enough. I then thought of Dr. Robert Brown for whom I had done some Japanese-to-English translation work in the first year and had earned some pocket money. I went to him, and was I lucky. He had just received some funds to do research on Japanese culture, especially on minority groups in Japan, and he was able to pay me monthly sums for translation work. So, I was all set to continue with my studies.

Soon after I enrolled at the University of Michigan, somehow word got around that I was a *kamikaze* pilot during World War II. Every once in a while, some of my dorm-mates kidded me about it. One of them said, "Shig, you're still alive today because you were so stupid you couldn't find your target, right?" On the other hand, there were some who very seriously wanted to find out from me how a person would ever voluntarily offer his life for the sake of his country. I was never able to give an answer to their satisfaction. Word got around to the outside too, and I began getting invitations to speak to church groups, school PTAs and other groups. One Sunday, I spoke to a church group. After I finished talking, a man came up to me and said, "I now understand why you had to do what you did. But you still were wrong. You fought against God." "But we had our own god too," I protested. "There is only one God, our God," he retorted and left in a huff. I felt hopeless and had the abominable thought that World War II was not going to be the last major war.

But on another occasion, a silver-haired old gentleman came to me after my talk and held my hands gently without saying a word for a moment. I saw tears in his eyes. After a while he said, "Forgive me. I have hated you Japanese for killing my only son in the war. Listening to you, I came to realize that there are old fathers like me in Japan too, who lost their sons in the war. I was wrong. It wasn't the Japanese who killed my son. It was the war that did it. Forgive me." I was deeply moved but no words came to my mouth. All I could do was grip his hands firmly in return.

Most of the courses I took at Michigan were in linguistics and the Teaching of English as a Foreign/Second Language (TEFL/ TESL). However, I had to be enrolled in some required courses in which I had no particular interest. One of them was Modern Diplomatic History of the United States. Until well into the semester, I did not realize that the professor was a former lieutenant commander in the U.S. Navy. As the course progressed, I began to feel that he was rather biased in his views on the causes of World War II. So, on several occasions, I attempted to present another view. That was a mistake. It was obvious that the professor did not like what I presented, even though my classmates seemed to appreciate my efforts. I thought I did a pretty good job on the final exam, but found that I earned a B minus grade for the course. That was the worst grade I got at the University of Michigan.

I got my BA degree in June 1953, and immediately set out for home. During vacations while at Michigan, I sometimes delivered cars for Detroit car dealers, a cheap way to travel to different parts of the country where I wanted to visit. Most often they were used cars, but the one I got to deliver to San Francisco on my way home was a brand new one. The first thing I did in San Francisco was to drop in at the office of the Institute for International Education there. I was told that I was to take the commercial liner *President Cleveland*. The cruise from San Francisco to Yokohama was very pleasant. When we arrived in Yokohama, I thought the air smelled strange. It smelled like a mixture of *takuan* (pickled radish, a common side dish) and soy sauce. Anyway it certainly smelled different from the air in America, which to me often smelled of Campbell soup.

On the second day home, I went to my office and went around thanking my colleagues for tolerating my two years of absence. Then I got right on to planning another inservice training program for English teachers for that summer. I had less than a month to get ready. This time, I chose a high school way up in the mountains, in a town called Kuma. The session earned the name "Kuma Seminar" that year. It was another big success. About 200 participants came and we attracted 20 native-speaker instructors. The seminar continued, always in Kuma in the summer and in other small towns in the spring, until I left for the United States again in 1961.

In 1955, I was invited to join the faculty at Ehime University. I became an assistant professor in the English Department of their College of Education. About a month after I made that move, I had a call from Dr. Robert Brown, for whom I did the translation work at Michigan. He had just come to Tokyo to head the Asia Foundation office there. He wanted me to come and work for him. I felt very obligated to do so because of the financial help he gave me in Michigan, but I had to say I could not make another move so shortly after I had taken a new job. He then said, "OK, if you can't come to us, we'll come to you," and explained that he was willing to fund whatever project I considered beneficial for education in Japan. He invited me to come to Tokyo to discuss the matter. The outcome of that discussion was that the Asia Foundation provided funds for all my future English seminars so that both the instructors and the participants could work in a more comfortable environment. We still slept on *tatami* mats on classroom floors, but the food got better and we had some heat for the spring sessions.

In the fall of 1956, we got an American instructor by the name of Ernest Richter at Ehime University. He was sent to us by the Asia Foundation, which also sent several other Americans to other universities in Japan. Ernie had a keen sense of humor and often made us all laugh. At first, though, there were many things about Japan that he did not understand. One morning, he came in and asked, "Shig, what does *"Dochirae"* mean?" I said it means, "Where are you going?" "That's what I thought. Why are the Japanese so nosy?" he said. I asked him what he meant, and he explained that his neighbors almost always asked him that when he met them leaving his house. "Why should they care where I'm going? It's none of their goddam business!" he said. As I explained that *"Dochirae?"* is not really a question but only a form of greeting, and that the usual reaction by the Japanese to it is *"Chotto sokomade,"* meaning "Oh, just around the corner," I felt I was at least more Japanese than Ernie was.

During the spring break of 1957, I was sent by the Asia Foundation to the University of the Ryukyus in Okinawa. I took with me a dozen tape recorders the Foundation had purchased and donated to the University. They were open-reel tape recorders, but tape recorders of any kind were a rarity in those days. The mission given to me by the Foundation was to help the University set up its first language laboratory. The University had an advisory commission made up of educators from Michigan State University and some Michigan secondary schools, including Drs. David Mead and Robert Geist. Drs. Mead and Geist took an interest in the seminars I was running in

Ehime and in the English Language Training Center I had established at Ehime University. The Training Center was where junior and senior high school English teachers on three-month leaves from their schools came to improve their language skills. The next summer, Bob Geist and Japanese professors from the University of the Ryukyus came to observe the Kuma Seminar and the Training Center, both of which were the only ones of their kinds in the whole country. They were impressed. It was through this connection that I was invited to Michigan State University (MSU) to help set up the English Language Center.

At Michigan State University, I assisted the director in organizing the curriculum and training the teachers. It was a challenge to start a new program at such a large American institution. Living in a university faculty apartment, I made many new friends and enjoyed my year in East Lansing, Michigan, very much. After returning to Japan and teaching a year at Ehime University, I resigned, and at the invitation of MSU returned to the English Language Center. Soon after, my wife Isako joined me in East Lansing. As soon as I started to work at MSU, I began to commute to Ann Arbor to pursue a master's degree in linguistics at the University of Michigan. It wasn't easy to drive the 60 miles each way, especially in deep winter when parts of the highways were frozen, but it paid off. I received my MA in December 1964. At my job at the English Language Center, I got along very well with everyone, including the director. But the director himself did not seem very happy with his work environment. At the end of the 1963-64 academic year, he left MSU for a similar position at another university down South. I was then asked to take over the directorship. When we first opened the Center in 1961, we started out with about 45 students. Each year the number increased. I think we reached the peak in the early 1970s when we had close to 300 students from about 30 different countries. I worked very hard to keep things running smoothly. But that was not all that I did. I joined national professional organizations such as the Linguistic Society of America (LSA), the National Association for Foreign Student Affairs (NAFSA), Administrators and Teachers of English as a Second Language (ATESL — a section of NAFSA), Teachers of English to Speakers of Other Languages (TESOL), and the Modern Language

Association (MLA), and attended most of their annual national conferences, which were held in cities all over the United States. I was elected chair of ATESL in 1966. I took the initiative in organizing the Consortium of Intensive English Programs (CIEP), involving some 20 major intensive English programs throughout the United States, and became its first chair from 1968 to 1970.

In the capacity of consultant for NAFSA on the Teaching of English as a Second Language, I visited many universities in the country, helping them plan or organize intensive English programs. One of the universities I visited was the University of San Francisco, where the dean said to me, "Why don't you take a leave from Michigan State and come and show us how to do it for a year?" I did that, but the stay there turned out to be for two years, from the fall of 1974 to the spring of 1976. I served as visiting professor and director of the English Language Center. That gave me plenty of time to revisit places dear to my childhood memories. Isako and I lived in an apartment in Japantown and did a lot of our shopping at Uoki, where I had gone with Mother. By the way, our Cedar Avenue house was completely gone, as were Taiseido, where Father worked and Sushigen, where he used to hang out.

When I left for San Francisco, the directorship of the English Language Center was passed on to a colleague of mine, Dr. Ralph Pat Barrett. When I returned to East Lansing in 1976, I worked as associate professor. At that time, MSU, along with three other U.S. institutions, participated in a program called the Konan-Illinois Center program, in which American college students went to Japan, specifically to Konan University in Kobe, to study Japanese language and culture for an academic year. During the 1978-1979 academic year, the director of the program from MSU died suddenly, so I was asked to take his place. Thus, I found myself living in Kobe for nine months. I lived in a Konan University-owned Japanese style house called the White House because it was painted white outside. I walked to Konan University to work 5 days a week and had 23 students to look after. They lived with their Japanese host families.

Shortly after returning to Michigan in 1979, I began to receive correspondence from Aoyama Gakuin University in Tokyo. They told me that they were going to establish a new college, to be named

School for International Politics, Economics and Business (SIPEB). Although there was not going to be an English major, the use of the English language was going to be the main emphasis for all students in that college. The Chancellor wanted me to join the SIPEB faculty and head the English program. SIPEB was to have its first class of students in the spring of 1982. I gave it much thought. There was no particular reason to leave Michigan. But to me, to start up another brand new program seemed like a good challenge, and I decided to take on that challenge. I flew back to Japan in September of 1981.

To find a place to live in Tokyo at a reasonable price was going to be a problem. Foreseeing that, Chancellor Oki suggested settling in Atsugi, about 30 miles southwest of Tokyo, where the University's new campus was being built and where most of our teaching was to be done. Until I found a suitable place in Atsugi, I had his permission to live in the dormitory for student athletes in northern Yokohama. I gladly accepted his generous offer. Isako and I bought into a condominium in Atsugi and moved into it in December of that year.

Aoyama Gakuin is one of the oldest private institutions of higher education in Japan. It attracts fairly high quality students, not only from Tokyo and its vicinity but also from all parts of the country. Partly because of the reputation it was able to build up prior to its opening, SIPEB drew some of the best applicants who would want to come to private universities. We were also able to get several good native speakers of English for our full- and part- time faculty, and got off to a good start in April of 1982.

Early in 1986, I was approached by Dokkyo Institute. This was the second time they tried to lure me away from my job and into their institution. The first time was while I was at Michigan State University and they planned to set up a new language institute at Dokkyo University north of Tokyo. This time they wanted me to head the English Department of the new university they planned to open in Himeji. I was attracted by the thought of helping to set up a brand new university. But there were arguments against the idea: a full professorship at a reputable institution like Aoyama would be a much better title than a professorship at a brand new institution of unknown quality. But Professor Shinomiya, the contact person for Dokkyo Institute, who was to be the Vice President of the new university, was very persuasive and persistent. We met several times in Tokyo and talked things over. One of his selling points was that mandatory retirement age at the new university was going to be 70, two years higher than at Aoyama Gakuin. Moreover, a limited number of those joining the new faculty at the age of over 60 would be given till age 75 to retire. I gave in.

I am sometimes asked where I would prefer to live in retirement, in the United States or in Japan. I am always hard put to answer that question, because I know I can live just as comfortably and pleasantly in either country. Besides, having visited some thirty countries around the world, I can think of several other places I might want to reside for the rest of my life. But such thoughts inevitably bring to my mind the sad fact that conflicts are still going on in various parts of the world, almost daily. The conflicts are brought on by reasons of politics, economics, religion, and race. Especially tragic are the ones that go way back in history.

As I look back on my wartime experience, I cannot help but wish that I knew then what I know now. It wasn't worth Japan and the United States fighting each other, not with the great losses of lives on both sides. Which leads me to wonder if there are any wars that are worth fighting, from an objective point of view. My experience and observation tell me that there aren't. I sincerely hope that this writing will help me to prove that point.

今村 茂男

Shigeo Imamura
April, 1994

Reprints of Tributes
In Memoriam

Shigeo Imamura

Shigeo Imamura died on December 24, 1998, in Himeji, Japan, at the age of 76. Throughout his life, "Shig" promoted international education and international understanding from both sides of the Pacific, beginning long before the term *Pacific Rim* was employed. He

helped shape the field of TESL in its formative years and continued to shape and promote professionalization of the field in the United States and Japan throughout his life.

Shig was born in San José, California, in August 1922 and lived in San Francisco until adolescence, when he and his family moved to Japan. He began his ESL career in the late 1940s and received his BA and MA in linguistics from the University of Michigan. In every sense of the word, he was an international scholar, holding academic positions in the United States and in Japan, publishing widely (more than 30 publications) on ESL topics both in English and in Japanese, presenting scholarly papers (more than 40) at conferences on both sides of the Pacific, and serving in leadership roles in U.S.-based and Japan-based professional organizations.

Numerous institutions have benefited from his professional contributions, including Michigan State University (1963–1981), where he served as director of the English Language Center for many years; Ehime University; University of San Francisco; Konan University; Aoyama Gakuin University; and Himeji Gokkyo University, where he taught most recently. In addition to being an exemplary and memorable instructor, Shig was a mentor to generations of young professionals, especially those starting out in their careers. His generosity and supportiveness are well known; he cared about those he had mentored, followed their careers, gave advice, guidance, and encouragement, and kept in touch with professionals all over the world. Shig's commitment to international understanding and international education are evident in his involvement in professional organizations and his service on advisory boards. He was active in professional organizations, holding appointed or elected positions in such organizations as TESOL, NAFSA, and the Japan Association for Language Teaching (JALT), most recently serving as president of JALT (1992–1993).

People who worked with Shig know that he was good company. He and Isako, his wife, hosted wonderful parties with delicious food and lively debates. Shig was always ready with an anecdote or joke and was always interested in good conversation over a good meal. His sense of humor was legendary.

On a personal note, I met Shig at Michigan State University in 1970, when I was a new graduate student in linguistics with a teaching assistantship at the English Language Center. Professor Imamura was my introduction to TESL and to internationalism. He assisted me in practical, on-the-job training and in theoretical learning about language teaching, but most important, he broadened my horizons and helped shape my philosophy about international education. Over the years, he grew to be a valued colleague and friend.

Mine is only one of many stories. Those who knew him and worked with him owe him much, as does the TESL profession. We miss Shig terribly! ❑

Johnnie Johnson Hafernik is a professor in the ESL department at the University of San Francisco.

From *TESOL Matters*, Vol. 9, #5, October/November 1999, p.9.

From *Himeji JALT News*, Vol. 2, No. 1, Winter 1999.

IN MEMORIAM: PROFESSOR SHIGEO IMAMURA

1922   1998

MR. SHIGEO IMAMURA

Shigeo Imamura was born and brought up in California and remained in the States until the age of ten. He then moved with his parents to Matsuyama in Ehime-ken and attended Middle School from 1935-1940 and Matsuyama College of Commerce from 1941-1943. His education was interrupted by the war years and during the Occupation of Japan by U.S. Forces Mr. Imamura served as a translator and interpreter for the U.S. Government Military team in Matsuyama.

When the Occupation was nearing an end he decided to focus his life on education and was able to continue his studies in America. He earned a Master's Degree in linguistics from the University of Michigan in 1953. After his studies were completed, he returned to Matsuyama and served as a teacher consultant for the Ehime Prefectural Board of Education and was also Instructor of English at Ehime University.

In 1962 he returned to America as assistant and associate professor of ESL at Michigan State University and also was director of the English Language Center there. From 1974 to 1976 he was visiting Professor at the English Language Center at the University of San Francisco and was Chair of ATESL (Association of Teachers of English as a Second Language) and Consortium of Intensive English Programs in NAFSA (National Association for Foreign Student Affairs).

Returning to Japan after 20 years in the U.S., Imamura was professor of English at the School of International Politics at Aoyama Gakuin University for six years. In 1987 he was the chair of the English Department and director of the Language Institute of Himeji Dokkyo University.

In 1996 he retired from teaching but remained active as a consultant to educators throughout Japan. Throughout his distinguished career he has enlightened and encouraged students and has been an active force in guiding them through their profession. He also leaves a rich legacy of writings and research in the field of language education.

****

REMEMBRANCES FROM THOSE WHO KNEW HIM:

I first met Shigeo Imamura more than twenty years ago at Michigan State University when I was a graduate student there and he was the head of the English Language Center. He was a great help and inspiration to me then and in later years and he had a profound influence on my life. If I had not me t him, my life would be very different than it is today. After leaving MSU, I was privileged to work with him for a period of two years at the University of San Francisco. He later helped me find my first job in Japan, and much later helped me obtain my current position at Himeji Dokkyo University. I also met him and his wife frequently over the years when I was not able to work with him. He was a good friend to me always. He was more than a friend, however. Through the years I have seen the influence he had on me, my colleagues, and generations of students from all over the world. I am sure that there are hundreds of people who remember him with affection and respect, as I do. As a friend of mine expressed it, the passing of Shigeo Imamura was the end of an era.

Ms. Susan Jackson
Himeji Dokkyo University

· ************

Dear members of Himeji JALT Chapter

When the late Professor Shigeo Imamura passed away on December 24, 1998 many of us lost an outstanding member of JALT, a beacon for the EFL profession, and a dear friend. He was a trusted teacher of English in both America and Japan. Born in America, but raised in both Michigan and Ehime he was able to successfully bridge communication between language teachers of both countries.

Prof. Imamura with David McMurray in Matsuyama

I first met him after he stepped down from the podium of a JALT meeting. It had been a packed and rather boisterous Annual General Meeting at Tokyo International University in Kawagoe. He served as the interim president and chair in 1992. Our meetings are perhaps quieter now thanks to his efforts at that turning point in JALT's administrative history. In 1994 he coined JALT's current name as the Japan Association for Language Teaching. I was also often able to talk with him in Matsuyama where he was mentor for many English students who had gone on to become excellent teachers of English at high schools and universities. His disciples regularly hosted parties in his honor. My fondest memory is when I delivered a box of winter oranges (mikan) from Matsuyama to his home in Himeji. Mrs. Imamura made chicken soup, and I thought I was visiting my own mother and father for the weekend.

With respect,
David McMurray
JALT Immediate Past-President and Treasurer
Fukui Prefectural University

****

I still remember vividly his fluency in English when he made a speech on English Education in the Convention of Sieban High School English Teacher's Association. I was also impressed with his passion for English Education. This was shown when he positively accepted my offer to ask him to send Asian students studying at Dokkyo University for the purpose of elevating my students' listening ability toward non-native speakers of English.

Koshi Kuroda
Kenmei Women's Junior College

****

I must have been one of the last students of Professor Imamura's. I first met him in his class for adults several years ago. He treated us all equally, regardless of age, title or length of friendship with him. His experience in teaching in two countries made him fair to everybody, liberal in opinion and generous in judgment.

I'm proud of having been one of his students.

Hiroko Hida
Kenmei Student

****

I felt remorse at hearing that Mr.Imamura passed away last month. It was Mr. Imamura that had started Himeji JALT, and he had continued to be a member of Himeji JALT for the past ten years. Mr. Imamura, please live in peace in heaven. and inspire us and give us assistance.

Shigeto Kinugasa
Miki Senior High School

. . . .

It must have been in 1961, or maybe 62. The place was The University of Michigan in Ann Arbor. It could have been at a linguistics meeting, or perhaps in a classroom. This young Japanese fellow (actually he was a few years older than me) spoke to me, or I to him, and we had a short get-acquainted conversation. His English was excellent; a native-speaker? He was born in San Jose (1922) and had a BA in English Language and Literature (1953) from the University of Michigan. But he grew up in Matsuyama and received his secondary school education there. In fact, he told me, for a number of years he forgot that he ever knew English. I saw him from time to time after that. He was studying for an M.A in linguistics too, and we had a class or two together. He came to Ann Arbor for classes from East Lansing, where he was an assistant professor and Director of the Michigan State University English Language Center (1963-74). In the following years he became active in NAFSA (National Association of Foreign Student Advisers) at about the same time that TESOL was being formed, and in 1966 he was elected Chair of ATESL (Association of Teachers of English as a Second Language), the NAFSA counterpart to TESOL. In 1968-70 he was Chair of CIEP (Consortium of Intensive English Programs), and from 1968 to 1978 he was a NAFSA Consultant for Intensive English Language Programs.

I left the U of M in 1965 and didn't have any contact with him again until 1987. By that time in addition to teaching at Michigan State University, he had taught at the University of San Francisco (1974-76) and Konan University in Kobe (1978-79). In 1981 he moved to Aoyama Gakuin and then in 1987 to Himeji Dokkyo. That year I met a long-time colleague of ours at a TESOL Convention and he mentioned that a position was open in Japan that he couldn't apply for. It was quite a surprise when a response to my inquiry came back from my friend of my graduate days.

During his career he published mostly on two themes, teaching English and Japanese students studying in the U.S. He was a bridge between Japanese and American societies, and he shared his perceptive insights about the learning difficulties of Japanese students through his articles. He was also a critic of English teaching in Japan. These themes he brought together in presentations when he was Vice President, then President of JALT (Japan Association of Language Teachers)(1991-93).

With the establishment of Himeji Dokkyo University in 1987 and its mandate to become an international university, he had an opportunity to create the type of English language program that was very successful in the U.S. during the 60s and 70s. But times and situations can differ, new trends can emerge, and educational traditions often are very slow to change. When he passed away in December, only a small part of his wish for improved English language instruction in Japan had been realized. Still the changes he advocated are gradually appearing – little achievements slowly, often imperceptibly being explored, accepted, and adopted. Perhaps from afar or from a broader time frame their importance will be clear.

Shig, you did your part! Now it is time for your kohai to nurture those wishes that you had for English teaching in Japan, and for the youth that are following in your footsteps.

The ashes of Shigeo Imamura will be accompanied by his wife, Isako, to San Francisco and met there by his ex-students and colleagues, then scattered from a chartered boat into San Franciso Bay -- into currents from the West flowing out and uniting with those from the East.

May Shig rest in Peace!

Mr. Jeris Strain
Himeji Dokkyo University

From T*he Japanese Association for Language Teaching*, Vol. 23, No. 3, March 1999.

Memorial to a Friend and Teacher

Shigeo Imamura

On December 24, 1998 many in the EFL profession lost a friend. Those of us in JALT also lost a valuable member. Our Past President passed away on after suffering from cardio-vascular complications. A quiet ceremony was held for his family, friends, and colleagues on December 25 in Himeji. The JALT membership was represented at the funeral and offered a remembrance to the grieving Imamura family.

Shigeo Imamura's life spanned two cultures. He was born and brought up in California until age ten. Then he travelled to Matsuyama, Japan and finished elementary school through college. He went back to the U.S. where he received an M.A. degree in Linguistics from the University of Michigan. He then took the position of instructor of English at Ehime University until he was offered a position as associate professor of ESL at Michigan State University. Returning once again to Japan after 20 years in the U.S., he taught as professor of English at Aoyama Gakuin University for six years, and then became director of the Language Institute of Himeji Dokkyo University. He remained teaching at Himeji Dokkyo University until the end.

The JALT electorate chose him to be their Vice President in 1991. When asked by the JALT executive board to fill a vacancy at the presidency he gracefully accepted. During his tenure with JALT he coined our current name in English, The Japan Association for Language Teaching.

Many members remember him best for his ability to bridge the Japanese and foreign members community in JALT. He happily celebrated with many at the 20th anniversary of JALT at JALT94 in Matsuyama and he also officiated at JALT95 in Nagoya. He was mentor for English students in America and all around Japan. Many of his students have gone on to be excellent teachers of English. We will all remember him well.

With respect,
David McMurray, Immediate Past President of JALT